A Complete Guide to Overcome

NO CANADIAN EXPERIENCE:

How and Where To

OBTAIN CANADIAN EXPERIENCE

For Foreign Trained Professionals
and Skilled Immigrants

On the Journey to Employment in Their Chosen Professions

Obi Orakwue

A Complete Guide to Overcome
NO CANADIAN EXPERIENCE:
How and Where To
OBTAIN CANADIAN EXPERIENCE
For Foreign Trained Professionals
and Skilled Immigrants

On the Journey to Employment in Their Chosen Professions

Obi Orakwue

Limit of Liability/Disclaimer

At the time this edition of this book was written/published, all the phone numbers, fax numbers Websites, email addresses, mailing addresses and names of coordinators, title of programs in this edition were accurate and functioning.

Although all the data and information in this book have been put through an undiscriminating and unsentimental sieve of accuracy and reliability of content, the author and publisher of this book are not liable for any disappointment, commercial, incidental and or consequential damages and or failure to deliver on the part of the host and coordinating organizations of the programs, schools and financial institutions. You may need to consult with a professional before employing the ideas, advice and strategies contained in this book. You are strictly advised to always purchase the most recent edition of this book.

Note for Librarians: A cataloguing record for this book is available from Library and Archives Canada at www.collectionscanada.ca/amicus/index-e.html
ISBN 1-4120-6198-9

Printed in Victoria, BC, Canada. Printed on paper with minimum 30% recycled fibre. Trafford's print shop runs on "green energy" from solar, wind and other environmentally-friendly power sources.

TRAFFORD
PUBLISHING

Offices in Canada, USA, Ireland and UK
This book was published on-demand in cooperation with Trafford Publishing. On-demand publishing is a unique process and service of making a book available for retail sale to the public taking advantage of on-demand manufacturing and Internet marketing. On-demand publishing includes promotions, retail sales, manufacturing, order fulfilment, accounting and collecting royalties on behalf of the author.

Book sales for North America and international:
Trafford Publishing, 6E–2333 Government St., Victoria, BC v8t 4p4 CANADA
phone 250 383 6864 (toll-free 1 888 232 4444)
fax 250 383 6804; email to orders@trafford.com
Book sales in Europe:
Trafford Publishing (uk) Ltd., Enterprise House, Wistaston Road Business Centre, Wistaston Road, Crewe, Cheshire cw2 7rp United Kingdom
phone 01270 251 396 (local rate 0845 230 9601)
facsimile 01270 254 983; orders.uk@trafford.com
Order online at: trafford.com/05-1099

10 9 8 7 6 5 4 3

DEDICATION

This book is dedicated to Echezona Santiago Orakwue and Deborah Godoy.

To the memory of Stephen, Nelson, Zebnaih, and Elizabeth.

And to the hopes and aspirations of all Foreign Trained Professionals and Skilled Immigrants on the journey to employment in their chosen professions in Canada.

ACKNOWLEDGMENTS

Thanks to all the people who were interviewed during the course of writing this book. Thanks to all Foreign Trained Professionals who shared their experiences, and to professional associations, professional regulatory bodies for offering information and details. Special thanks to all the facilitators at the Center For Foreign Trained Professionals And Tradespeople, Etobicoke (Humber College) for their endeavour in helping hundreds of Foreign Trained Professionals annually.

CONTENTS

PART 2

PART 3

PART 4

PART 5

Author's Note

There is something overwhelmingly romantic about the idea of living and working in Canada. But the romanticism surrender's it's lustre as soon as you step into the ambush and find yourself guilty of the phrase: 'No Canadian Experience'.

The aim of writing this book is to elaborate the most direct and lasting ways to overcome the most formidable barrier faced by Foreign Trained Professionals and Skilled Immigrants in Canada, in finding a job in their field of study and or expertise. To arm you—the Foreign Trained Professional and Skilled Immigrant in and or outside of Canada with the most lethal strategy to humiliate the 'beast' "No Canadian Experience" in ambush.

The author is quite aware of the fact that when you purchase this book you undoubtedly expect to find the most authentic and insightful information to overcome the most formidable barrier Foreign Trained Professionals and or Skilled Immigrants encounter on engressing into the Canadian territory.

All the data and information in this book have been

put through an undiscriminating and unsentimental sieve of accuracy and reliability of content. The Author, a Foreign Trained Professional used his first hand encounter with the bully barrier "No Canadian Experience" and insight gained by closely following the plight of other Foreign Trained Professionals and or Skilled Immigrants in weaving this book to equip the reader with all necessary information and facts needed in getting established in your field of expertise in Canada. Some of the information in this book you may not find in official information sources, thus leaving you to figure it out for yourself. By buying this book, you have taken a step in the positive direction to figure things out.

Welcome to this unofficial bank and or bible of information on how to:

The Complete Guide to Overcome 'No Canadian Experience': *How and Where to Obtain 'Canadian Experience'.*

If this book for any reason doesn't provide the solution to your employment related problems as a foreign trained professional in Canada. If this book for all reasons provide you with the most needed guide to overcoming the barriers faced by most foreign trained professionals in Canada. Please contact the author for further suggestions and or to give your testimony.

Contact the author at: Obiorakwue@yahoo.com

Visit: www.Obtaincanadianexperience.com

"There is something overwhelmingly romantic about the idea of living and working in Canada. But the romanticism surrender's it's lustre as soon as you step into the ambush and find yourself guilty of the phrase: 'No Canadian Experience', and sentenced to innumerable hours of 'survival job'".

"A country where being human, is to inherit a life long opportunity for being whatever you want to be. Where those who reach out for excellence are promised and rewarded with a gift of support and success".

"Majority of Foreign Trained Professionals, are into 'survival jobs' because of lack of information, lack of centralized source of information. Coming into a multicultural and on-your-own type of society as Canada, could be intimidating".

"This 'Guide' weaved information related to several fields of expertise in a scrupulous precise format that it is a no-miss 'Bible of Information' for the Foreign Trained Professionals and or Skilled Immigrants in Canada who wants to get into their field of expertise as quickly as possible without going through the rigours of 'survival jobs'".

"Uprooting from home, from the comfort of well established social structure and protection—abandoning family, friends, a cherished knowledge of how the mechanics of things work in your native home to make a leap of faith into a strange land is sheer bravery, courage and adventure. It also takes flexibility, hard work, determination, money, time and emotional upheaval to relocate".

"Whether your hopes are oversize or regular, and you have a normal or extravagant expectation, this scrupulously researched guide book will give you factual guide you need to attain your hopes and expectations without tears. Without seeing the face of the 'beast' christened 'No Canadian Experience'".

"'No Canadian Experience' ambushes you as soon as you set out to search for a job. It dashes your hope of landing a befitting job as quickly as you had expected. But certainly it doesn't land a knockout punch on your focus if you really have one. It is only a barrier you must figure out how to overcome".

"You made a choice to come to Canada to pursue your dreams. And you have a right to success and happiness. All the necessary resources are available, but enforcing what it takes to succeed and be happy rests on you".

"Nowadays, unfortunately your foreign experience and particularly the lack of Canadian experience locks you out from the corporate corridors. And when it doesn't lock you out, which happens very seldom, it attracts you less pay and some measure of professional relegation".

"'No Canadian Experience' as a phrase, is a beast, a monster. A dignity-consuming and deprivative enemy of inclusion"—a South African Chemist.

"'No Canadian Experience' is a bully phrase that labels one

as a professional freak and misfit that needs some kind of rehabilitation and upgrading"—a Pakistani Doctor

"'No Canadian Experience' is a bully phrase that renders the shelf life of ones academic credentials and professional experience obsolete at face value"—a Romanian Engineer.

"'No Canadian Experience' is a very competitive disclaimer. It beats you at your own trade"—a Chinese Acupuncturist.

"'No Canadian Experience' is a faceless bully phrase, an untamed enemy of the Foreign Trained Professional"- an Argentine Agronomist.

"An existential reality that desperately needs to be exterminated from the Canadian corporate workplace"—an Indian Chemical Engineer.

"'No Canadian Experience' is an un-Canadian disclaimer phrase that condemns the Foreign Trained Professionals and Skilled Immigrants to innumerable hours of heart-wrenching 'survival jobs' in the factory floors. It desperately needs to be caged, away from the Canadian corporate corridors"—a Ukrainian Accountant.

"Uno monstro that ambushes most Foreign Trained Professionals on arrival in Canada. It humiliated me in every interview I attended. I can't wait to attend it's funeral"—a Chilean Architect.

"One good thing about the phrase 'No Canadian Experience' is that it is neither vindictive, an enigma nor entirely elusive. It could be put out of your way for good. This guide tells why and how?"

INTRODUCTION

Many atimes professionals come to Canada harbouring hopes and expectations. Hopes that sometimes could be oversize, and extravagant expectations. Hopes are oversize and expectations extravagant when they are not hedged, guided with a real and functional plan. Although hope is good, it is in itself not a strategy. Expectations become extravagant when they are practically unattainable. Whether your hopes are oversize or regular, and you have a normal or extravagant expectation, this scrupulously researched book will give you the factual guide you need to attain your hopes and expectations without tears, without seeing the face of the 'beast' christened "No Canadian Experience".

Who is this book for?

This book is for all Foreign Trained Professionals and Skilled Immigrants on the journey to employment in their chosen professions in Canada. Without going through the frustration, stress, angst and the inevitable self doubt of hearing time and over that he/she has 'No Canadian Experience'—that the shelf life of his/her academic credential and professional experience are obsolete. A lot of foreign trained professionals who arrive in Canada just do not know where and how to start and need help, information and guidance. This book provides you with the most up to date and comprehensive information, help and guidance you may need.

What is the book's approach?

This book is scrupulously direct and factual. It is designed to save you time, stress and money.

What is in this book?

In this book you will find a step-by-step guide to circumvent the barriers, the roadblocks and the deterrents that keep Foreign Trained Professionals from securing a job in their area of expertise within a reasonable time of arriving in Canada.

Steps that will save *you* the doctor from driving a taxi for years before knowing what to do to be able to practice in Canada...

- You the lawyer from being a security guard.
- You the Chemist from stocking shelves in some supermarket.
- You the Engineer from working in the Butchery.
- You the Architect from being a bar tender in some bar.

And all Foreign Trained Professionals and Skilled Immigrants from doing all sorts of survival jobs when it is not necessary.

Why was this book written?

There is something overwhelmingly romantic about the idea of living and working in Canada. But the romanticism surrender's it's lustre as soon as you set out to hunt for a job, and step into the ambush and find yourself guilty of the phrase: 'No Canadian Experience', and sentenced to innumerable hours of tawdry 'survival job' in the factory floor.

It is disturbing to find people who spent years in institutions of higher learning albeit not in Canada and or North America, people who have worked as professionals all their lives, outside Canada and or United States, doing 'survival jobs':

Medical doctors working as security guards, Chemists stocking shelves in some superstores, Lawyers driving taxis, Psychologists working in a grocery stores, Engineers working as general labourers in the factory floors, Accountants cleaning hotel lobbies and washrooms. And much more professionals doing all sorts of 'survival jobs' in various places across Canada as witnessed in the factual fiction book— *Overqualified Labourer: No Canadian Experience.*

Disturbing because you see Talents wasting, Egos bruised, Pride tortured. And worse still you see Canada— "the meeting place", the fastest growing economy of the G-8 nations, the highest standard of living for numerous consecutive years by UNO standards. A country where being human, is to inherit a life long opportunity for being whatever you want to be. Where those who reach out for excellence are promised and rewarded with a gift of support and success. Being projected as an endangered place for the Foreign Trained Professional.

Majority of Foreign Trained Professionals are into 'survival jobs', because of lack of information, lack of centralized source of information. Coming into a multicultural and on-your-own type of society as Canada, could be intimidating.

Additionally, the lack of a centralized bank of information, pinpointing specific information related to a particular field and coordinating several bits of information from the multi channels of information: websites, newspapers, magazines and centers could be daunting especially to someone who is not used to an over-informed Society.

Many Foreign Trained Professionals, who were unable to find jobs in their field of expertise, pack bag and baggage and return to their country of origin after spending years in Canada sentenced to survival jobs. They leave heart broken, sad and undoubtedly with little love left for Canada—a country they once fell in love with, a country of their dreams.

Lack of concise and timely information on the particular line of action to follow on arriving in Canada contributes greatly to the 'angst and frustration' that many Foreign Trained Professionals undergo.

This 'Guide' weaved information related to several fields of expertise in a scrupulously precise format, that it is a no-miss 'Bible of Information' for the Foreign Trained Professionals and or Skilled Immigrants in Canada who wants to get into their field of expertise as quickly as possible without going through the rigours of 'survival jobs'. For that professional who wants to jump all the hurdles he/she is bound to meet on the journey to employment in his/her chosen profession. Who wants to render void, the ambush of, 'No Canadian Experience'.

This book is written to help.

PART 1

1

COMING TO CANADA

Canada admits about 220,000 immigrants every year. A big percentage of these immigrants, about 60%, are highly *education* educated professionals and skilled workers from different countries around the world.

Immigration has been as old as mankind. And people relocate for several reasons that may include planned and forced immigration. Forced immigration may be caused by war, natural disasters, and persecution. But notwithstanding the reason that prompted your emigration, you immigrated because you are the type who doesn't want to keep hanging only onto your inherited culture, language, situation and environment. When you can reach out for the better, more variety and safety.

Uprooting from home, from the comfort of well established social structure and protection—abandoning family, friends, a cherished knowledge of how the mechanics of things work in your native home to make a leap of faith into a strange land is sheer bravery, courage and adventure. It also takes flexibility, hard work, determination, money, time and emotional upheaval to relocate.

Most immigrants come from monocultural, monoracial

and sometimes unjust societies to Canada—a multicultural, multiracial, organized, coherent, highly industrialized, just and transparent society of literate culture. Engressing on the Canadian soil, you feel buoyed and satisfied for having accomplished one phase of the dream and or agenda. And satisfaction from ones effort is an essential component of happiness. But arriving in Canada brings you closer to the onset of the struggle than to the end of it.

Some immigrants and professionals come to Canada armed with their academic degrees, foreign experience/expertise, hopes and expectations, sometimes with big, little or no plan. Well, welcome to Canada, a place where being human is to inherit a lifelong opportunity for being whatever you want to be. A place where those who reach out for excellence are promised and rewarded with the gift of support and success.

You made a choice to come to Canada to pursue your dreams. And you have a right to success and happiness. All the necessary resources are available, but enforcing what it takes to succeed and be happy rests on you. And that is why you must have a sustainable action plan.

Preliminary challenges you may encounter on coming to Canada may include:

- New Environment—Personal adjustments
- Climate
- Language—if you are not from English or French speaking Country
- Settling

But armed with determination and excellent guide, you are bound to overcome all challenges.

2

LANGUAGE

If you do not speak English or French, language will be the first challenge you will face in Canada because most things you will do on hourly and daily bases have to be expressed in words, verbal or written.

Most Immigrant settlement Agencies listed below under **settling** offer English as Second Language course (ESL) and French as a second language (FSL). Another program that offer English and French is the Language Instruction for Newcomers (LINC).

In British Columbia the program is called English Language Services for Adults (ELSA) and Francisation in Quebec.

The program is offered in Colleges and Institutes around Canada. Studying English/French in Colleges and Institutes is very advantageous because it exposes the participant to career/technical/diploma/degree programs offered in the College or Institute. And the participants may pursue any of the programs after the language program.

The following is a list of provinces and Colleges that offer LINC.

- **Alberta—LINC**
  Bow Valley College, Calgary
  Norquest College, Edmonton

- **British Columbia—ELSA**
  Camosun College, Victoria
  Northwest Community College, Terrace
  Vancouver Community College, Vancouver
  North Island College, Courtenay

- **Ontario—LINC**
  Algonquin College, Ottawa
  Centennial College, Toronto
  Mohawk College, Hamilton
  Sir Sanford Fleming College, Peterborough

- **Quebec—Francisation**
  Cegep du Vieux-Montreal, Montreal
  Cegep Andre-Laurendeau, Montreal
  Cegep Maria-Victorin, Montreal
  Cegep de Saint-Laurent, Saint-Laurent
  College de Bois-de-Boulogne, Montreal

- **Prince Edward Island—LINC**
  Holland College, Charlottetown

- **Saskatchewan—LINC**
  Saskatchewan Institute of Science and Technology, Regina
  Saskatoon
  Cypress Hills Regional College, Swift Current

Settling

There are numerous community settlement services in Canada in general and Ontario in particular. And you can use any of the agencies nearest to you or located in the community you will like to settle.

The following is a list of some Community Settlement Agencies:

- **Ontario (Toronto)**

  Ontario Council of Agencies Serving Immigrants (OCASI)
  110 Eglinton Avenue West, Suite 200
  Toronto, On
  M4R 1A3
  Phone: 416-322 4950 ext. 227
  Email: generalmail@ocasi.org
  Website: www.ocasi.org

  COSTI Immigrant Services
  Offices in Toronto includes:
  1710 Dufferin Street,
  Toronto, On
  M6E 3P2
  Phone: 416- 658-1600

  1700 Wilson Ave, Suite 114
  Toronto, On
  M3L 1B2
  Phone: 416- 244-0379

  700 Caledonia Road at Eglinton Ave W
  Toronto, On
  M6B 3X7
  Phone: 416- 789-7925

For information about COSTI services in other communities, visit the COSTI Website at: www.costi.org

- Settlement.Org
  Website: www.settlement.org/

- Canadian Ukrainian Immigrant Aid Society
  2150 Bloor Street West, Suite 96
  Toronto, On
  M6S 1M8
  Phone: 416-767-4595

- Arab Community Center of Ontario
  4002 Sheppard Avenue East, Suite 501
  Scarborough, On
  M1S 4R5
  Phone: 416-299-8118

  1 Resurrection Road, Toronto
  Phone: 416-533-3292

  5468 Dundas Street West, Suite 324
  Etobicoke
  Phone: 416-231-7746

- Afghan Association of Ontario
  28 Pemican Court, Unit 6
  North York, On
  M9M 2Z3
  Phone: 416- 744-6671

- Catholic Cross-Culture Services
  780 Birchmount Road, Unit 11
  Toronto, On
  M1K 5H4
  Phone: 416-644-0816

- Center for Information & Community Services of Ontario
  58 Cecil Street at Spadina
  Toronto, On
  M5T 1N6
  Phone: 416-598-2022

- Center for Spanish Speaking People (CSSP)
  2141 Jane Street, 2nd Floor
  Toronto, On
  M3M 1A2
  Phone: 416-533-5731

- Center for Francophone de Toronto Metropolitain (CFTM)
  20 Lower Spadina Avenue
  Toronto, On
  M5V 2Z1
  Phone: 416-203-1220

- Ethiopian Association in Toronto
  2064 Danforth Avenue
  Toronto, On
  M4C 1J8
  Phone: 416-694-1522

- Jamaican Canadian Association
  995 Arrow Road
  North York, On
  M9M 2Z5
  Phone: 416-746-5772

- Jewish Immigrant Aid Services Toronto
  4600 Bathurst Street, Suite 325
  Willowdale, On
  M2R 3V3
  Phone: 416-630-6481

- Midaynta Association of Somali Service Agencies
  1992 Yonge Street, Suite 203
  Toronto, On
  M4S 1Z8
  Phone: 416-544-1992

- Skills for Change
  791 St. Clair Ave. West
  Toronto, On
  M6C 1B8
  Phone: 416-658-3101

- South Asian Women's Center
  1332 Bloor St. west
  Toronto, On
  M6H 1P2
  Phone: 416-537-2276

- Toronto Chinese Community Services Association
  721 Bloor St. West, Suite 303
  Toronto, On
  M6G 1L5
  Phone: 416-538-9412

- Vietnamese Association Toronto
  1364 Dundas St. West
  Toronto, On
  M6J 1Y2
  Phone: 416-536-3611

- YMCA- Korean Community Services
  721 Bloor St. west., Suite 303
  Toronto, On
  M6G 1L5
  Phone: 416538-9412

For more Information visit the Website at www.atwork. settlement.org

British Columbia (Vancouver)
- Abbotsford Community Services
  2420 Montrose Avenue
  Abbotsford, B.C. V2S 3S9
  Phone: 604-859-7681
  Website: www.abbotsfordcommunityservices.com/

- Immigrant Services Society of British Columbia
  501—333 Terminal Avenue
  Vancouver, B.C. V6A 2L7
  Phone: 604 684-2561
  Website: www.issbc.org

- Burnaby Multicultural Society
  6255 Nelson Avenue
  Burnaby, B.C. V5H 4T5
  Phone: 604- 431-4131
  Website: www.bby-multicultural.ca/

- Challiwack Community Services
  46293 Yale Road
  Chilliwack, B.C V2P 2P7
  Phone: 604-792-7376
  Website; www.comserv.bc.ca/

- SUCCESS Richmond Office
  220—7000 Minoru Blvd.
  Richmond, B.C. V6Y 3Z5
  Phone: 604-279-7160
  Website; www.rmcs.bc.ca

For more information on settlement services in British Columbia (Vancouver) visit the Website: www.mcaws.gov. bc.ca/

Other Immigrant Service Agencies in BC includes:
- Central Vancouver Island Multicultural Society— Nanaimo

- Inland Refugee Society of BC—Vancouver
- Inter-Cultural Association of Greater Victoria
- Mennonite Central Committee—BC—Vancouver and the Fraser Valley
- MOSAIC (Multilingual Orientation Services Association for Immigrant Communities)
- Options: Services to Community Society—Surrey
- Pacific Immigrant Resources Society—Vancouver
- Progressive Inter-Cultural Community Services Society—Surrey
- SUCCESS—United Chinese Community Enrichment Services Society—Vancouver
- Surrey Delta Immigrant Society—Surrey
- Vernon & District Immigrant Services Society.

Nova Scotia (Halifax)
- Metropolitan Immigrant Settlement Association
  7105 Chebucto Road, Suite 201
  Halifax, NS, B3L 4W8
  Phone: 902-423-3607
  Fax: 902-423-315
  Email: Info@misa.ns.ca
  Website: www.misa.ns.ca

Alberta
- Alberta Association of Immigrant Serving Agencies
  3rd Floor, 120-17 Avenue S. W.
  Calgary, Alberta
  T2S 2T2
  Phone: 403-290 5763
  Fax: 403- 262-2033
  Email: contact@aaisa.ca
  Website: www.aaisa.ca

- Brooks Global Friendship Immigrant Center
  2nd Floor, 120 –1st Avenue East

Brooks, Alberta
TIR 1C5
Phone: 403-362 6115
Fax: 403-362-6337
Email: gfic@monarch.net

Calgary

*   Calgary Bridge Foundation for Youth
    #201, 1112B—40 Avenue N .E.
    Calgary, Alberta
    T2E 5T8
    Phone: 403- 230- 7745
    Fax; 403- 230- 7745
    Email: yeecalgary@hotmail.com

*   Calgary Catholic Immigration Society
    3rd Floor, 120—17 Avenue, S. W.
    Calgary, Alberta
    T2S 2T2
    Phone: 403- 262- 2006
    Fax: 403- 262- 2033
    Email: contact@ccis-calgary.ab.ca
    Website: www.ccis-calgary.ab.ca

*   Calgary Immigrant Aid Society
    12th Floor, 910- 7 Avenue, S. W.
    Calgary, Alberta
    T2P 3N8
    Phone: 403-265-1120
    Fax: 403-266-2486
    Email: info@calgaryimmigrantaid.ca
    Website: www.calgaryimmigrantaid.ca/

*   Calgary Immigrant Women's Association
    #200, 138-4th Avenue S. E.
    Calgary, Alberta

T2G 4Z6
Phone: 403-263-4414
Fax: 403-264- 3914
Email: general@ciwa-online.com
Website: www.ciwa-online.com

• Calgary Mennonite Center for Newcomers
#125, 920- 36th Street N.E.
Calgary, Alberta
T2A 6L8
Phone: 403-569-3325
Fax: 403-248-5041
Email: newcomer@cmcn.ab.ca
Website: www.cmcn.ab.ca/

Edmonton
• ASSIST Community Services Center
9653- 105A Avenue
Edmonton, Alberta
T5H 0M3
Phone: 780-429-3111
Fax: 780-424-7837
Website: www.telusplanet.net/public/eccsc/
english/main.htm

• Catholic Social Services
10709—105 Street
Edmonton, Alberta
T5H 2X3
Phone: 780-424-3545
Fax: 780-425-6627
Website: www.catholicsocialservices.ab.ca/

• Changing Together—A Center for immigrant
Women
3rd Floor, 10010—105 Street

Edmonton, Alberta
T5J 1C4
Phone: 780-421-0175
Fax: 780-426-2225
Email: changing@interbaun.com
Website: www.changingtogether.com/

- Edmonton Immigrant Services Association
Suite 201, 10720—113 Street
Edmonton, Alberta
T5H 3H8
Phone: 780-474-8445
Fax: 780-477-0883
Email: eisa@compusmart.ab.ca
Website: www.compusmart.ab.ca/eisa/

- Edmonton Mennonite Center for Newcomers
101, 10010—107A Avenue
Edmonton, Alberta
T5H 4H8
Phone: 780- 424-7709
Fax: 780-424- 7736
Email: mcnedm@emcn.ab.ca
Website: www.emcn.ab.ca

3

PLANNING

You need an Action Plan

Planning has always been the key to success. Everybody understand and cherishes the importance of planning, but unfortunately not everyone has the discipline and wisdom of spending quality time to layout an action plan, even when the consequence of not planning is imminent and inevitable.

"When you fail to plan. You are planning to fail"

And nothing fails like failure while nothing succeeds like success. Failure has the most ugly face under the sun, while success has the most beautiful and attractive face. Though when intelligent people fail, it offers them a window of opportunity to sit back to re-evaluate and readjust. But the time it takes to ignore planning, the eventual failure caused by not planning, to recollect, re-evaluate and readjust and set out to conquer may be enormous and sometimes devastating.

In all, don't wait to fail before succeeding. Rise early and start succeeding and succeed all the way.

Some people often confuse hope with strategy. Hope and expectation alone are not strategies. But hope armed with a good and functional plan is a lethal strategy. Remember, your plan must be functional. It is not enough to have a plan. A plan must be functional to morph into success.

Importance of Planning

a. **Set Goals**
When we plan, we set goals. Goals add purpose and direction to our lives. Your goals help you stay on course. And when we set goals we adhere to our plans to achieve our goals.

b. **Planning gives you structure:**
Having structure is like being set to go. It's being ready, it's being prepared, and nothing substitutes preparation.

c. **Time Management:**
When you plan, you are simply allotting tasks to every bit of your time. And your time is therefore used judiciously. Judicious usage of time increases productivity.

d. **Staying Positive**
Planning makes you stay upbeat. And being positive is an important employable component in overcoming barriers, and hitting targets.

e. **Dissecting the Pros and Cons.**
While in the process of planning, you will stumble into things that are pro and against your plan. Understanding the positives and negatives of your game plan is to acknowledge where you are coming from, where you are, where you are headed, and you never get confused or lost along the way.

f. **Purpose, Control, Focus**
The sense of purpose and control has always been

an indispensable ingredient of having a clear focus. It keeps your eyes on the target.

g. **Stress Reduction**
Work related stress has been blamed for up to 60% of under-productivity. But when you have structure, manage your time effectively, acknowledges the pros and cons of your action plan and knows where and why all your negatives are coming. When you have a goal and reduced sense of uncertainty. When you possess purpose and control, and invariably a sense of accomplishment. You obviously will keep stress at bay.

Undoubtedly before most immigrants and especially professionals leave their native country where they are well rooted to pursue their dreams in Canada, they have a vision, hope, expectations, and sometimes a plan, hopes and expectations centered on finding a job in their fields of expertise. And they often have an idea of where and how to go about it: Search for jobs in the Companies, Businesses, Industries related to their fields of study.

Some immigrants know that it will not be a roller coaster and as such must have envisioned some sort of barriers, but little do most of the immigrants think and or know about the heavy weight barrier christened 'No Canadian Experience'- a barrier that acts best in ambush.

People, especially victims of the phrase, have described this phrase as bigoted, snobbery and xenophobic. We will get to the meaning of this phrase in detail later on.

"No Canadian Experience" ambushes you as soon as you set out to search for a job. It dashes your hope of landing a befitting job as quickly as you had expected. But certainly it doesn't land a knockout punch on your focus if you really have one.

It is only a barrier you must figure out how to overcome.

4

HUNTING FOR A JOB

Job search is a skill and you need to acquire this skill in other to have an effective job search. There are many job search centers where you will acquire job search skills and knowledge as they are related to Canadian employment and business practices.

Some of the skills you will learn from the centers include the following:

Resume Writing

A resume is a summary of your education and training, professional experience, work history, technical and soft skills, accomplishments, interests and activities/hobbies as they relate to the job position you are targeting.

In Canada when you set out to search for a job, you must have a resume. The main purpose of writing and sending out a resume is to attract an interview. And sometimes the Professionals that finally secure a particular job may not be the best brain for the job, but rather the ones that presented the best resumes and subsequently the best interview skills.

Resumes help to give you a competitive edge because it demonstrates that you are prepared about the job. It is the preliminary step of marketing yourself and abilities to your employer. At job search centers and organizations listed in this chapter, you will be taught the art of resume writing.

Cover Letter

A cover letter is a letter to be sent with your resume and must be addressed to the person who is hiring. Cover letters stipulates particular information about your experience, achievements that relates to the establishment and the job in question.

References

References are the people who will attest to the qualities, abilities and experiences stated in your resume, and or during interview.

We have different types of References:

Character Reference, Personal Reference, Professional Reference

Letters of Reference

A letter of reference is a written attestation from previous employers or a person who knows you well.

Thank you letter

Thank you letters are sent after an interview or a contact.

Business cards

Interview skills

Interview preparation

Follow up letter

A follow up letter is a letter sent after making some form of contact with a person.

Labour Market

National Occupation Classification

Goal Setting

Academic Credentials Assessment

Networking

Networking is the act of making and establishing contacts and exchanging information for the purpose of career advancement. It is the most effective tool of job searching and securing a job in Canada and elsewhere in the world. Truly, whom you know, fetches you jobs much more easier than what you know.

Developing job leads

Hidden job market

About 80% of jobs are not advertised. They are said to be in the hidden job market.

Directories

Developing telephone script

Cold Calls

Making contact with a company, organization and a person through telephone, email, and letter or in person, without prior introduction, invitation, or referral is called Cold Call.

Accepting a job offer

Some Job Search Centers include the following:

- Skills For Change
  791 St. Clair Ave W.
  (St. Clair & Christie)
  Phone: 416-658-3101
  Website: www.skillsforchange.ca

- CanWorkNet
  Website: www.workinfonet.ca/

- COSTI Immigration Services
  Website: www.costi.org

- ONESTEP Links
  Website: www.onestep.on.ca

- Center For Foreign Trained Professionals And
  Tradespeople—Etobicoke
  Phone: 416-745-0281
  Fax: 416-745-5718
  E-mail: cftpt.etobicoke@humber.ca
  Website: www.cftpt.org

- Center for Foreign Trained Professionals and
  Tradespeople—Caledonia
  Address: 700 Caledonia Road
  (Caledonia & Glencairn)
  Phone: 416-789-3420

- ACCES—Toronto
  489 College Street, Suite 100
  Toronto, On
  M6G 1A5
  Phone: 416- 921-1800

- ACCES—Scarborough
  2100 Ellesmere Road, Suite 250
  Scarborough, On
  M1H 3B7
  Phone: 416-431-5326

- Community Microskills Development Center
  1 Vulcan St
  (Martin Grove & Rexdale)
  Phone: 416-247-7181

- Culturelink
  474 Bathurst St. 3rd Floor
  (Bathurst & College)
  Phone: 416-923-4678

- IWJPC
  2221 Yonge St. Suite 201
  Yonge & Eglinton)
  Phone: 416-488-0084

- JVS Toronto
  1280 Finch Ave W
  Suite 607
  (Finch & Keel)
  Phone: 416-661-3010 ext. 303
- Northwood Neighbourhood Services
  2524A Jane St.
  (Jane & Sheppard)
  Phone: 416-748-0788

- Durgham Region Unemployment Help Center
  15 Colborne Street East
  Oshawa, On
  L1G 1M1
  Phone: 905-579-1821

- London Unemployment HelpCenter
  114 Dundas Street, 2nd floor
  London, On
  N6A 1G1
  Phone: 519-439-0501

- Lutherwood-CODA-Guelph
  30 Wyndham Street North
  Guelph, On
  N1h 4E5
  519-822-4141

- Niagara Falls Employment Help Center
  6100 Thorold Stone Road, Unit 7
  Niagara Falls On
  L2J 1A3
  Phone: 905-358-0021

- St. Catherines Unemployed Help Center
  122 B Queenston Street
  St. Catherines, On
  L2R 2Z3
  Phone: 905-685-1353

- The Working Center
  58 Queen Street South
  Kitchener, On
  N2G 1V6
  Phone: 519-743-1151

- Windsor Unemployed Help Center
  6955 Cantelon Drive
  Windsor, On
  N8T 3J9
  Phone: 519-944-4900

Some of the centers listed above may help to find a

co-op placement or an internship, but they are not under any obligation to find you a job. They arm you with all the necessary tools you need to find yourself a job.

For more information, call; 1-888-562-4769 or 416-326-5656

Academic Credentials Assessment Services in Canada includes the following:

Ontario

- World Education Services (WES)
  Address: 45 Charles Street East, Suite 700
  Toronto, Ontario,
  M4Y 1S2
  Phone: 416-972-0070
  Fax: 416- 972-9004
  Toll Free: 866-343-0070 (from outside the 416 area code)
  Email: Ontario@wes.org
  Website: www.wes.org/ca
- Academic Credentials Evaluation Service (ACES)
  York University
  Website: www.yorku.ca/admissions/aces.asp
- Ontario Comparative Education Services
  University of Toronto
  Address: 315 Bloor Street West
  Toronto, On,
  M5S 1A3
  Phone: 416-978-2185
  Fax: 416-978-7022
  www.adm.utoronto.ca/ces/

- **Canadian Information Center For International Credentials**
  Address: No 95 St. Clair Avenue West
  Suite 1106
  Toronto, Ontario

M4V 1N6
Phone: 416-962-9725
Fax: 416-962-2800

- **International Credential Assessment Service of Canada**
  Address: 147 Wyndham Street North, Suite 409
  Guelph, On,
  N1H 4E9
  Phone: 519-763-7282
  Toll Free: 800-321-6021
  Fax: 519-763-6964
  Email: info@icascanada.ca
  Website: www.icascanada.ca/

- **Engineering International-Educational Assessment Program (EIEAP)**
  Address: 180 Elgin Street, Suite 1100
  Ottawa, On,
  K2P 2K3
  Phone: 613- 232-2474
  Fax: 613-230-5759
  Email: evaluation@ccpe.ca
  Website: www.ccpe.ca/

British Columbia
- **International Credential Evaluation Service (ICES)**
  Address: 3700 Willingdon Avenue
  Burnaby, BC,
  V5G 3H2
  Phone: 604-432-8800
  Toll Free: 1-866-434-9197 (from within North America)
  Fax: 604-435-7033
  Email: icesinfo@bcit.ca

Website: www.bcit.ca/ices/

Alberta

- **International Qualifications Assessment Service (IQAS)**
  Alberta Learning
  9th Floor, Sterling Place
  9942-108 Street
  Edmonton, Alberta
  T5K 2J5
  Phone: 780-427-2655
  Toll Free: 310-0000 ext. 427-2655 (within Alberta)
  Website: www.learning.gov.ab.ca/iqas/iqas.asp

Quebec

- **Service des Evaluations Comparatives (SEC)**
  Centre de reconnaissance des formations et des competences
  Ministere des Relations avec les citoyens et de l'Immigration
  255, boulevard Cremazie Est, 8e etage
  Montreal (Quebec)
  H2M 1M2
  Phone: 514-864-9191 ou 877-264-6164
  Fax: 514-873-8701
  Email: equivalences@mrci.gouv.qc.ca
  Website: www.immigration-quebec.gouc.qc.ca/anglais/edcation/educational-report.html

Manitoba

- **Academic Credentials Assessment Service-Manitoba (ACAS)**
  Manitoba Labour and Immigration
  Settlement & Labour Market Services Branch
  213 Notre Dame Avenue

Winnipeg, Manitoba
R3B 1N3
Phone: 204-945-6300
Fax: 204-948-2148
Email: glloyd@gov.mb.ca
Website: www.gov.mb.ca.labour.immigrate/
newcomerservices/7a.html

Northwest territories
• **International Qualifications Assessment Service**
Alberta Learning
9th Floor, Sterling Place
9942- 108 Street
Edmonton, Alberta
T5K 2J5
Phone: 780-427-2655
Toll Free: 1-866-692-7057 (within the Northwest
Territories)
Website: www.learning.gov.ab.ca/iqas/iqas.asp

Saskatchewan
• **International Qualifications Assessment Service**
Alberta Learning
9th Floor, Sterling Place
9942- 108 Street
Edmonton, Alberta
T5K 2J5
Phone: 780-427-2655
Toll Free: 1-866-692-7057 (within the Northwest
Territories)
Website: www.learning.gov.ab.ca/iqas/iqas.asp

The Provinces of Northwest Territories and Saskatchewan
provide this service through an inter-provincial agreement
with the Province of Alberta.
Other Provinces including: New Brunswick,

Newfoundland and Labrador, Nova Scotia, Prince Edward Island, Nunavut, and Yukon provide the academic assessment service by using the services of any of the above mentioned centers.

It is important to note at this point that the service provided by the above mentioned Assessment Centers is in accordance with the General Guiding Principles for Good Practice in the assessment of Foreign Credentials and the Recommendation on Criteria and Procedures for the Assessment of Foreign Qualifications adopted under the 1997 Lisbon Recognition Convention.

However, if for any reason you wish to challenge the assessment given to your credential, there is an Appeal Process for such challenges.

Contact Canadian Information Center For International Credentials for advise on such Appeal Process, and for more information about International Academic Credentials Assessment:

- **Canadian Information Center For International Credentials**
  95 St. Clair Avenue West, Suite 1106
  Toronto, On
  M4V 1N6
  Phone: 416-962-9725
  Fax: 416-962-2800

The centers listed above evaluate your academic credentials for employment and educational purposes only. It is important to note that the bodies do not evaluate non-academic credentials obtained from professional organizations.

The following is the list of some Network Organizations/Groups:

- Canadian Associations list
  Website: www.canadainfo.com/associations.html

- Maclean's Career Forum:
  Website: www.canoe.ca/macleans/linkup/
  forumsetup.html
- The Ontario Network for International
  Professional Online
  Website: www.onip.ca
- National Business Employment Forum
  Website: www.nbew.com/forum
- Netjobs Links and Resources
  Website: www.netjobs.com:800/sefuljob.html
- Chatelaine sources (networking for women)
  Website: www.canoe.ca/chatelainedestinationswork
  /home.html
- Links to job-related Newsgroups
  Website: www.netjobs.com:8000/jwnews.html
- Toronto Board of Trade
- EARN Networking Group
  Website: http://web.idirect.com/-earn/
- ConnectUs Communications Canada
  Website: www.connectuscanada.com
- Management Accountants Discussion Group
  Website: www.purdyswharf.com/cma
- Liszt- communicate via email on various topics
  Website: www.liszt.com
- Canadian women Internet Association
  Website: www.women.ca
- Creando Puentes—Hispanic Women Network
  Website: www.creandopuentes.net
  www.hispanicwomennetwork.com
- Girls International
  Website: www.webgrrls.com
- Deja News- News-Group Listings
  Website: www.dejanews.com
- New Experiences For Newcomer Women—N.E.W
  745 Danforth Avenue, Suite 401

Toronto, On
M4J 1L4
Phone: 416-469-0196

The following is a list of Directories

- Yellow Pages
- Ontario Business Directory
- Canadian Key Business Directory
- Duns Regional Business Directory, Toronto—(has 3 volumes)
- Blue Book of Canadian business
- The Dunn &Bradstreet National Directory of Canadian Service Companies

General Manufacturing Directories:

- Canadian Trade Index
- Fraser's Canadian Trade directory
- Metropolitan Toronto, Ontario, Atlantic, Western, Quebec
- Scott's Industrial directories
- B.O.S.S Products and Companies (Business Opportunities Sourcing System)

General and Special Guides and Directories

- Consulting Engineers of Canada/Consulting engineers of Ontario
- Canada's Money Managers
- Career Directory/Financial Post 500
- Directory of Canadian Associations
- Advanced Technology Companies in Greater Metropolitan Toronto
- Directory of Community Services in Metropolitan Toronto
- Who's Who in Super Sites—LAN Installation + MIS Manager
- Directory of Retail Chains
- Canadian Wholesale Drug Association

Membership Directory
- Directory of Canadian Management Consultants
- Directory of Automotive & Automotive Parts Manufacturing in Greater Toronto
- General Insurance Register
- Guide to Toronto Regions Top Employers
- Who is Hiring
- Directory of Toronto Area Business recruiters
- Guide to the Canadian Financial Services Industry—(Stocks, Bonds, Trust, Credit Union)
- Directory of Canadian Marketing Research Organizations

Job Information From Government Sources:
- Federal Government
  Public service Commission
  Address: No 1 Front Street West
  Toronto, Ontario
  M5J 2X5
  Program and services
  Phone: 1-800-667-3355
  Job Information Line
  Phone: 416-973-4636
  Website: www.jobs.gov.ca
  Website: www.psc-cfp.gc.ca/recruit/dtoe.htm
- Provincial Government—Ontario
  Queen's Park
  Human Resources
  Address: No 25 Grosvernor Street, (17th Floor)
  Toronto, Ontario
  Employment information Line
  Phone: 416- 326-1234
  Website: www.gojobs.gov.on.ca
- Municipal Government—City of Toronto
  Metro Hall
  Employment Services, Metro Hall, (5th Floor)

55 John Street, Toronto, On
M5V 3C6
Employment information Line
Phone: 416- 392-8665
Fax: 416-397-9818

The Following is a List of other Information Line for Job Lead

- Canada Post Information Line
  416-462-5200
- Nestle Canada Human Resources Staffing Line
  416-218-3030 ext.
- North York General Hospital Employment Center
  416-756-6732
- E.A.R.N—Executive for Advanced Resource Network
  416-466-6891
- Epson Job Hotline (Epson is a Computer Printer manufacturer)
  1-800-822-0313
- IBM Canada Limited—Employment Enquiry Line
  905-316-2000
- Human Resources Development Canada
  416 954-5107
- City of Toronto Job Hotline
  416-392 8665
- Federal Government Job Hotline
  416-073-4636
- Regional Municipality of Peel Employment Hotline
  905-791-7800 ext.5510
- Regional Municipality of Halton Employment Hotline
  905-825-6202
- National Life Insurance Employment Information Line

    416-585-8090
- Metro Toronto Police Job Hotline
  416-808-7134
- Rogers Cable Human Resources External Hotline
  416-446-6512
- Holiday Inn Toronto Airport Job Opportunity Hotline
  416-674-4390
- Club Monaco Career Information Hotline
  416-585-4896
- Business Deport /Staples Human Resources Info Line
  905-678-4200 ext.: 4203
- Apotex
- Pfizer
- Air Canada
- Wal-Mart

Other Places You Can Turn To For Job Search
- ACCES—Toronto
  No 489 College Street, Suite 100
  Toronto, On
  M6G 1A5
  Phone: 416-921-1800
- ACCES—Scarborough
  No 2100 Ellesmere Road, Suite 250
  Scarborough On, M1H 3B7
  Phone: 416- 431-5326
- COSTI—Caledonia
  No 700 Caledonia Road
  Toronto, On, M6B 4H9
  Phone: 416-789-7925
- COSTI—Vaughan
  No 7800 Jane Street, Unit 1
  Concord On, L4K 4R6

Phone: 905-669-5627
- Durham Region Unemployed Help Center
  No 15 Colborne Street East
  Oshawa On, L1G 1M1
  Phone: 905-579-1821
- London Unemployment Help Center
  No 114 Dundas Street, 2nd Floor
  London On, N6A 1G1
  Phone: 519-439-0501
- Lutherwood-CODA—Guelph
  No 30 Wyndham Street North
  Guelph On, N1H 4E5
  Phone: 519-822-4141
- Niagara Falls Employment Help Center
  6100 Thorold Stone Road, Unit
  Niagara Falls, On, L2J 1A3
  Phone: 905-358-0021
- St. Catharines Unemployment Help Center
  No 122 B Queenston Street
  St. Catharines On, L2R 2Z3
  Phone: 905-685-1353
- The Working Center
  No 58 Queen Street South
  Kitchener, On, N2G 1V6
  Phone: 519- 743-1151
- Windsor Unemployed Help Center
  No 6955 Cantelon Drive
  Windsor, On, N8T 3J9
  Phone: 519-944-4900

Some Websites For Job Leads
University And College Career Service/Employment Related Sites:
- University of Toronto Career Center
  Website: www.utoronto.ca/career

- York University Career Center
  Website: www.yorku.ca/admin/careers
- University of Guelph Career Center
  Website: www.uoguelph.ca/career
- University of Western Ontario Career Center
  Website: www.uwo.ca/career
- Ryerson University Career Center
  Website: www.ryerson.ca/career
- Queens University Career Center
  Website: www.career.queensu.ca
- University of British Columbia Career Center
  Website: www.ubc.ca/career
- University of Alberta Career Center
  Website: www.ualberta.ca/CAPS/
- Humber College Career Services
  Website: www.admin.humber.on.ca:80/-careerc/
- Seneca College Career Center
  Website: www.senecacareerlink.com
- George Brown College Career Center
  Sheridan College Career Center
- Website: www.sheridanc.on.ca/career
  www.campusaccess.com

Services you will get from the above Colleges and Universities Career centers include:

Assisted job searches, resume/cover letter advice, career counseling, interview tips, internet access, information on internships, co-op, volunteer work, job postings within the schools and or from outside employers that call/fax/email job positions in their companies that need to be filled.

Federal And Provincial Government Sites

- Public Service Commission
  Website: www.psc-cfp.gc.ca/recruit/jobse.htm
- HDRC National Job Bank
  Website: www.jb-ge.hdrc-drhc.gc.ca

- Work Search Canada
  Website: www.worksearch.gc.ca
- Canada WorkInfoNet
  Website: www.workinfonet.ca
- Workwire
  Website: www.workwire.com

City Government sites
- City of Toronto
  Website: www.city.toronto.on.ca
  www.metrotor.on.ca
- City of North York
  Website: www.city.north-york.ca
- Etobicoke Business Development
  Website: www.busdev.city.etobicoke.on.ca
- Mississauga
  Website: www.city.mississauga.on.ca/home.html
- City of Brampton
  Website: www.city.brampton.on.ca
- City of Scarborough
  Website: www.city.scarborough.on.ca
- City of Vaughan
  Website: www.city.vaughan.on.ca
- City of Oakville
  Website: www.town.oakville.on.ca
- Burlinghton
  Website: www.city.burlinghton.on.ca

Newspaper Websites
- The Globe and Mail
  Website: www.theglobeandmail.com/
  careerconnect/globe
- The Toronto Star
  Website: www.thestar.com/thestar/classified/
  plmonster.html
- National Business Employment Weekly

Website: www.nbew.com

Library Sites
- **Metro Toronto Reference Library**
  Website: www.mtrl.toronto.on.ca
- North York Public Library
  Website: www.nypl.north.york.on.ca

Now you have graduated from the job search centers. Armed with every necessary skills and information to secure a job. But something, a bully still stands between you and your dream job. A bully christened 'No Canadian Experience'— the most formidable of all roadblocks to securing a job in Canada as a Foreign Trained Professional.

PART 2

5

ROADBLOCKS/BARRIERS
TO SECURING A JOB

Canadian Corporate Culture

The corporate culture of different regions and countries differ. For example, the corporate culture of Asian countries like Japan, China, Indonesia, Malaysia, Singapore, India, Pakistan and others differ from the corporate cultures of countries in East Europe, West Europe, North America, South America, Central America, Africa and the Caribbean.

You may have the expertise for a position in a company but if you don't fit into the corporate culture of the company, you are bound to be shown the way out. Being in the corporate corridors of a country and or region imbibes one with the corporate culture of such a place. Having the corporate culture of Canada is part of having the elusive Canadian Experience. Sometimes when employers say you don't have Canadian Experience, they are afraid you may not fit into the corporate culture of the company.

License

Being unlicensed and or not registered to practice a profession could be another barrier to getting a job in Canada in general, and Ontario particularly. Regulated professions are the professions that are regulated by the national, regional and or provincial regulatory laws and are regulated by their respective professional bodies. The professional bodies act in accordance with the provincial laws. Laws established by the provincial government are meant to maintain a certain level of standard and competence to protect the public. The professions that fall within the regulatory laws and licensing are called regulated professions. It is noteworthy to know that it is not only illegal to practice in a regulated profession without first registering with the appropriate body and getting licensed but it may also be illegal to use the title of the profession without proper registration and licensing. To practice in a regulated profession in Canada and in Ontario particularly, you have to apply to the regulatory body of such profession, pay the necessary registration fee and submit all credentials and or documents required for licensing. The Registration Committee of such a body will evaluate your credentials/qualifications and make a decision. And if they are satisfied with it and subsequently issue a positive evaluation decision, then you are qualified to take a certification/qualifying/registration examination. If you successfully write and pass the examination, the body will:

    a.   License

    b.   Register

    c.   Certify

You to practice.

There are some other professions that are not regulated by law, but may have a professional body. And the professional body offers certification courses and registration. But you are not obliged by any law to be a member of such professional body, though getting certified and licensed by such a professional body may give you more professional clout and credibility to find a job and to practice.

It is important to note at this point that no single body regulates all the professions. Rather each and every profession has its own professional and regulatory body.

The Task Of Professional Bodies

The provincial regulatory laws armed the professional bodies with the authority to:

- a. Assess/evaluate professional qualifications and academic credentials including: theoretical, practical and general experience.
- b. Offer provisional license and or certificate of registration/certification when need be.
- c. Register and certify qualified applicants
- d. Offer advise about upgrading courses and or programs to professionals that they deem not qualified enough to sit for the certification/ qualifying/registration examinations
- e. Offer certification/registration/qualifying examination where necessary.
- f. Set entry and training requirements
- g. Set standards of practice
- h. Discipline members when need be

Registering with a Professional Regulatory Body

The process of registering with a professional regulatory body takes time and money. The time and money it takes may vary depending on the profession and the professional body. The process of registration may also vary depending on the province. It is therefore very important that you check with the respective professional regulatory body in the province you want to practice, before you set out to register. In cases where the documents/credentials required by the professional body is not originally issued in English or French, you may need to translate such a document into English and or French, and have a notary public or a lawyer notarize it.

To translate your document, you may need the services of a community settlement agency and or the services of an accredited private translation agency.

Check to see the community settlement agency nearest to you. (See Chapter 2)

The following Associations may help you with a list of accredited translators

- **Association of Translators and Interpreters of Ontario (ATIO)**
  Phone: 613-241-2846
  Toll free: 1-800-234-5030
  Website: www.atio.on.ca

- **Association of Translators and Interpreters of Manitoba (ATIM)**
  200 Ave de la Cathedrale, BOX 83
  Winnipeg, Manitoba
  R2H 0H7
  Phone: 204-797-3247
  Email: info@atim.mb.ca
  Website: www.atim.mb.ca

- **Association of Translators and Interpreters of Alberta (ATIA)**
  P.O.BOX 546
  Main Post Office
  Edmonton AB
  T5J 2K8
  Phone: 780-434-8384
  Website: www.atia.ab.ca

- **Society of Translators and Interpreters of British Columbia (STIBC)**
  Website: www.stibc.org

- **Translators and Interpreters Association of**

Quebec
Ordre des Traducteurs et Interpretes Agrees du Quebec (OTIAQ)
Website: www.otiaq.org
- **Association of Visual Language Interpreters of Canada**
  Website: www.avlic.ca
- **Association of Translators and Interpreters of Saskatchewan (ATISK)**
  Website: www.atis-sk.ca

The following is a list of some private translation agencies:
- Translators Café.Com
  1425 Bodmin Road, Suite 407
  Mississauga, On
  L5J 3T4
  Phone: 905-823-2156
  Fax; 905-823-2156
  Email: Info@translatorscafe.com
  Website: www.translatorscafe.com
- Transnet Multilingual services
  43—19034 Mcmyn Road
  Pih Meadows,
  Vancouver, B.C
  V3Y 2N8
  Phone: 604-460-8677
  Fax: 604-4608675
  Email: transnet@idmail.com

Depending on the profession and the regulatory body, after submitting you documents and completed application form you may be required to:
- Submit a resume outlining your work experience
- Write professional examination(s)
- Take some training/upgrading courses

The examination(s) is mostly conducted in English language.

The Following is a List of Regulated Professions and the respective Regulatory Bodies:

- **Ontario**
  a. Architect
  Ontario Association of Architects
  111 Moatfield Drive
  Toronto, On
  M3B 3L6
  Phone: 416-449-6898
  Fax: 416-449-5756
  Email: oaamail@oaa.on.ca
  Website: www.oaa.on.ca
  b. Audiologist and Speech Patholigist
  College of Audiologists and Speech-Language pathologists of Ontario
  160 Bloor Street East, Suit 1125
  Toronto, On
  M4W 1B9
  Phone: 416-975-5347
  Toll Free: 1-800-993-9459
  Fax: 416-975-8394
  Email: saslpo@caslpo.com
  Website: www.caslpo.com
  c. Certified General Accountant
  Certified General Accountants Association of Ontario
  240 Eglinton Avenue East
  Toronto, On
  M4P 1K8
  Phone: 416-322-6520
  Fax: 416-322-6481
  Email: nfo@cga-ontario.org
  Website: www.cga-ontario.org

d. Certified Management Accountant
The Society of Management Accountants of Ontario
70 University Avenue, Suite 300
Toronto, On
M5J 2M4
Phone: 416-977-7741
Fax: 416-977-6079
Email: info@CMA-Ontario.org
Website: www.cma-ontario.org
e. Chartered Accountant
The Institute of Chartered Accountants of Ontario
69 Bloor Street East
Toronto, On
M4W 1B3
Phone: 416-962-1841
Fax: 416-962-8900
Email: custserv@icao.on.ca
Website: www.icao.on.ca

The addresses of the three major National Accounting Organizations in Canada are:

- Canadian Institute of Chartered Accountants (CICA)
  277 Wellinghon Street West
  Toronto, On,
  M5V 3H2
  Phone: 416-977-3222
  Fax: 416- 977-8585
  Email: peter.Wilkinson@cica.ca
  Website: www.cica.ca/
- CGA-Canada
  1188 West Georgia Street, Suite 700
  Vancouver BC,
  V6E 4A2
  Phone: 604-669-3555

Toll Free: I-800-663-1529
Fax: 604-689-5845
Email: public@cga-canada.org
Website: www.cga-online.org/servlet/custom/
publicView?region=ca
• CMA Canada (CMA-Canada)
One Robert Speck Parkway, Suite 1400
Mississauga, On
L4Z 3M3
Phone: 905-949-420Toll Free: 1-800-263-7622
Fax: 905-949-0038
Email: info@cma-canada.crg
Website: www.cma-canada.org/index.cmf.ci_
id/15/la_id/l.htm

For information on the Association of Professional
Accountants and the Regulatory body in other Provinces,
visit the website at: www.cicic.ca/professions/1111en.asp

f. Chiropodist
College of Chiropodists of Ontario
180 Dundas Street West, Suite 2102
Toronto, On
M5G 1Z8
Phone: 416-542-1333
Toll Free: 1-877-232-7653
Fax: 416-542-1666
Email: adminassistant@cocoo.on.ca
Website: www.cocoo.on.ca
g. Chiropractor
College of Chiropractors of Ontario
130 Bloor Street West, Suite 902
Toronto, On
M5S 1N5
Phone: 416-922-6355
Fax; 416-925-9610

Email: cco.info@cco.on.ca
Website: www.cco.on.ca
h. Dental Hygienist
College of Dental Hygienists of Ontario
69 Bloor Street East, Suite 300
Toronto, On
M4W 1A9
Phone: 416-961-6234
Fax: 416-961-6028
Email: deputyregistrar@cdho.org
Website: www.cdho.org
i. Dental Technologist
College of Dental Technologists of Ontario
2100 Ellesmere Road, Suite321
Scarborough, On
M1H 3B7
Phone: 416-438-5003
Toll Free: 1-877-391-2386
Fax: 416-438-5004
Email: info@cdto.ca
Website: www.cdto.ca
j. Dentist
Royal College of Dental Surgeons of Ontario
6 Crescent Road, 5th Floor
Toronto, On
M4W 1T1
Phone: info@rcdso.org
Website: www.rcdso.org
k. Denturist
College of Denturists of Ontario
180 Bloor Street West, Suite 903
Toronto, On
M5S 2V6
Phone: 416-925-6331
Toll Free: 1-888-236-4326

Fax: 416-925-6332
Email: info@denturists-cdo.com
Website: www.denturists-cdo.com
l. Dietitian
College of Dieticians of Ontario
438 University Avenue, Suite 1810
Toronto, On
M5G 2K8
Phone: 416-598-1725
Fax: 416-598-0274
Email: beharis@cdo-on.ca
Website: www.cdo.on.ca
m. Engineer
Professional Engineers of Ontario
25 Sheppard Avenue West, Suite 1000
Toronto, On
M2N 6S9
Phone: 416-224-1100
Toll Free: 1-800-339-3716
Fax: 416-224-8168
Toll free Fax: 1-800-268-0496
Email; webmaster@peo.on.ca
Website: www.peo.on.ca
n. Engineering Technician or Technologist
Ontario Association of Certified Engineering
Technicians & Technologists (OACETT)
10 Four seasons Place, Suite 404
Etobicoke, On
M9B 6H7
Phone: 416-621-9621
Fax: 416-621-8694
Email: info@oacett.org
Website: ww.oacett.org
o. Forester
Ontario Professional Foresters Association

8000 Yonge Street, Unit #3
Innisfil, On
L9S 1L5
Phone: 705-436-2226
Fax: 705-436-1151
Email: opfa@on.aibn.com
Website: www.opfa.on.ca
p. Funeral Director
Board of Funeral Services
777 Bay Street, Suite 2810
Toronto, On
M5G 2C8
Phone: 416-979-5450
Fax: 416-979-0384
Toll Free: 1-800-387-4458
Email: info@funeralboard.com
Website: www.funeralboard.com
q. Geoscientist
Association of Professional Geoscientists of
Ontario
67 Yonge Street, Suite 1500
Toronto, On
Phone: 416-203-2746
Fax: 416-203-6181
Email: info@apgo.net
Website: www.apgo.net
r. Insurance Broker
Registered Insurance Brokers of Ontario
401 Bay street, suite 1200
Toronto, On
M5H 2Y4
Phone: 416-365-1900
Toll Free: 1-800-265-3097
Fax: 416-365-7664
Email: Lillian@ribo.com

Website: www.ribo.com
s. Land Surveyor
Association of Ontario Land Surveyors
1043 McNicoll Avenue
Scarborough, On
M1W 3W6
Phone: 416-491-9020
Fax: 416-491-2576
Email: admin@aols.org
Website: www.aols.org
t. Lawyer
Law Society of Upper Canada
Osgoode Hall, 130 Queen Street West
Toronto, On
M5H 2N6
Phone: 416-947-3300
Toll Free: 1-800-668-7380
Fax: 416-947-5263
Email: lawsociety@lsuc.on.ca
Website: www.lsuc.on.ca
u. Massage Therapist
College of Massage Therapists of Ontario
1867 Yonge Street, Suite 810
Toronto, On
M4S 1Y5
Phone: 416-489-2626
Toll Free: 1-800-465-1933
Fax: 416-489-2625
Email: Registration@cmto.com
Website: www.cmto.com
v. Medical Laboratory Technologist
College of Medical Laboratory Technologists of
Ontario
10 Bay Street, Suite 330
Toronto, On

M5J 2R8
Phone: 416-861-9605
Fax: 416-861-0934
Email: mail@cmlto.com
Website: www.cmlto.com
w. Medical Radiation Technologist
College of Medical Radiation Technologists of
Ontario
170 Bloor Street west, Suite 1001
Toronto, On
M5S 1T9
Phone: 416-975-4353
Toll Free: 1-800-563-5847
Fax: 416-975-4355
Email; igough@cmrto.org
Applicants from abroad: clewis@cmrto.org
Website: www.cmrto.org
**Canadian Association of Medical Radiation
Technologists**
Suite 500—1095 Carling Avenue
Ottawa, On
K1Y 4P6
Phone: 603-234-0012
Toll Free: 1-800-463-9729
Fax: 613-234-1097
Website: www.camrt.ca
x. Midwife
College of Midwives of Ontario
2195 Yonge Street, 4th Floor
Toronto, On
M4S 2B2
Phone: 416-327-0874
Fax: 416- 327-8214
Email; admin@cmo.on.ca
Website: www.cmo.on.ca

y. Nurse
College of Nurses of Ontario
101 Davenport Road
Toronto, On
M5R 3P1
Phone: 416-928-0900 ext. 207
Toll Free: 1-800-387-5526
Fax: 416-928-6507
Email: cno@cnomail.org
Website: www.cno.org
z. Occupational Therapist
College of Occupational Therapists of Ontario
10 Bay Street, Suite 340
Toronto, On
M5J 2R8
Phone: 416-214-1177
Toll Free: 1-800-890-6570
Fax: 416-214-1173
Email: registration@coto.org
Website: www.coto.org
Optician
College of Opticians of Ontario
85 Richmond street West, Suite 902
Toronto, On
M5H 2C9
Phone: 416-368-3616
Toll Free: 1-800-990-9793
Fax: 416-368-2713
Email; ghyland@coptont.org
Website: www.coptont.org
Optometrist
College of Optometrists of Ontario
6 Crescent Road, 3rd Floor
Toronto, On
M4W 1T1

Phone: 416-962-4071
Toll Free; 1-888-825-2554
Fax: 416-962-4073
Email: registration@collegeoptom.on.ca
Website: www.collegeoptom.on.ca
Physiotherapist
College of Physiotherapists of Ontario
230 Richmond Street West, 10th Floor
Toronto, On
M5V 1V6
Phone: 416 591-3828
Toll Free: 1-800-583-5885
Fax: 416- 591-3834
Email: info@collegept.org
Website www.collegept.org
Pharmacist
Council of the Ontario College of Pharmacists
483 Huron Street
Toronto, On
M5R 2R4
Phone: 416- 962-4861
Fax: 416- 703-3100
Email: jmckee@ocpharma.com
Website: www.ocpinfo.com
Physician or Surgeon (Medical Doctors)
College of Physicians and Surgeons of Ontario
80 College Street
Toronto, On
M5G 2E2
Phone: 416-967-2600
Fax: 416-961-3330
Website: www.cpso.on.ca
Psychologist
College of Psychologists of Ontario
1246 Yonge Street, Suite 201

Toronto, On
M4T 1W5
Phone: 416-961-8817
Fax; 416-961-2635
Email: cpo@cpo.on.ca
Website; www.cpo.on.ca
Real Estate Agent
Real Estate Council of Ontario
3250 Bloor Street West, Suite 600
Toronto, On
M8X 2X9
Phone: 416-207-4800
Fax: 416-207-4820
Email: information@reco.on.ca
Website: www.reco.on.ca
Respiratory Therapist
College of Respiratory Therapists of Ontario
180 Dundas Street west, Suite 2103
Toronto, On
M5G 1Z8
Phone: 416-591-7800
Toll Free: 1-800-261-0528
Fax: 416-591-7890
Email: crto@crto.on.ca
Website: www.crto.on.ca
Social Worker
Ontario College of Social Workers and Social
Services Workers
80 Bloor Street West, Suite 700
Toronto, On
M5S 2V1
Phone: 416-972-9882
Toll Free: 1-877-828-9380
Fax: 416-972-1512
Email: info@ocswssw.org

Website: www.ocswssw.org
Teacher
Ontario College of teachers
121 Bloor Street East, 6th Floor
Toronto, On
Phone: 416-961-8800
Toll Free: 1-888-534-2222
Fax: 416-961-8822
Email: info@oct.on.ca
Website: www.oct.on.ca
Veterinarian
College of Veterinarians Of Ontario
2106 Gordon Street
Guelph, On
N1L 1G6
Phone: 519-824-5600
Fax: 519-824-6497
Email: Kgamble@cvo.org
Or questions@cvo.org
Website: www.cvo.org
The national Association of Veterinarian is the:
Canadian Veterinary Medical Association (CVMA)
339 Booth St.
Ottawa, On
K1R 7K1
Phone: 613-236-1162
Fax: 613-236-9681
Email: info@canadianveterinarians.net
Website: www.cvma-acmv.org/

For more information on Professional Associations and their respective Regulatory bodies in other Provinces, visit the Website at: www.cicic.ca/professions/profession-en.asp

And click on the profession you need information about.

Also visit other Websites:

- www.ola.bc.ca/ices/organizations.html
- www.micromedia.ca/CIRC/overview.htm.
- www.learnandearn.bc.ca/learnandearn.htm
- www.red-seal.ca
- www.charityvillage.com
- www.canadiancareers.com/sector.html
- www.mcaws.gov.bc.ca/amip/iqp

Once you decide where you will settle and practice your profession, do not hesitate to contact the appropriate Professional Association and the Regulatory body for information on licensing procedures.

6

NO CANADIAN EXPERIENCE

At this point, you have gone through job search programs, you are a registered professional in your field of expertise, but still most of you cannot get a job. The same old story, the same excuse, the same roadblock keep bumping up at your interviews, cold calls and corporate corridors. The same old bully- "No Canadian Experience" refuses to cut you a slack. It is time we dissect this bully.

As you may have witnessed first hand, this is the most frustrating, the master of all barriers. Before 1990, having an international experience earned people extra dollars, according to Statistics Canada—(STATCAN) report of 2004. In 1969, during their first year in Canada, immigrants from western countries enjoyed 2% in extra earnings for every year of foreign experience. In 1999, the figure was 1.8%. In comparison, in 1969, immigrants from Asian and African countries enjoyed 1% in extra earnings for each year of foreign experience in their first year of stay in Canada. In 1999, their earnings for foreign experience were zero.

But nowadays, unfortunately, your foreign experience and particularly the lack of Canadian work experience, locks you out from the corporate corridors. And when it doesn't lock you out, which happens very seldom, it attracts you less pay and some measure of professional relegation.

Some victims of the phrase "No Canadian Experience" have described the phrase as:

- "A bully phrase that labels one as a professional freak and misfit that needs some kind of rehabilitation and upgrading"—a Pakistani Doctor
- "A thoughtfully hewn polite snobbery to keep Foreign Trained Professionals at bay, from the bountiful Canadian corporate circles and corporate welfare"—a Jamaican Business Analyst.
- "It is a beast, a monster. A dignity-consuming and deprivative enemy of inclusion"—a South African Chemist.
- "An existential reality that desperately needs to be exterminated from the Canadian corporate workplace"—an Indian Chemical Engineer.
- "A very competitive disclaimer. It beats you at your own trade"—a Chinese Acupuncturist.
- "You have not gone through a detoxification process to be cleansed of a presumed professional and academic ignorance, mediocrity and quackery"—a Nigerian Sociologist.
- "A bully phrase that renders the shelf life of ones academic credentials and professional experience obsolete at face value"—a Romanian Engineer.
- "A faceless bully phrase, an untamed enemy of the Foreign Trained Professional"—an Argentine Agronomist.
- "An un-Canadian disclaimer phrase that condemns the Foreign Trained Professionals and Skilled Immigrants to innumerable hours of heart-wrenching 'survival jobs' in the factory floors. It desperately needs to be caged away from the Canadian corporate corridors"—a Ukrainian Accountant.

- "Uno monstro that ambushes most Foreign Trained Professionals on arrival in Canada. It humiliated me in every interview I attended. I can't wait to attend it's funeral"—a Chilean Architect.

Objective meaning of the phrase "No Canadian Experience"

From the objective point of view, the phrase 'No Canadian Experience' could mean the following:

a. We Trust You, but not enough/You have not been evaluated

Business and genuine employer–employee relationship is all about trust. When there is no trust, there is no business. It is that simple. Lack of trust may arise from lack of adequate information about the prospective employee. An example is in the case of an employer who wants to hire a manager for his establishment. This employer may not have proper information about the corporate culture, scope of responsibilities, and conduct of a manager in the country say X, where you the prospective manager earned your academic qualifications and managerial experience as shown in your resume or said in the interview. And very seldom will the employer go out of his/her way to look for this information. Due to lack of this information and fear that you might mess things up, though you may have been an excellent manager who may have made great achievements in your former company. But you were that great and excellent in a monoculturacial society, of unstable democracy and probably non-transparent business ethics. This employer may not hire you and may cite 'No Canadian Experience' as his reason for not hiring you. He has an interest to protect.

b. Nobody Vouches For You/You have not been vetted

The use of the phrase 'No Canadian Experience' as a reason for not giving you a job could simply mean: 'nobody vouches for you in Canada'.

Credibility and referral has been the North American way. The Canadian University or College one attended, which issued ones academic degree, the professional association you are a member of, the certificate of registration issued by a regulatory body all stand as a source of your academic and professional credibility. The company where one did his/her internship/co-op placement as a student. The company(s) one worked for after graduation, all acts as a ready reference to the employer. The employer doesn't need to do so much and or reach out too far for the information he/she needs to make a hiring decision.

An employer, who wants to hire a Medical/Pharmaceutical laboratory technologist/technician for example, will like to hire someone with complete and demonstrated knowledge of the regulatory laws and ethics in that field. Very few employers have the patience to build or strengthen your backbone.

One good thing about the phrase 'No Canadian Experience' is that it is neither vindictive, an enigma, nor entirely elusive. It could be put out of your way for good.

For some victims who described the phrase 'No Canadian Experience' as snobbery, well, being a snob is somewhat wanting the best. The best and only way of overcoming such snobbery is to be and or possess the best. And one good and sure thing about the snob is that it forever craves the best.

So?

Reach out to upgrade and enhance your professional experience and academic credentials. You international experience is already an asset, never mind if it earns you fewer dollars. Obtaining a Canadian academic credential from one of the numerous Canadian Universities or Colleges, having work experience through paid or unpaid internship/co-op placement arms you with all you need to put the 'bully' at bay forever. In addition, it gives you a worldview of your profession.

PART 3

7

HOW AND WHERE TO OBTAIN CANADIAN EXPERIENCE

Career Bridge Program

This program as the name implies, bridges the gap, between you and the Canadian job market. The program provides you with the opportunity to earn the most elusive Canadian experience through paid internship.

The Career Bridge program was started in November 2003, but was officially launched on June 17th 2004. The program was created to provide paid internship for Foreign Trained Professionals. It is an initiative by the Toronto Region Immigrant Employment Council (TREIC), and is funded by the Ontario provincial government.

The program started with 51 interns after screening 1300 Professionals. The author of this book was screened in 2004 during the second phase of the program. The selected interns filled paid internship ($16670/mth), offered by 30 employers.

The coordinators of the program promised to increase the number of interns in the program to 150 in 2005, and to 250 in 2006. So far, about 150 companies are participating, with more companies joining and others dropping out for some undisclosed reasons. The internship lasts for an upward of 4 to 6 months, but the host company can extend it to one year.

At the end of the internship, the company may or may not retain the intern for permanent employment. In the case where the intern is not given a permanent position, she/he will include the host in his/her resume as a reference (Canadian Experience) in a fresh job search.

The Career Bridge Program is an excellent initiative and helps hundreds of the many foreign trained professionals who arrive in Canada in hundreds of thousands every year.

To qualify for the Career Bridge Program you need:

a. At least three years of work experience in your field of expertise in an organization or company outside of Canada.

b. A post-secondary education from a country other than Canada

c. You must not have resided in Canada for more than three years.

And you will be screened for:

1. English language proficiency
2. Assessment of international academic credentials
3. Workplace communications training
4. An email resource to provide support to interns during their placement

The program claims that 85% of interns secured permanent employment after completing the program.

As at the year 2004, some companies that participated in the Career Bridge Program includes:

• Bell Canada
• BMO Financial Group

- Hospital for Sick Children
- Motorola
- Procter & Gamble
- General Electric
- Toronto Hydro
- Humber College
- Municipal governments: Toronto City, Markham and York region

The Career Bridge Program is under the coordination of Career Edge—a Toronto-based youth internship program.

The CEO of Career Edge Program is Lucille Joseph

The Honorary Chairperson of Career Bridge Program is John Tory

The Director of Career Bridge Program is Barbara Nowers

Contact: Barbara Nowers

Phone: 1-888-507-3343

Email: info@careerbridge.ca

Website: www.careerbridge.ca

Toronto City Government Mentorship Program

The Metro Hall Mentorship Program started in February 2004. The program matches Foreign Trained Professionals with Professionals in their similar field from the Toronto City Hall, for mentoring and assistance to secure a job in their field of expertise. The City Hall Professionals help new Immigrants to:

a. Identify the skills necessary in the Canadian Job market
b. Understand some Canadian corporate ethics
c. Understand how the Canadian workplace functions
d. Network

The participants in this mentorship program communicate with the mentor in person, over the phone and through email.

It is a four months program. During the four months duration, the program gears the participants to a co-op placement or volunteering in a company related to their fields of expertise. This may lead to contract or permanent position in the company. At other times when the participants could not secure a permanent position, they leave the company with the most elusive Canadian Experience, an experience that they will explore to enrich their resumes for a fresh Job search.

Eligibility for this program includes:

a. At least three years of work experience in your field of expertise in an organization or company outside of Canada.

b. A post-secondary education from a country other than Canada.

c. You must not have resided in Canada for more than three years.

Like the Career Bridge program, this City Hall initiative helps hundreds of participants in a year. Recently, Skills For Change—a Job search/ Settlement organization joined with the City Hall initiative.

Mr. David Miller- the honorable Mayor of Toronto founded the Toronto City Hall Mentorship Program.

The program is coordinated by the Toronto City Hall Employment Equity Unit, and is headed by Jo-Anne Banard.

The program claims that 1/3 to 2/3 of the Participants secure permanent jobs after completing the four months program, co-op and volunteering in various companies.

Contact: Jo-Anne Banard
Phone: 416-392-8665
Website: www.city.toronto.on.ca
www.metrotor.on.ca

TREIC/Maytree Foundation Mentorship Program

This program is coordinated by the Toronto City Summit Alliance and the Maytree Foundation. The program aims at bringing top executives, employers and decision makers together with Foreign Trained Professionals and Skilled Immigrants.

For more information, visit the website: **www.triec.ca**

Professional Enhancement and Career Bridge Programs For Specific Professions

Engineering Technicians and Technologists:

The professional enhancement and career bridge program for Foreign Trained Engineering Technicians and Technologists, coordinated by Ontario Association of Certified Engineering Technicians and Technologists provides the following services:

a. Assessment of academic qualifications and professional experience
b. Referrals to appropriate academic qualification courses and OACETT examination preparation
c. Job-specific language and terminology training
d. Mentoring and networking opportunities
e. Enhanced certification process and certification
f. Information about employment opportunities
g. Internship/co-op placement

Contact: Tony DaSilva, Director
Phone: 905-949-0049 ext. 2226
Email: tdasilva@clta.on.ca

Teachers

The enhancement and career bridge program for Foreign Trained Teachers, coordinated by the Ontario College of Teachers in conjunction with Skills For Change provides the following services:

a. Facilitate the entry of foreign trained Teachers into Ontario's publicly funded schools as classroom teachers or other positions in the education system.

b. Certify and channel foreign trained Teachers towards areas/subjects of high demand including French as a second and or foreign language (in primary and secondary schools), Chemistry, Physics, Computer Sciences, Mathematics, and Technology subjects in places of intermediate and higher learning.

c. Assistance for obtaining required documents for evaluation process.

d. One- week classroom visits to witness classroom practices and school program.

e. Training in sector/occupation-specific language and terminology.

f. Examination preparation course for Ontario Teachers Qualification Test (OTQT).

Contact Linda Zaks-Walker, Project Manager
Phone: 416-961-8800 ext. 420
Email: info@teachinontario.ca

Alternative Teacher Accreditation Program

This program for Internationally Trained Teachers is geared towards providing an alternative way of delivery of the Bachelor of Education program currently offered at Queens University, Kingston, Ontario. The program is designed to allow participants to continue working while attending the training program delivered over one summer and one spring period.

The program is coordinated by the Faculty of Education at the Queen's University with the participation of Ottawa-Carleton District School Board and Local Agencies Serving Immigrants (LASI) World Skills.

Contact: Sue Lloyd, Project Manager
Phone: 613-533-6000
Email: lloyds@educ.queensu.ca
Website: www.educ.queensu.ca/-ataptie/

Health Care Professionals—Medical Radiation Technologist, Radiological Technologist, Magnetic Resonance Imagist, Medical Laboratory Technologist, Diagnostic Cytologist and Respiratory Therapist

The professional enhancement and career bridge program for these Professionals is coordinated by the Michener Institute for Applied Health Sciences, with the participation of George Brown College and Skills For Change to provide:

a. Canadian workplace experience.
b. Guidance needed to pass the Licensing and Certification (CAMRT national exam) exam.
c. Liaise with the regulatory bodies to ensure that the time spent in the course of the program is accepted as part of the required clinical hours.
d. Mentorship
e. Occupation-specific didactic and practical trainings
f. Clinical placements

This program that began in the early months of 2003 is also offered through distance education and e-learning support to ensure access throughout the province of Ontario

Contact: Cecil Canteenwalla, Project Manager
Phone: 416-596-3154
Email: ccanteenwalla@michener.ca
Website: www.michener.ca/access/

Another Program designed especially for Medical Laboratory Technologists, is coordinated by Mohawk College in conjunction with College of Medical Laboratory Technologists of Ontario, Canadian Society for Medical Laboratory Science, Hamilton Health Sciences and MDS

Laboratories, Ontario Society of Medical Technologists and, Settlement and Integration Services Organization (SISO) to provide:

a. Gear participants towards gaining Clinical Skills and preparation for licensure in Ontario
b. Orientation to Canadian workplace practices
c. Mentorship
d. Occupation-specific Language training
e. Clinical placement

Contact: Mary Golba-Bilhouwer, Mowhawk College
Phone: 905-540-4247 ext. 26706
Email: golbam@mail.mohawkc.on.ca
Website: www.mohawkc.on.ca/dept/cehs/fml/index.html
* Note this program may need tuition

Pharmacists

The enhancement and career bridge program for Foreign Trained Pharmacists is called the International Pharmacy Graduate Program (IPGP). The program is coordinated by the Faculty of Pharmacy at the University of Toronto, with the participation of the Ontario college of Pharmacists to provide:

a. Skills and knowledge necessary to meet Ontario's pharmacy practice standards and requirements for licensing
b. Mentorship and Networking
c. Link participants with practicing pharmacists and the pharmacy community
d. Educational and clinical training

Contact: Marie Rocchi-Dean, Faculty of Pharmacy
Phone: 416-946-5586, 416-946-5779
Email: marie.dean@utoronto.ca
Website: www.newontariopharmacists.com/IPG

Biotechnologists

The enhancement and career bridge program for Biotechnologists and Life Sciences Professionals is coordinated by Vitesse Re-skilling Canada Inc., with the participation of Canadian Bioprocess Institute and Local Agencies Serving Immigrants (LASI) World Skills to provide

a. Canadian workplace experience
b. Training
c. Internship/Co-op placement (paid)

Contact: Dr. Taras Hollyer
Pone: 613-254-9880 ext. 224
Email: taras.hollyer@vitesse.ca
Website: www.vitesse.ca/site/programs_bridge.htm

Engineers

The enhancement and career bridge program for Foreign Trained Engineers is coordinated by Ontario Society of Professional Engineers (OSPE), with the participation of Professional Engineers of Ontario (PEO) and Consulting Engineers of Ontario (CEO), Workplace Training & Services Inc. (WTS Inc.), Progress and Associates (P&A), Speakwell, Archer Resource Solutions Inc., Multicultural Business Solutions, Walsh & Co. Accountants to provide:

a. Licensure as a Professional Engineer in Ontario
b. Six-week full time in class communications/ employability training
c. Coaching support
d. One-year paid Canadian work placement experience under the supervision of a licensed Professional Engineer

This program stretches for 58 weeks.
Contact: Hana Jibry, Project Manager
Phone: 416-223-9961
Email: hjibry@ospe.on.ca
Website: www.pathways.ospe.on.ca

Nurses

The professional enhancement and career bridge program for Foreign Trained Nurses is coordinated by Alonquin College, with the participation of University of Ottawa, Ottawa Civic Hospital, Local Agencies Serving Immigrants (LASI) World Skills and College of Nurses of Ontario to:

a. Gear participants toward employment as registered Nurses (RNs)
b. Give participants an alternative occupation and or training in the Health Care field including: Personal Support Worker (PSW), Registered Practical Nurse (RPN), or Post RN baccalaureate
c. Clinical placements that will provide on-the-job training and exposure to Canadian workplace culture and practices
d. Give employment counseling

Contact:
Carmen Hust, Project Manager, Algonquin College
Phone: 613-727-4723 ext. 7263
Email: hustc@algonquincollege.com
Website:
www.algonquincollege.com/foreign-trainednurseproject

Another bridge program for Nurses called CARE enlists participants that include:

- College of Nurse of Ontario
- Centennial College
- Ryerson University
- George Brown College
- St. Micheal's Hospital
- Sick Children's Hospital
- Sunnybrook & Women's College Health Sciences
- Diverscare
- YeeHong Center for Geriatric Care

- Mt. Sinai Hospital

To provide:

a. Orientation to Nursing in Ontario
b. English communication for Nurses (CLB 6-8)
c. Enhanced language training for Nurses (CLB 8-10)
d. Process for recognition of prior knowledge and experiences
e. Academic bridge to BScN
f. Examination preparation and support
g. Work placement

Contact: Dawn Sheppard, Project Manager
Phone: 416-415-5000 ext. 6686
Email: dsheppard@care4nurses.org
Website: www.care4nurses.org/

You may want to contact Certinurse.ca for other information at:
Email: info@certinurse.ca (email query)
Email: service@certinurse.ca (customer service)
Website: www.certinurse.ca

Information Technologist, Health Informatics & Financial Services

The professional enhancement and career bridge program for the Foreign Trained Information Technologists is coordinated by George Brown College, with the participation of Skills For Change and COSTI to provide:

a. Training leading to diploma in Computer programming
b. Training with specialization in Health Informatics and Financial Services
c. Training geared towards work place knowledge and experience.

Contact:
Phone: 416-415-5000, ext.4401
Email: jli@gbc.gbrownc.on.ca
Website: www.gbrownc.on.ca/Marketing/FTCal/
infotech/T202.html

Midwives

The professional enhancement and career bridge program
for Foreign Trained Midwives is coordinated by Ryerson
University Continuing Education Department in conjunction
with College of Midwives of Ontario to provide:

a. Preparation for Licensure with the College of
    Midwives of Ontario
b. Introduction to general practice, cultural and
    regulatory aspect of Midwifery in Ontario
c. Occupation -specific language training
d. Training in Clinical Skills
e. Mentorship
f. Examination preparation seminars
g. Clinical placements

Contact: Alison Gaul
Phone: 416-979-5000-1, ext. 7681
Email: agaul@ryerson.ca
Website: www.ryerson.ca/ce/midwife

Precision Machining And Tooling, General Machinist, Tool & Die Maker

The enhancement and career bridge program to address the
need of Foreign Trained Machinist, Tool and Die makers
is coordinated by Georgian College, with the participation
of Simcoe County Training Board, Automotive Parts
Manufacturers' Association, Global Placement Services, to
provide:

a. Cultural and workplace training

b. Language training
c. Academic review and upgrade
d. Training in the Trade Theory
e. Training in Practical Skills
f. Eight-week work placement

Contact:
Charles Craig, Project Manager, Georgian College
Phone: 705-728-1968, ext. 1221
Email: ccraig@georgianc.gov.on.ca
Website: www.georgianc.on.ca/technology/bridges/

Construction And Manufacturing Trades (Industrial Maintenance Mechanic, Welder)

The professional enhancement and career bridge program for people in Skilled Manufacturing Trades is coordinated by Fanshawe College of Applied Arts & Technology. It is a Preparation for Apprenticeship, Trades & Technology (PAT) program to provide:
a. Training in Occupational language
b. In-class and shop technical training
c. Information on Canadian workplace practices
d. A work placement (minimum of eight weeks)

Contact: Monte Black, Fanshawe College
Phone: 519-452-4430, ext. 4586
Email: mblack@fanshawec.ca

Ontario Government's Loan For Tools Program

This program funded by the provincial government of Ontario aims to provide new apprentice with:
a. Loan to buy the necessary tools and equipment he/she may need to practice the trade in which he/she is registered.

Contact:
Phone: 1-888-562-4769 or 416-326-5656

Medical Doctors (Physicians & Surgeons)

The professional enhancement and career bridge program for International Medical Graduates (IMG) is offered by IMG-Ontario.

IMG-Ontario is an initiative developed with the help of Royal College of Physicians and Surgeons of Canada (RCPSC), College of Family Physicians Of Canada (CFPC) and Medical Council of Canada (MCC). The program is coordinated by Council of Ontario Faculties of Medicine (COFM) in conjunction with College of Physicians and Surgeons of Ontario (CPSO), Ontario Ministry of Health and Long-Term Care (MOHLTC).

The program aims to provide:

Access to professional practice in Ontario for International Medical Graduates (IMGs) who meet the Ontario regulatory requirements.

*It is important at this point to note that admittance into the IMG-Ontario program does not guarantee a license from the College of Physicians and Surgeons of Ontario (CPSO). The CPSO has regulatory requirements beyond those of IMG-Ontario.

For information about the CPSO regulatory requirements, please visit the
Website at: www.cpso.on.ca
Or phone: 416-967-2600.

Also see Chapter 5 of this book and the section in that chapter that lists regulatory professions and the respective regulatory bodies, and turn to Physicians and Surgeons for address and fax number of CPSO.
Contact: IMG-Ontario
Phone: 416-946-0550

Fax: 416-946-0572
Email: img.resources@utoronto.ca
Website: www.oimgc.utoronto.ca/
Mailing Address: IMG-Ontario
700 Bay Street, Suite 200
P.O.Box 332
Toronto, On
M5G 1Z6

It may also be useful to contact the Association of International Physicians and Surgeons of Ontario (AIPSO). This Association helps international trained Physicians integrate into the Canadian health care system.

Some members of the AIPSO are not licensed to practice in Ontario, while others are at different stages of licensing.

Contact:
Address: 2 Carlton Street, Suite 820
Toronto, On
M5B 1J3
Phone: 416-979 8611
Fax: 416-979-9853
Email: info@aipso.ca

The National Medical Body in Canada is:
Medical Council of Canada
Box 8234, Ottawa
On, K1G 3H7
Phone: 613-521-6012
Fax: 613-521-9417

Finance and Office Assistant Program
This 26-week enhancement and bridging program is coordinated by Skills for Change to provide:
a.   Comprehensive clerical skills
b.   Improve communication skills
c.   Six weeks job placement
Eligibility:

1. Social Assistance recipient
2. Must successfully complete a numeracy test
3. Average level of English language
4. Keyboard typing at 25wpm
5. Must be eligible to work in Canada

Contact: 416-658-3101 ext. 0 or ext. 227

Accountants and Bookkeepers

This 26-week enhancement and bridging program for Foreign Trained Accountants and Bookkeepers is coordinated by Skill For Change to provide:

a. Bookkeeping and Accounting Principles
b. ACCPAC (version 5.0)
c. Simply Accounting (version 9.0)
d. Income Microsoft Word
e. Excel and Access
f. Office procedures
g. Business writing
h. Tax preparation
i. 5 weeks job placement

Eligibility:

1. Above average level of English language
2. Must successfully complete a bookkeeping test
3. Social Assistance recipient
4. Keyboard typing at 25wpm
5. Must be eligible to work in Canada

Contact:
Phone: 416-658-3101 ext. 0 or ext.227

Trades—

Electromechanical Sector (Construction & Maintenance Electrician, Industrial Electricians, Industrial Mechanics or Millwrights)

This 12-week enhancement and bridging program for Foreign Trained Tradespeople is coordinated by Skills for Change in conjunction with an Electromechanical school to provide:

    a.   Occupational Terminology
    b.   Labour Market information
    c.   Job placement (may be)
    d.   Training in Technical skills
    e.   Preparation to write Certification/Qualification examination

Eligibility:

1. Average level of English language (CLB 7)
2. Five years of international experience in the field
3. Landed Immigrant, Convention Refugee or Canadian Citizen

Contact:
Phone: 416-658-7090 or 416-658-3101 ext. 0

Retail Services

This 15-week enhancement and bridging program is coordinated by Skill for Change to provide:

    a. Corporate Terminology
    b.   Retail Skills
    c.   Workplace communication skills
    d.   Conflict Resolution
    e.   Six weeks work placement

Eligibility:

1. Average level of English Language
2. Must successfully complete a numeracy test

3. Must be eligible to work in Canada
4. Keyboard typing at 25wpm
Contact:
Phone: 416-658-3101 ext. 0 or ext. 227

Microelectronics Manufacturing Techniques
Contact:
Canadian Association of Microelectronics Corporation
210A Carruthers Hall
Queens University
Kingston, On
K7L 3N6
Phone: 613-530-4666
Fax; 613-5488104
Website www.cmc.ca

Now Program

This 8-week enhancement and career bridge program is for newcomers to Canada. The program is coordinated by the Brickford Center to provide:
   a. Four weeks of assessment
   b. Career planning
   c. Job search techniques
   d. Four weeks of unpaid Co-op/internship placement
Contact: 416-393-0378, 905-764-3334

Professional Enhancement and Bridging Programs in other Provinces

For information on Professional Associations and their respective Regulatory bodies in other Provinces, visit the Website at: www.cicic.ca/professions/profession-en.asp
   And click on the profession you need information about. Also visit other Websites:
   • www.ola.bc.ca/ices/organizations.html
   • www.micromedia.ca/CIRC/overview.htm

- www.learnandearn.bc.ca/learnandearn.htm
- www.red-seal.ca
- www.charityvillage.com
- www.canadiancareers.com/sector.html
- www.mcaws.gov.bc.ca/amip/iqp

Alberta

Some Professional Association And Professional Regulatory Bodies in Alberta includes:

- College of Physicians & Surgeons of Alberta
  #900 Manulife Place,
  10180-101 Street NW, Edmonton
  Alberta, T5J 4P8
  Phone: 780-423-4764
  Fax: 780-420-0651
  Email: info@cpsa.ab.ca
  Website: www.cpsa.ab.ca/

- Alberta Dental Association and College
  Suite 101, 8230—105 Street
  Edmonton, Alberta
  T6E 5H9
  Phone: 780-432-1012
  Fax: 780-433-4864
  Toll Free Phone: 1-800-843-3848
  Email: adaadmin@telusplanet.net
  Website: www.abda.ab.ca/

- Alberta Association of Registered Nurses (AARN)
  11620—168 Street
  Edmonton, Alberta
  T5M 4A6
  Phone: 780-451-0043
  Toll Free Phone: 1-800-252-9392
  Fax: 780-452-3276
  Email: aarn@nurses.ab.ca
  Website: www.nurses.ab.ca/

- Registered Psychiatric Nurses Association of
  Alberta (RPNAA)
  9711- 45 Avenue, Suite 201
  Edmonton, Alberta
  T6E 5V8 Canada
  Phone: 780-434-7666
  Toll free Phone: 1-877-234-7666
  Fax: 780-436-4165
  Email: rpnaa@rpnaa.ab.ca
  Website: www.rpnaa.ab.ca/
- College of Physical Therapists of Alberta (CPTA)
  5555 Calgary Trail South, Suite 1350
  Edmonton, Alberta
  T6H 5P9 Canada
  Phone: 780-438-0338
  Fax: 780-436-1908
  Email: cpta@cpta.ab.ca
- The National association is:
  Canadian Physiotherapy Association (CPA)
  2345 Yonge Street, Suite 410
  Toronto, On
  M4P 2E5 Canada
  Phone: 416- 932-1888
  Toll free Phone: 1-800-387-8679
  Fax: 416-932-9708
  Email: information@physiotherapy.ca
  Website: www.physiotherapy.ca
- College and Association of Respiratory Therapists
  of Alberta
  Suite #370, 6715- 8th Street N.E.,
  Calgary, Alberta
  T2E 7H7
  Phone number: 403-274-1828
  Toll Free Phone: 1-800-205-2778
  Fax: 403-274-9703

Email: carta1@telusplanet.net
Website: www.carta.ca/
- Alberta Association of Registered Occupational Therapists
Suite 302, 8657- 51 avenue
Edmonton, Alberta
T6E 6A8 Canada
Phone: 780-436-8381
Toll Free Phone: 1-800-561-5429
1-800-561-5429
Fax: 780-434-0658
Email: info@aarot.ca
Website: www.aarot.ca/
- Midwifery Health Disciples Committee
Alberta Health and Wellness
10025 Jasper Avenue 22nd Floor
Edmonton Alberta
T5J 2N3 Canada
Phone: 780-422-2733
Fax: 780-415-2800
Email: heather.Cameron@gov.ab.ca
- Alberta Association of Midwives (AAM)
Main P.O.BOX 11957
Edmonton, Alberta
T5J 3L1 Canada
Email: albertamidwives@shaw.ca
Website: www.albertamidwives.com
- Alberta Association of Medical Radiation Technologists
#501, Center 104, 5241 Calgary Trail
Edmonton, Alberta
T6H 5G8 Canada
Phone: 780-487-6130
Toll Free: 1-800-282-2165
Fax: 780-432-9106

Email: info@aamrt.org
Website: www.aamrt.org
The discipline covered by this association includes:
* Radiological Technology (RTR)
* Radiation Therapy (RTT)
* Nuclear Medicine Technology (RTNM)
* Magnetic Resonance Imaging (RTMR)
* Electroneurophysiology (ENP)

For more information on Professional Associations and Regulatory Bodies in Alberta (health sciences), visit the website: www.hsaa.ca/ (Health Sciences Association of Alberta) and click on the profession you wish to know about.
* The Alberta Association of Architects
  Duggan House, 10515 Saskatchewan Drive
  Edmonton Alberta
  T6E 4S1 Canada
  Phone: 780-432-0224
  Fax: 780-439-1431
  Email: info@aaa.ab.ca
  Website: www.aaa.ab.ca
  The above list is not definitive and or exhaustive.

CAREER BRIDGE PROGRAMS

Accounting Professionals

The professional enhancement and career bridge program for Foreign Trained Accountants is coordinated in the City of Edmonton Alberta by Edmonton Mennonite Center for Newcomers (EMCN) in conjunction with Northern Alberta Institute of Technology (NAIT), Certified General Accountants of Alberta (CGA) and Certified Management Accountants of Alberta (CMA). The program spans 10 months (April to January)

Eligibility for participation:

a. Have a Bachelor's degree in Accounting from a University outside of Canada.

b. Work experience in the field of Accounting outside of Canada.

c. Be a resident of the Province of Alberta for a minimum of three months prior to the commencement of the program.

d. Be a Landed Immigrant/Permanent Resident of Canada or a Canadian Citizen

e. Be unemployed or a recipient of EI or income Support or working for not more than 20hour/week.

The program provides:

a. Refreshes to increase your knowledge of Accounting

b. Laws, Standards, Workplace practices and expectations of the Accounting practice in Canada.

e. Eligibility for membership in CGA and CMA

f. Mentorship

g. Accounting training

h. Co-op Placement

Contact:

Luella Gaultier, Manager for Immigrant Professionals

Phone: 780-945-2285

Email: igaultier@emcn.ab.ca

OR

Octavian Bosonea, Program coordinator

Phone: 780-945-2279 or 780-421-7400

Email: obosonea@emcn.ab.ca

Website: www.emcn.ab.ca/

Another Bridging Program for Accounting Professionals in Alberta:

• Accounting Assistant—ESL Certificate

This 44-week professional enhancement and career bridge program is especially designed for Foreign Trained

Accounting Professionals who are willing to start off working at entry-level position. The program is coordinated by Bow Valley College, Calgary to provide:

a. Occupational Terminology
b. English as a Second Language (ESL) training
c. Theory of Accounting Principles
d. Practice of Accounting principles
e. Computerized accounting software training.
f. Preparation of financial statements.
g. General office procedures.
h. Training in Microsoft Word and Excel.
i. Training in common accounting software programs.

Contact:
Bow Valley College,
332—6 Avenue SE
Calgary, Alberta.
T2G 4S6
Canada
Phone: 403-410-1400
Toll Free: 1-866-428-2669
Email: info@bowvalleycollege.ca

Work Experience For Immigrants

This is another program offered by the Bow Valley College Calgary, Alberta.

It is a 16-week program designed to provide:

a. - 10 weeks of training in Canadian workplace culture
b. Canadian workplace functionality and communication
c. Six weeks work placement

Contact the College to find information on a specific field.

Contact:

Bow Valley College, Calgary, Alberta.

Engineers

The professional enhancement and career bridge program for Foreign Trained Engineers is coordinated in the city of Edmonton Alberta by Edmonton Mennonite Center for Newcomers (EMCN). The program spans 10 months, from January to October.

Eligibility to participate:

a. The participant must have an Engineering degree from a University outside of Canada.

The program provides:

a. Technical communication, presentation skills, and Technical Writing Skills
b. Canadian Engineering workplace experience
c. Training in AutoCAD
d. ASET (Alberta Society of Engineering Technologists) membership Training
e. Full certification in C.E.T (Certified Engineering Technologist)
f. One-year work placement

Contact: Octavian Bosonea, Program Coordinator
Phone: 780-421-7400
Email: obosonea@emcn.ab.ca
OR
Liella Gaultier, Manager
Phone 780- 945-2285
Email lgaultier@emcn.ab.ca

Paid Work Experience Opportunities for Youth

This is another Professional enhancement and career bridging program offered by the Edmonton Mennonite Center for Newcomers (EMCN)

The program provides:

a. Six weeks of Canadian workplace training
b. 16-weeks of paid work placement
Eligibility
1. Participant must be between 17 and 30 years
2. Unemployed and looking for a job
3. Participant must be a high school graduate or have post secondary education
4. Participant must be a resident of Canada six months prior to the commencement of the program
5. Participant must be a Landed Immigrant or a Canadian citizen
6. Participant must not be receiving Employment Insurance benefit or a reach-back candidate

Contact:
Ninfa Castellanos
Phone: 780-421-7400

Career Options for New Canadians

This 20 weeks professional and career bridging program is coordinated by Norquest College, Edmonton, Alberta. The program provides:

a. Three months training in computer literacy and communications
b. Job safety training
c. Training in Science and English
d. Seven months supervised on-the- job training.

Contact
Norquest College,
10215–108 Street
Edmonton, Alberta
T5J 1L6
Phone: 780-422-202-
Fax: 780-427-4211

Email: info@norquest.ab.ca

Other programs offered by the Norquest College include

a. Re-entry Program for Nurses
b. Bridge to Business program

Business, Employment and Training

This professional enhancement and career-bridging program is coordinated by Calgary Catholic Immigration Society (CCIS) in conjunction with Alberta Human Resources and Employment, Calgary Community Adult Learning Association, Citizenship and Immigration Canada. The program offers various training in different field of expertise.

The program provides:

a. Career planning
b. Occupational training
c. Technical training
d. Business English training
e. Computer Skill upgrading
d. Access improvement
f. Industry work experience
h. Job leads
i. Job placement.

The Training Programs are as follows:

Commercial Baking Decorator

This program takes in 15 participants in every batch. The program provides:

a. Job related English terminology
b. Basic computer skills
c. Trade calculations
d. Management skills

    e.   Occupational training at SAIT

    f.   One-month job placement

Contact:

Canadian Catholic Immigration Society (CCIS)

Phone: 780-262-2006

Email: cbd@ccis-calgary.ab.ca

For more information contact:

Daniel Hirschkorn—Manager

Canadian Catholic Immigration Society (CCIS)

Phone: 780-262-2006

Email: dhirschkorn@ccis-calgary.ab.ca

Website: www.ccis-calgary.ab.ca/

Drilling Training

This 13-week program takes in 15 participants in every batch. It is designed for individuals who are willing to start off at the entry-level position. This program provides:

    a.   Employment preparation for people in the drilling industry

Contact:

Canadian Catholic Immigration Society (CCIS)

Phone: 780-262-2006

Email: drill@ccis-calgary.ab.ca

For more information contact:

Daniel Hirschkorn—Manager

Canadian Catholic Immigration Society (CCIS)

Phone: 780-262-2006

Email: dhirschkorn@ccis-calgary.ab.ca

Website: www.ccis-calgary.ab.ca/

Electrician

This 22-week program takes in 15 participants (Foreign Trained Electricians) in every batch. The program provides:

    a.   Journeyman Certification
    b.   Canadian work experience
    c.   Communication support training
    d.   Job search skills
    e.   Job placement

Contact:
Canadian Catholic Immigration Society (CCIS)
Phone: 780-262-2006
Email: ele@ccis-calgary.ab.ca
For more information contact:
Daniel Hirschkorn—Manager
Canadian Catholic Immigration Society (CCIS)
Phone: 780-262-2006
Email: dhirschkorn@ccis-calgary.ab.ca
Website: www.ccis-calgary.ab.ca/

Engineering Technology and Technology Upgrading

This APEGGA (Association of professional Engineers, Geologists, and Geophysicists of Alberta) endorsed program takes in 15 participants in every batch. The primary aim of this program is to act as a bridge between local Engineering firms and the Foreign Trained Engineers, and provides:

    a.   Technical training
    b.   Interpersonal communication (English verbal grammar)
    d.   Canadian workplace culture
    e.   Intensive Technical/Technological skills upgrading
    f.   AutoCAD training at SAIT (3 levels)
    g.   Project Management
    h.   Presentation
    i.   Computer training (MS Office)
    j.   Job search Techniques
    k.   Technical communication
    f.   Job placement

Contact:
Canadian Catholic Immigration Society (CCIS)
Lynn Merrithew—Program Coordinator
Heidi Tegart—Assistant Coordinator
Phone: 780-262-2006
Email: eng@ccis-calgary.ab.ca
For more information contact:
Daniel Hirschkorn—Manager
Canadian Catholic Immigration Society (CCIS)
Phone: 780-262-2006
Email: dhirschkorn@ccis-calgary.ab.ca
Website: www.ccis-calgary.ab.ca/

Millwright

This 8-month program coordinated by CCIS in conjunction with SAIT, aims to bridge the career gap for professionals who work in industries like, Pulp and Paper Mills, Steel & Saw Mills, Refineries, Breweries, Chemical Plants. The program provides:

    a.   Technical and workplace training
    b.   One-month job placement

Contact:
Canadian Catholic Immigration Society (CCIS)
Phone: 780-262-2006
Email: mrp@ccis-calgary.ab.ca
For more information contact:
Daniel Hirschkorn—Manager
Canadian Catholic Immigration Society (CCIS)
Phone: 780-262-2006
Email: dhirschkorn@ccis-calgary.ab.ca
Website: www.ccis-calgary.ab.ca/

Trowel Trade

This 5-month program coordinated by CCIS in conjunction with SAIT, aims to bridge the career gap for professionals who work in the industry as tile setter, concrete finisher, or bricklayer. The program takes in 15 participants in every batch. The program provides:

a. Occupational training
b. One-month practical experience

Contact:
Canadian Catholic Immigration Society (CCIS)
Phone: 780-262-2006
Email: trwl@ccis-calgary.ab.ca
For more information contact:
Daniel Hirschkorn—Manager
Canadian Catholic Immigration Society (CCIS)
Phone: 780-262-2006
Email: dhirschkorn@ccis-calgary.ab.ca
Website: www.ccis-calgary.ab.ca/

Signpost For Youth Program

As the name implies, this program is designed for youths, and provides:

a. Skills enhancement
b. Management skills
c. Job search skills
d. 16-week wage-subsidy
e. Job placement

Contact:
Canadian Catholic Immigration Society (CCIS)
Phone: 780-262-2006
Email: ypgm@ccis-calgary.ab.ca

For more information contact:
Daniel Hirschkorn—Manager

Canadian Catholic Immigration Society (CCIS)
Phone: 780-262-2006
Email: dhirschkorn@ccis-calgary.ab.ca
Website: www.ccis-calgary.ab.ca/

You may reach the CCIS through
CCIS Contact Info
CCIS Main Office:
3rd Floor, 120 –17 Avenue SW
Calgary, Alberta
T2S 2T2
Phone: 780-262-2006
Fax: 780-262-2033
Email: contact@ccis-calgary.ab.ca
Website: www.ccis-calgary.ab.ca

Training Centers:

a. 3rd Floor, 120-17 Avenue SW
Calgary, Alberta
T2S 2T2
Phone: 780-262-5695
Fax:
780-261-0955

b. 610, 1509 center Street South
Calgary, Alberta
T2G 2E6
Phone: 780-264-4850
Fax: 780-264-4858
Email: contact@ccis-calgary.ab.ca

• Margaret Chisholm Resettlement Center:
23 McDougall Court NE
Calgary, Alberta
T2E 8R3
Phone: 780-264-8132
Fax: 780-264-8743

Email; mcrc@ccis-calgary.ab.ca
- Immigrant Youth Outreach Project
  100A, 315—10 Avenue SE
  Calgary, Alberta
  T2G 0W2
  Phone: 780-268-8131
  Fax: 780-268-5470
  Email: iyp@ccis-calgary.ab.ca
- North of McKnight Community Resource Center
  Falconridge/Castleridge
  Community Association
  Lower Floor, 95 Falshire Dr., NE
  T3J 1P7
  Phone: 403-293-0424
  Fax: 403-293-0027
- Cross Cultural Children's Center
  100, 120—17 Avenue SW
  Calgary, Alberta
  T2S 2T2
  Phone: 780-262-5695
  Fax: 780-262-2033
  Email: rbray@ccis-calgary.ab.ca

Nurses

Professional enhancement and career bridge programs for Nurses are offered at:

1. Norquest College
   This Program is named: Re-entry Program for Practical Nurses
   Contact:
   Norquest College
   10215–108 Street
   Edmonton, Alberta
   T5J 1L6
   Phone: 780-422-202-

Fax: 780-427-4211
Email: info@norquest.ab.ca
2. Grant McEwan College
This program at the Grant McEwan College for Nurses is specifically designed to offer credentials to Nurses at the end of their successfully attending the full Course.
Contact:
Grant McEwan College, Alberta
3. Mount Royal College
At the Mount Royal College in Alberta, there is a Prior Learning Assessment and Recognition—PLAR program for Nurses
Contact:
Mount Royal College Alberta

Health Care Professionals

The Robertson College in Alberta offers professional enhancement and career bridging programs for healthcare professionals including:
a. Personal Support Workers Challenge Program
b. Pharmacy Technician Program
Contact:
Robertson College Alberta

Other Health Care programs in Alberta Include:
1. Geriatric Nursing Care Attendant
2. Homecare Attendant Training Program

Medical Graduates

In the province of Alberta:
The Program for IMGs is funded by Alberta Health and Wellness (AHW).
A professional enhancement and career bridge program for International Medical graduates (IMGs) is offered by Alberta

Medical Graduates Program. This program enlists:

a. Family Medicine Residency

b. Part 5 Registered Physicians program
   Under this program, IMGs whose credentials allow provincial registration under Part 5 are granted temporary registration with a validity of thirty months

c. J-1 Visa Sponsorship Program
   Under this program, Medical doctors who are Canadian Citizens or Landed Immigrants can undertake post-graduate specialist training in the United States

d. Rural Physician in Action Plan (RPAP) This program has various initiatives for Part 5 immigrant physicians

e. Regional Health (RHA) International Medical Graduates Initiatives
   The initiatives includes:

   a. The IMG Preceptorship Program
   b. The Capital Health Critical Care Clinical Preceptorship Program
   c. IMG Physician Assistant Program—for the internal medicine and diagnostic imaging department

   Contacts:
   Alberta Learning, Community Programs
   Phone: 780-427-5624

- Alberta Human Resources and Employment, Labour, Force, Partnership and Skills Policy Branch
  Phone: 780-644-4306
  Website: www.learning.gov.ab.ca/

- College of Physicians and Surgeons of Alberta
  900 Manulife Place,
  10180-101 Street
  Edmonton, AB

T5J 4P8
Phone: 403-423-4764
* The National Medical Body in Canada is:
  Medical Council of Canada
  Box 8234, Ottawa
  On, K1G 3H7
  Phone: 613-521-6012
  Fax: 613-521-9417
  See general information on IMG's.

Other Career Bridging Programs in Alberta Include:
* Glazier First Year Apprenticeship Training
* Transition to Technical and Trades career

Also Bredin Institute offers Professional and Career bridging program that provides:
a. Credential evaluation
b. Pre-employment training
c. Monthly networking sessions
d. Job leads

Contact:
Bredin Institute
Center For Learning
Capital Place
9707—110 Street
Edmonton, AB
T5K 2L9
Phone: 780-425-3730
Email: foreign@bredin.ab.ca

Employer—Employee Assistance Program

This program is offered by McBride Career Group Inc. The program provides:
a. Free workshops in planning career moves
b. Labour market research
c. Computer training

d. Personal development programs
e. Employer support services
f. Resume preparation
g. Co-op placement—towards permanent employment at the end of the internship

Contact: Ronald Cooke—Program Coordinator
McBride Career Group Inc.
910, 10045-111 Street
Edmonton, Alberta
T5K 2M5
Phone: 780- 488-2541
Email: Ronc@mcbridecareers.com

BRITISH COLUMBIA

The following is a list of Regulatory Bodies in British Columbia

Accountancy

- Institute of Chartered Accountants of BC
  Suite 500, One Bentall Centre
  505 Burrard Street
  Box 22,
  Vancouver, BC
  V7X 1M4
  Canada
  Phone: 604-681-3264
  Toll Free: 1-800-663-2677 (within BC)
  Fax: 604-681-1523
  Website: www.ica.bc.ca
- Certified General Accountants Association of BC
- Certified Management Accountants Society of BC

- **Computer Professionals**
- Software Human Resources Council
- Canadian Information Processing Society

Law

- Canadian Bar Association (BC Branch)
  The Law Society of BC
  845 Cambie Street
  Vancouver, BC
  V6B 4Z9
  Phone: 604-669-2533
  Toll Free: 1-800-903-5300 (within BC)
  Fax: 604-669-5232
  Email: memberinfo@isbc.org (credential and member services)
  pltc@isbc.org
  (professional legal training course—PLTC)
  professionalconduct@isbc.org
  (professional conduct and discipline)
  ethics@isbc.org (ethics)
  insurance@isbc.org (lawyers insurance fund)
  specialfund@isbc.org (special compensation fund)
  advisor@isbc.org (practice advice)
  standards@isbc.org
  (practice standards and remediation)
  counsel@isbc.org (policy and legal services)
  policy@isbc.org (policy and legal services)
  diversity@isbc.org (policy and legal services)
  personnel@isbc.org (human resources)
  communications@isbc.org
  (communications and website)
  archives@isbc.org (archives)
  uap@isbc.org (unauthorized practice)
  foipp@isbc.org (freedom of information and protection of property)
  Website: www.lawsociety.bc.ca

Medicine and Therapy

- BC Medical Association

115—1665 W. Broadway
Vancouver, BC
V6J 5A4
Phone: 604-736-5551
Toll Free: 1-800-665-2262
Email: communications@bcma.bc.ca
Website: www.bcma.org/

- College of Physicians and Surgeons of BC
  400-858 Beatty St.
  Vancouver, BC
  V6B 1C1
  Phone; 604-733-7758
  Toll Free: 1-800-461-3008
  Fax: 604-733-3503
  Website: www.cpsbc.ca

- Association of Naturopathic Physicians of BC
  2238 Pine Street
  Vancouver BC,
  V6J 5G4
  Phone: 604-736-6646
  Toll Free: 1-800-277-1128
  Fax: 604-736-6048
  Email: bcna@bcna.ca
  Website: www.bcna.ca

- National Board of Examiners in Optometry
- Board of Hearing Aid Dealers and Consultants

Dentistry

- College of Dental Hygienists of BC
  Suite 219, Yarrow Building
  645 Fort Street
  Victoria, British Columbia
  V8W 1G2
  Canada
  Phone: 250-383-4101

Toll Free: 1-800-778-8277 (within BC)
Fax: 250-383-4144
Email: cdhbc@cdhbc.com
Website: www.cdhbc.com
- College of Dental Surgeons of BC
Suite 500—1765 West Avenue
Vancouver, BC
Phone: 604-736-3621
Fax: 604-734-9448
Email: postmaster@cdsbc.org
Website: www.cdsbc.org/
- Denturist Association of BC
9801 King George Hwy. 312c
Surrey, BC,
V3T 5H5
Canada
Phone: 604-582-6823
Fax: 604-582-0317
Email: info@denturist.bc.ca
Website: www.denturist.bc.ca/
- Denturist Association of Canada
P.O.BOX 46114 RPO Westdale
Winnipeg, MB
R3R 3S3
Canada
Phone: 204-897-1087
Toll Free: 1-800-773-0099
Fax: 204- 895-9595
Email: DACDenturist@mts.net
Website: www.denturist.org

Pharmacy

- College of Pharmacists of BC
200—1765 West 8th Ave
Vancouver, BC V6J 5C6

Canada
Phone: 604-733-2440
Toll Free: 1-800-663-1940
Fax: 604-733-2493
Toll Free Fax: 1-800-377-8129
Website: www.bcpharmacists.org

Nursing

- College of Midwives of BC
  Suite 210, 1682 West 7th Avenue
  Vancouver, BC
  V6J-4S6
  Phone: 604-742-2230
  Fax: 604-730-8908
  Email: information@cmbc.bc.ca
  Website: www.cmbc.bc.ca
- College of Licensed Practical Nurses of BC
- College of Registered Psychiatric Nurses of BC
- Registered Nurses Association of BC
  2855 Arbutus Street
  Vancouver, BC
  V6J 3Y8
  Canada
  Phone: 604-736-7331
  Toll Free: 1-800-565-6505
  Fax: 604-738-2272
  Email: info@rnabc.bc.ca (for general inquiry)
  register@rnabc.bc.ca (to register as a nurse in BC)
  exams@rnabc.bc.ca (nursing registration examinations)
  practice@rnabc.bc.ca (nursing practice advice)
  Website: www.rnabc.bc.ca/

Therapy

- College of Physical Therapists of BC

302—1765 West 8th Avenue,
Vancouver, BC
V6J 5C6
Canada
Phone: 604-730-9193
Fax: 604-730-9273
Email: info@cptbc.org
Website: www.cptbc.org

- BC Society of Respiratory Therapists
BCSRT
P.O.BOX 4760
Vancouver BC,
V6B 4A4
Canada
Phone: 604-623-2227
Toll Free: 1-800-2673422
Website: www.bcsrt.com/

- College of Massage Therapists of BC (CMTBC)
#103—1089 West Broadway,
Vancouver, BC
V6H 1E5
Phone: 604-736-3404
Fax: 604-736-6500
Email: office@cmtbc.bc.ca
Website: www.cmtbc.bc.ca

- BC Society of Occupational Therapists
- BC Association of Speech –Language Pathologists
and Audiologists
9912 Lougheed Highway
Burnaby, BC
V3J 1N3
Phone: 604-420-2222
Toll Free: 1-877-BCASLPA (222-7572)
Fax: 604-420-4896
Email: admin@bcaslpa.ca

Website: www.bcaslpa.bc.ca/
- BC College of Chiropractors
- BC Chiropractic Association
125-3751 Shell Road
Richmond, BC
V6X 2W2
Phone: 604-270-1332
Fax: 604-278-0093
Email: info@bcchiro.com
- BC Association of Podiatrists
1400—1500 West Georgia Street
Vancouver, BC
V6G 2Z6
Phone: 604-602-0400
Fax: 604-602-0399
Email: bcap@foothealth.ca
Website: www.foothealth.ca
- College of Acupuncturists of BC
2nd Floor, 5050 Kingsway
Burnaby BC
V5H 4H2
Canada
Phone: 604-638-3108
Fax: 604-638-3103
Email; info@ctcma.bc.ca
Website: www.ctcma.bc.ca
- BC Board of Examiners in Podiatry

Psychology

- College of Psychologists of BC
1755 West Broadway
(#404)
Vancouver, BC
V6J 4S5
Phone: 604-736-6164

Toll Free: 1-800-665-0979 (within BC)
Fax: 604-736-6133
Website: www.collegeofpsychologists.bc.ca/

Nutrition

- BC Dieticians and Nutritionists Association

Veterinary

- BC College of Veterinary Medical Association
  107—828 Harbourside Drive,
  North Vancouver, BC V7P 3R9
  Phone: 604-929-7090
  Toll Free in BC: 1-800-463-5399
  Fax: 604-929-7095
  Email: info@bcvma.org

Engineering

- Association of Professional Engineers and
  Geoscientists of BC
- Canadian Council of Engineers (BC Branch)

Architecture

- Architectural Institute of BC
- BC Society of Landscape Architects
- Planning Institute of BC
- Corporation of Land Surveyors of BC

Science

- BC Institute of Agrologists
- BC Association of Professional Foresters

Technology

- Applied Science Technologists and Technicians of
  BC
- BC Society of Medical Technologists

- BC Association of Medical Radiation
  Technologists
  19941—39A Avenue
  Langley, BC
  V3A 7G3
  Canada
  Phone: 604-530-0612
  Toll Free: 1-800-990-7090
  Fax: 604-530-0622
  Email: bcamrt@intergate.ca
  Website: www.bcamrt.bc.ca
- Canadian Association of Medical Radiation
  Technologists
  Suite 500—1095 Carling Avenue
  Ottawa, On
  K1Y 4P6
  Phone: 603-234-0012
  Toll Free: 1-800-463-9729
  Fax: 613-234-1097
  Website: www.camrt.ca
- Board of Registration for Social workers in BC
  302—1765 West 8th Ave.
  Vancouver, BC
  V6J 5C6
  Canada
  Phone: 604-737-4916
  Fax: 604-737-6809
  Email: brsw@brsw.bc.ca
  Website: www.brsw.bc.ca
- British Columbia College of Teachers
  400—2025 W Broadway
  Vancouver BC
  V6J 1Z6
  Canada
  Phone: 604-731-817Fax: 604-731-9142

Toll Free: 1-800-555-3684
Email: communication@bcct.ca
Website: www.bcct.ca
The above list is not definitive and or exhaustive.

Career Bridging Programs in British Columbia

Engineers

- Engineer-in-Training (EIT) Program
  This two-year professional and career bridge
  program is coordinated by BC Hydro to provide
  a. On-the-job training with competitive
     salary
  b. Necessary skills, knowledge and
     experience to channel the participant to
     become a junior Engineer in BC Hydro
  c. Training geared towards obtaining P.
     Eng.

During the course of the program, the participant
may be required to relocate to different regions in
and around the province British Columbia.
Eligibility
  1. A University/College degree in Electrical,
     Mechanical, or Civil Engineering
  2. The participant must be eligible for
     registration with APEGBC
  3. The participant must be legally eligible to
     work in Canada
  4. The participant must be able and or
     willing to relocate to different regions
     in and around the province of British
     Columbia

Contact:
BC Hydro
Employment Center, 14th Floor

333 Dunsmuir Street
Vancouver, BC
V6B 5R3
Phone: 604-623-4348
Email: hr.services@bchydro.com

- Internationally Trained Engineers Pilot Program
This professional enhancement and career bridge program aims to make a speedy integration of internationally trained Engineers into the Canadian workplace as registered professionals. It is initiated by different bodies that includes:
  1. MOSIAC
  2. Chilliwack Community Services
  3. SUCCESS
  4. TuturEd
  5. Possibility Concept
  6. Immigrant Services Society of BC
  7. Business Council of BC
  8. Inter-Cultural Association of Greater Victoria
  9. Citizenship and Immigration Canada
  10. Hecate Strait Employment Society
  11. Central Vancouver Island Multicultural Society
  12. Community Futures Development Corporation of North Fraser
  13. YMCA of Greater Vancouver
  14. School District
  15. Community Futures Development Corporation of Greater Trial

The program provides:
  a. Professional work experience
  b. Review of the policies and procedures for the regulatory body

c. Improve the international qualification issues

d. Improve the realities of the job market

For more information, contact any of the participating institutions listed above

Nurses

There are various Pilot initiatives for the Nursing professionals in British Columbia

1. Nurses Cultural Orientation

This professional enhancement and career bridge program is coordinated by the Registered Nurses Association of BC in conjunction with the University of British Columbia Center for Intercultural Studies. The main aim of the program is to:

Prepare the participants to write and pass the Canadian Nurses Examination.

Success in the Canadian Registered Nurses Examination is a gateway into the Nursing Profession for all Nursing professionals.

2. Language Assessment Tool for the Nursing Profession

This professional enhancement and career bridge program is coordinated by the Center Canadian Language Benchmarks and Citizenship and Immigration Canada to provide:

Tool to assess the language skills of foreign trained Nurses

3. Prior Learning Assessment for Licensed Practical Nurses

This professional enhancement and career bridge program is coordinated by Vancouver Community College in conjunction with the College of Licensed Practical Nurses of BC to provide:

Skill and knowledge assessment of International

trained Nurses
4. PLA Tools for the Nurse Practitioner
   This professional enhancement and career bridge program is coordinated by Registered Nurses Association of British Columbia with the participation of the Ministry of Advanced Education and Ministry of Health of Services to provide:
   Assessment of professional capabilities related to 'Nurse Practitioner' as underlined in the BC provincial new Health Professions Act.
5. Transition into Nursing Series
   This professional enhancement and career bridge program is coordinated by the Registered Nurses Association of British Columbia in conjunction with the Center for Curriculum, Transfer and Technology, the Open Learning Agency and the Ministry of Advanced Education. The program aims to provide:
   a. An educational curriculum that will sate the need of Foreign Trained Nurses as they transit to nursing practice in the province of British Columbia
   b. A web-based course that can be completed by the Foreign Trained Nurses before they come to Canada

For more information on any of the programs, contact the coordinators of each program
6. Canadian Language Benchmarks Assessment for Nurses (CELBAN)
   This professional enhancement and career bridge program which is recognized by the College of Licensed Practical Nurses of British Columbia is offered at
   The Assessment Center,
   King Edward Campus
   Vancouver Community College

1155 East Broadway,
Vancouver, BC.
The program is designed for foreign trained Nurses whose first language is not English. For those Nurses who need to meet the English language requirements of the Nursing regulatory bodies in Canada.
The program is designed to provide:

    a.   Assessment of language proficiency in four skills that includes: speaking, listening, reading, and writing

    b.   Training in the language used in the nursing profession

Eligibility

    1.   Prospective participants need to have a minimum of Canadian Language Benchmark (CLB) level 6 language proficiency skills with scores as follows:
        Speaking: CLB 8,
        Listening: CLB 9
        Reading: CLB 8
        Writing: CLB 7
        Contact:
        Jane Sheil—jsheil@vcc.ca
        Patricia Mahler—pmahler@vcc.ca
        Susan Vellutini—svellutini@vcc.ca
        Website: www.celban.org

General questions may be sent to the Canadian English Language Assessment Services (CELAS) Center at celas@rrc.mb.ca

Dieticians

This professional enhancement and career bridge program is coordinated by Langara College and the Dieticians and Nutritionists Association of BC. The program aims to provide:

   a.   The 500 hours of Canadian workplace experience
        required of foreign trained Dieticians for Licensure
        in British Columbia
   b.   Coordinated workplace practice
For more information, contact the coordinators of the
program.

Dental Laboratory Technicians

This professional enhancement program and career bridge
program is coordinated by the Vancouver Community
College, the College of Dental Technicians of British
Columbia and Ministry of Advanced Education. The program
aims to provide:
   a.   Prior Learning Assessment and Recognition
        (PLAR) student guide for Dental Laboratory
        Technicians
   b.   PLA tools for program courses
   c.   PLAR tools for the theory and practical courses
        related to Orthodontics 1, Orthodontics 2 and
        Orthodontics 3
For more information on the program, contact the
coordinators of the program.

International Medical Graduates (IMG's)
In the Province of British Columbia

It is noteworthy to say British Columbia has the lowest IMG
residencies per capita in Canada.
   Pre-Residency Orientation Program for International
Medical Graduates
   This 12-week professional enhancement and career bridge
program is coordinated by the UBC School of Medicine,
College of Physicians and Surgeons of British Columbia and
the Ministry of Health Services of British Columbia. The
program aims to:
   a.   Introduce IMGs to Medical practice within the

context of BC healthcare

b. Prepare IMGs for the Spring and Fall CAERMS selection process

For more information on the program, contact the coordinators.

Obtaining a Residency in British Columbia

1. Canadian Resident Matching Service (CaRMs)
   The percentage of IMGs who obtain residency through CaRMs is about 10%. The CaRMs is one of the ways to get residency in British Columbia.
2. Clinical Trainee
   This method has always proven to be one of the 'easiest' ways of getting residency in BC. To become a clinical trainee, the IMG has to:
   a. Find a practicing medical doctor who will take him/her into the medical practice as a helper/volunteer in a specific practice.

Before taking the IMG on, the medical doctor has to sign the Clinical Traineeship Agreement that is obtainable from the College of Physicians and Surgeons of BC. The College may charge a fee of $75 for educational licensing.

In the form provided by the College, the host/ sponsoring Canadian physician must request and affirm for the following:

i. Registration of the IMG as a clinical trainee
ii. State the duration of traineeship (usually not longer than 3 years)
iii. Procedures and Parameters of the traineeship
iv. The host Physician's and the IMG's responsibilities
v. Aims and benefits of the traineeship
vi. The extent and mode of supervision of the traineeship program
vii. Any clinical contact with patients by the IMG trainee must be closely monitored/supervised by

the host/sponsoring Canadian physician

viii. During the course of the traineeship, the host/ sponsoring Canadian physician must ensure that the IMG trainee complies with the ethical responsibilities set out in the Canadian Medical Association's Code of Ethics.

If the traineeship will be conducted in a hospital environment and or will involve clinical contact with the patients in the hospital, the prospective trainee will provide a document signed by the chief of staff of the hospital. The document must show clear support for the application for temporary registration.

b. The IMG has to obtain Malpractice Insurance Coverage from the Canadian Medical Protection Agency—CMPA. This insurance may cost $100 per month

c. Document confirming success in MCCEE must be submitted

d. Document showing immigration status must be submitted

e. Document confirming success in TOFEL

f. The IMG has to supply the college of Physicians and Surgeons of BC with certified copies of his/her medical diploma, school transcripts, permanent license and proof of registration with the appropriate medical body/council of the country where he/she obtained his medical degree. If the documents are not in English language, it has to be translated to English. Then both the original translation and the original document must be submitted.

After a successful review of all documents submitted by the IMG, the College of Physicians and Surgeons of BC may issue an "Educational License as a Clinical Trainee", for a fee of $75. The license will grant a limited authority to the IMG to access the patients professionally and in so doing will gain Canadian medical/hospital workplace experience.

At the end of the traineeship the IMG will receive a good reference letter from the host medical doctor.

Eligibility for Traineeship Program:

There are two eligible factors to qualify for the traineeship program

1. The IMG applicant must affirm that he/she has received, reviewed and understood the Canadian Medical Association Code of Ethics approved by the College of Physicians and Surgeons of BC. The IMG applicant must successfully demonstrate to the Registrar of the College that he/she understands the different ethical issues and principles especially as regards the respect to patient confidentiality.

2. The IMG applicant must comply completely with Rule 80.1 of the Medical Practitioners Act. Rule 80.1 includes:

    a. The IMG must possess a medical degree issued by a medical school that is in the list of the council's approved medical schools.

    b. The IMG applicant must have successfully undertaken the Medical Council of Canada Evaluating Examination (MCCEE)

    c. Provide a written proof of intended sponsor/supervision by a Canadian physician member who is in good standing and acceptable to the College of Physicians and Surgeons.

Contact:

College of Physicians and Surgeons of BC
400-858 Beatty St.
Vancouver, BC
V6B 1C1
Phone; 604-733-7758
Toll Free: 1-800-461-3008
Fax: 604-733-3503
Website: www.cpsbc.ca

3. St. Paul's Hospital IMG Program
    The St. Paul's Hospital IMG program is designed
    to offer Family Practice Residencies only. The
    program is funded by the Provincial Government
    of BC and is very competitive. This program runs
    for a total duration of 2 years and six months.
Eligibility
a. The prospective participant must have a favourable
    reference letter from a Canadian Doctor
b. Be a Canadian Citizen, a Landed Immigrant, a
    UNO Convention Refugee
c. A minimum score of 250 on the computer-based
    TOEFL and a pass mark on the MCCEE and
    MCCQE, Part I.
d. Must participate and be successful in the
    evaluation process, the Objective Structured
    Clinical Examination (OSCE)
e. Must undertake the 6-8 weeks clinical evaluation
    at the St. Paul's Hospital.
The program is divided into:
                a. Six months of clinical introductory
                    program
                b. Two years of Family Practice Residency
                    program.
For more information contact St. Paul's Hospital in BC.
See general information on IMG's.

Pharmacists

Canadian Pharmacy Practice Program

This 12-week professional enhancement and career bridge program for Foreign Trained Pharmacy Graduates is coordinated by the Division of Continuing Pharmacy Professional Development (CPPD) at the University of British Columbia (UBC). The program aims to provide:

a. Training to gain the required competencies for practice in Canada and British Columbia
b. Communication Skills
c. Therapeutics
d. Patient Dialogue Skills
e. Health Care Systems Overview
f. Practice Skills Laboratory
g. An opportunity to practice performance assessments of the Objective Structured Clinical Examination (OSCE)—this is commonly used in the licensure examinations
h. Preparation for the national Pharmacy licensure examination

Eligibility

1. Prospective participant must have successfully completed the Evaluating Examination of the Pharmacy Examination Board of Canada (PEBC) For more information about PEBC visit the Website at: www.pebc.ca/ (click at the link for the Evaluating Examination)
2. The prospective participant must have successfully completed the English Language Fluency Requirements set out by the college of Pharmacists of British Columbia or a CELPIP score of 4L.

For more information about the language fluency requirements visit the website at: www.bcpharmacists.org/registration/ or www.ares.ubc.ca/CELPIP.

Note: A registration fee may apply to this program

Contact:
Catherine Ekeland
Coordinator, Canadian Pharmacy Practice Program
  The Division of Continuing Pharmacy Professional
  Development
Faculty of Pharmaceutical Sciences
The University of British Columbia
105—2194 Health Sciences Mall
Vancouver, BC
V6T 1Z3
Canada
  Phone: 604-827-5781
  Email: cekeland@interchange.ubc.ca
  Website: www.ubcpharmacy.org/cpe/programs

Immigrant Loan Program

This program is coordinated by MOSIAC, Vancity Credit Union and, Vancity Community Foundation. The program aims to provide:

Access to small loans to cover expenses associated with Licensure, credential assessment, language and skills upgrading.

For more information contact the coordinators of the program.

Access to Trades Project

This enhancement program is coordinated by Kwantlen University College. The program is designed to cover four trade areas for the Foreign Trained Tradespeople: carpentry, refrigeration, plumbing and electrical trades. The program aims to:

a. Guide the Foreign Trained Tradespeople applying for apprenticeship and writing trades qualification examinations.

b. Develop a success oriented assessment methods for

the Foreign Trained Tradespeople
Contact:
Kwantlen College, BC

The Bamboo Network Host Mentoring Program

This professional enhancement program is coordinated by Multicultural Helping House Society (MHHS) and funded by the BC Ministry of Community, Aboriginal and Women's Services. The program matches Foreign Trained Professionals with Professionals in their similar field from the community for mentoring and assistance. The program aims to provide:

a. General introduction to Canadian lifestyle, work habits and corporate culture
b. Introduction to professions and trades
c. Introduction to continuing education and educational requirements in the field
d. The importance of accreditation and registration with professional bodies
e. Introduction to job search strategies
f. Introduction to the similarities and differences between the Canadian professional and trade practices and the foreign professional and trade practices
g. Contacts, references and referrals for employment
h. Information about apprenticeship, internships and or volunteer opportunities
i. Information about accreditation and education
j. Advice on resumes, portfolios, job interviews and interview skills
k. Information about alternative places for employment in the field

Eligibility for the Program

1. The participant must be in Canada for not more than three years
2. The participant must have studied outside of

Canada
3. The participant must have professional work experience outside of Canada
4. The participant must be prepared to work with a mentor for up to six months and complete a program evaluation form

Contact:

Bamboo Network Host Mentoring Program
Phone: 604-8793277

PART 4

8

ACADEMIC BRIDGE

Short Period Academic Programs with Internship/Co-op placements (Post Graduate Certificate/Diploma)

Post graduate certificate and diploma programs with duration not longer than one year with internship/co-op placement is another way of professional enhancement, career bridging and positioning oneself for employment in Canada. You will empower your foreign earned degree with this Canadian graduate certificate with (in some cases) internship/co-op hands-on experience. After completing the program, your new resume will include a postgraduate certificate/diploma earned in a Canadian school and a four to five months internship/coop placement (work experience)—a real prop.

Post-graduate certificate/diploma program is advocated in this edition, so that I will not be advocating that you duplicate an academic qualification you already possess by going for an undergraduate diploma/certificate and or degree in your field of expertise or in a related field. A post-graduate certificate/diploma is an added upward notch to your experience, expertise and academic stance.

In Ontario

The programs are arranged under colleges in an alphabetical order

* ALGONQUIN COLLEGE
  <u>Post-graduate Certificate/Diploma Programs</u>

  Advanced Care Paramedic
  > Duration of Program: 36 weeks
  > Start date: August
  > On completion: Postgraduate diploma/certificate
  > * Note: This program is new in Algonquin
  >   College, it is still waiting the ministry approval

  Event Management
  > Duration of Program: 1 year
  > Start Date: August
  > On completion: Postgraduate diploma/certificate

  Geographic Information System
  > Duration of Program: 1 year
  > Start Date: August
  > On completion: Postgraduate diploma/certificate

  Information System Security
  > Duration of Program: 1 year
  > Start Date: August
  > On completion: Postgraduate diploma/certificate

  Interactive Multimedia
  > Duration of Program: 1 year
  > Start Date: August and January
  > On completion: Postgraduate diploma/certificate

  Registered Nurse-Refresher
  > Duration of Program: 26 weeks
  > Start Date: August
  > On completion: Postgraduate diploma/certificate

  Registered Practical Nurse
  > Duration of Program: 16 weeks
  > Start Date: August and January

On completion: Postgraduate diploma/certificate
Sport Business Management
    Duration of Program: 1 year
    Start Date: August
    On completion: Postgraduate diploma/certificate
Teacher of English as a Second/Foreign Language
    Duration of Program: 1 year
    Start Date: August
    On completion: Postgraduate diploma/certificate
Technical Writer
    Duration of Program: 1 year
    Start Date: August
    On completion: Postgraduate diploma/certificate

Contact:

Website: www.algonquincollege.com

Woodroffe Campus
1385 Woodroffe Avenue
Ottawa, On
K2G 1V8
Phone: 613-727-0002
Toll Free: 1-800-565-4723
Fax: 613-727-7632

Louise Mitchell
Phone: 613-727-4723 ext. 5482
Toll Free: 1-800-565-4723
Email: mitchel@algonquincollege.com

Christine Summers
Phone: 613-735-4700 ext. 2709
Email: summer@algonquincollege.com
Pembroke Campus
315 Pembroke Street East
Pembroke, On
K8A 3K2

Phone: 613-735-4700
Perth Campus
3 Craig Street
Perth, On
K7H 1X7
Phone: 613-267-2859

Admission requirements
Eligibility

The minimum requirements for the
Postgraduate programs is a University degree or
College diploma
Each program may have additional admission
requirement(s), as such it is advisable that you
visit the specific admission requirements section
of each program

- BOREAL COLLEGE
Post-graduate Certificate/Diploma Programs
Gerontology

Duration of program: 1 year
Start Date: September
On completion: Postgraduate Certificate/
Diploma

Alcoholism and Toxicology

Duration of program: 1 year
Start Date: September
On completion: Postgraduate Certificate/
Diploma

Contact:

21, Boulevard Lasalle
Sudbury, On
P3A 6B1
Phone: 705-560-6673
Toll Free: 1-800-361-6673
Fax: 705-560-7641

Or
Louise Descoteaux (Admissions)
Phone: 705-560-6673
Toll Free: 1-800-361-6673
Email: lodescoteaux@borealc.on.ca
Website: www.borealc.on.ca

Admission requirements
Eligibility
The minimum requirements for the
Postgraduate programs is a university degree or
College diploma
Each program may have additional admission
requirement(s), as such it is advisable that you
visit the specific admission requirements section
of each program.

- CAMBRAIN COLLEGE
Post-graduate Certificate/Diploma
Advertising
Duration of Program: 1 year
Start Date: September
On completion: Postgraduate Certificate/
Diploma
Human Resources Management
Duration of program: 3 semesters (1 year)
Start Date: September
On completion: Postgraduate Certificate/
Diploma
Public Relations
Duration of program: 1 year
Start Date; September
On completion: Postgraduate Certificate/
Diploma
Contact
1400 Barrydowne Road

Sudbury, On

P3A 3V8

Phone: 705-566-810

Toll Free: 1-800-461-7145

Fax: 705-525-2087

Or

Brenda Bouchard, Marcel Laforest

Phone: 705-524-7303

Toll Free: 1-800-461-7145

Email: info@cambrianc.on.ca

Website: www.cambrianc.on.ca

<u>Admission requirements</u>

Eligibility

The minimum requirements for the
Postgraduate programs is a University degree or
College diploma

Each program may have additional admission
requirement(s), as such it is advisable that you
visit the specific admission requirements section
of each program.

- CANADORE COLLEGE

<u>Post-graduate Certificate/Diploma Programs</u>

Business Management

Duration of Program: 1 year

Start Date: September and January

On completion: Postgraduate Certificate/
Diploma

Community Resource Consultant

Duration of Program; 12 weeks

Start date: May

On completion: Postgraduate Certificate/
Diploma

Interactive Multimedia

Duration of program; 1 year

Start Date: September
On completion: Postgraduate Certificate/
Diploma

Contact:

100 College Drive
P.O.Box 5001
North Bay, On
P1B 8K9
Phone: 705-474-7600
Fax: 705-494-7462
Website: www.canadadorec.on.ca

Admission requirements

Eligibility

The minimum requirements for the
Postgraduate programs is a University degree or
College diploma
Each program may have additional admission
requirement(s), as such it is advisable that you
visit the specific admission requirements section
of each program.

- CENTENNIAL COLLEGE

Post-graduate Certificate/Diploma Programs

Advertising-Account Management

Duration of Program: 1 year
Start Date: September
On completion: Postgraduate Certificate/
Diploma

Automation Robotics
(Electro-Mechanical Engineering Technician)

Duration of Program: 1 year
Start Date: May
On completion: Postgraduate Certificate/
Diploma

Biotechnology Technician (Industrial Microbiology)

Duration of Program; 1 year
Start Date: September
On completion: Postgraduate Certificate/
Diploma

Book and Magazine Publishing
Duration of Program: 1 year
Start date; September
On completion: Postgraduate Certificate/
Diploma

Corporate Communication
Duration of Program; 1 year
Start Date: September and January
On completion; Postgraduate Certificate/
Diploma

Electronic Commerce
Duration of Program: 1 year
Start date: September
On completion; Postgraduate Certificate/
Diploma

Environmental Protection Technician
Duration of Program: 1 year
Start Date: September
On completion: Postgraduate Certificate/
Diploma

Human Resources Management
Duration of Program: 1 year
Start Date: September
On completion of Program: Postgraduate
Certificate/Diploma

International Business Management
Duration of Program: 1 year
Start Date: September
On completion of Program: Postgraduate
Certificate/Diploma

Marketing Management

Duration of Program: 1 year
Start Date: September
On completion of Program: Postgraduate
Certificate/Diploma

Mechanical Engineering Technician-Design
Duration of Program: 1 year
Start Date: September
On completion of Program: Postgraduate
Certificate/Diploma

Network Specialist
Duration of Program: 1 Semester
Start Date: September and January
On completion of Program: Postgraduate
Certificate/Diploma

Network Specialist Level ll
Duration of Program: 1 Semester
Start Date: September
On completion of Program: Postgraduate
Certificate/Diploma

Registered Nurse-Perioperative Nursing
Duration of Program: 1 Semester
Start Date: September and January
On completion of Program: Postgraduate
Certificate/Diploma

Workplace Wellness and Health Promotion
Duration of Program: 1 year
Start Date: September
- On completion of Program: Postgraduate
Certificate/Diploma

Contact:
Centennial College
P.O.BOX 631, Station A
Scarborough, On
M1K 5E9
Phone: 416-289-5300

Toll Free: 1-800-268-4419
Fax; 416-694-1503
Email: success@centennialcollege.ca
Or
Diane Gooch
Phone: 416-289-5000 ext. 2367
Email: dgooch@centennialcollege.ca
Vicky Choy
Phone: 416-289-5000 ext. 2361
Email: vchy@centennialcollege.ca
Website: www.centennialcollege.ca

Admission requirements
Eligibility
The minimum requirements for the
Postgraduate programs is a University degree or
College diploma
Each program may have additional admission
requirement(s), as such it is advisable that you
visit the specific admission requirements section
of each program

- CONESTOGA COLLEGE
Postgraduate Certificate/Diploma Programs
Accounting and Information Management
Duration of Program: 1 year (3 Semesters)
Start Date: September
On completion of Program: Postgraduate
Certificate/Diploma
Career Development Practitioner
Duration of Program: 1 year
Start Date: September and January
On completion of Program: Postgraduate
Certificate/Diploma
Computer Numerical Control
Duration of Program: 14 weeks

Start Date: July
On completion of Program: Postgraduate
Certificate/Diploma

Early Child Resource Consultant
Duration of Program: 16 weeks
Start Date: May
On completion of Program: Postgraduate
Certificate/Diploma

Environmental Engineering Applications
Duration of Program: 1 year (co-op)
Start Date: September
On completion of Program: Postgraduate
Certificate/Diploma

Human Resource Management
Duration of Program: 1 year (co-op)
Start Date: September
On completion of Program: Postgraduate
Certificate/Diploma

Teaching English as a Second Language
Duration of Program: 25 weeks
Start Date: September
On completion of Program: Postgraduate
Certificate/Diploma

Woodworking Manufacturing Management
Duration of Program: 1 year
Start Date: January
On completion of Program: Postgraduate
Certificate/Diploma

Youth Recreation Leadership
Duration of Program: 16 weeks
Start Date: September
On completion of Program: Postgraduate
Certificate/Diploma

Contact:
Conestoga College

299 Doon Valley Drive
Kitchener, On
N2G 4M4
Phone: 519-895-1097
Fax: 519-748-5926
Email: wwwed@conestogac.on.ca
Or
College information center;
Phone: 519-748-5220 ext. 3656
Email: geninfo@conestogac.on.ca
Website: www.conestogac.on.ca

Admission requirements
Eligibility
The minimum requirements for the
Postgraduate programs is a University degree or
College diploma
Each program may have additional admission
requirement(s), as such it is advisable that you
visit the specific admission requirements section
of each program.

- CONFEDERATION COLLEGE
Post-graduate Certificate/Diploma Programs
Corporate Communications
Duration of Program: 1 year
Start Date: September
On completion of Program: Postgraduate
Certificate/Diploma
Entrepreneurship
Duration of Program: 1 year
Start Date: September
On completion of Program: Postgraduate
Certificate/Diploma
Human Resource Management
Duration of Program: 1 year

Start Date: September
On completion of Program: Postgraduate
Certificate/Diploma
International Business Management
Duration of Program: 1 year
Start Date: September
On completion of Program: Postgraduate
Certificate/Diploma

Contact
Confederation College
P.O.BOX 398
1450 Nakina Drive
Thunder Bay, On
P7C 4W1
Phone: 807-475-6110
Toll Free: 1-800-465-5493
Fax: 807-623-4512 or 807-623-3956
Or
Bob Griffiths
Phone: 807-475-6112
Email: liaison@confederationc.on.ca
Website: www.confederationc.on.ca

Admission requirements
Eligibility
The minimum requirements for the
Postgraduate programs is a University degree or
College diploma
Each program may have additional admission
requirement(s), as such it is advisable that you
visit the specific admission requirements section
of each program

• DURHAM COLLEGE
Post-graduate Certificate/Diploma Programs
Addictions Counsellor

Duration of Program: 1 year
Start Date: September
On completion of Program: Postgraduate
Certificate/Diploma

Communications Disorders Assistant
Duration of Program: 1 year
Start Date: September
On completion of Program: Postgraduate
Certificate/Diploma

Computer Animation-Filmmaking Studio Arts
Duration of Program: 1 year
Start Date: September
On completion of Program: Postgraduate
Certificate/Diploma

E-Commerce
Duration of Program: 1 year
Start Date: September
On completion of Program: Postgraduate
Certificate/Diploma

Financial Planning
Duration of Program: 1 year
Start Date: September
On completion of Program: Postgraduate
Certificate/Diploma

Human Resources
Duration of Program: 1 year
Start Date: September
On completion of Program: Postgraduate
Certificate/Diploma

Paramedic-Advance Care
Duration of Program: 1 year
Start Date: August
On completion of Program: Postgraduate
Certificate/Diploma

Penology and Youth

Duration of Program: 1 year
Start Date: September
On completion of Program: Postgraduate
Certificate/Diploma

Public and Private Investigations
Duration of Program: 1 year
Start Date: September
On completion of Program: Postgraduate
Certificate/Diploma

Sports Business Management
Duration of Program: 1 year
Start Date: September
On completion of Program: Postgraduate
Certificate/Diploma

Supply Chain Management
Duration of Program: 1 year
Start Date: September
On completion of Program: Postgraduate
Certificate/Diploma

Training and Adult Education
Duration of Program: 1 year
Start Date: September
On completion of Program: Postgraduate
Certificate/Diploma

Contact
Durgam College (Oshawa Campus)
P.O.BOX 385
200 Simcoe Street North
Oshawa, On
L1H 7L7
Phone: 905-721-2000 (general)
905-721-3033 (admissions, liaison, and student
recruitment)
Fax: 905 721-3113 (admissions, liaison, and
students recruitment)

Email: https://myplace.durhamcollege.ca
Website: www.durhamcollege.ca
Skills Training Center
1610 Champlain Avenue
Whitby, On L1N 6A7
Phone: 905-721-3300 (general)
905-721-3033 (admissions, liaison and student
   recruitment)
Fax: 905-721-3338
Email: https://myplace.durgamcollege.ca

<u>Admission requirements</u>

Eligibility

The minimum requirements for the
Postgraduate programs is a University degree or
College diploma

Each program may have additional admission
requirement(s), as such it is advisable that you
visit the specific admission requirements section
of each program

- FANSHAWE COLLEGE

<u>Post-graduate Certificate/Diploma programs</u>

Advanced Care Paramedic

Duration of Program: 45 weeks
Start Date: September
On completion of Program: Postgraduate
   Certificate/Diploma

Broadcast Journalism-Television News

Duration of Program: 1 year
Start Date: September
On completion of Program: Postgraduate
   Certificate/Diploma

Broadcast Television Digital Post Production

Duration of Program: 1 year
Start Date: September

On completion of Program: Postgraduate
Certificate/Diploma
Concierge Services-Guest Relations Specialist
Duration of Program: 1 year
Start Date: September
On completion of Program: Postgraduate
Certificate/Diploma
Corporate Communication and Public Relations
Duration of Program: 1 year
Start Date: September
On completion of Program: Postgraduate
Certificate/Diploma
Photography-Advanced
Duration of Program: 1 year
Start Date: September
On completion of Program: Postgraduate
Certificate/Diploma
Recording Industry-Digital Applications
Duration of Program: 1 year
Start Date: September
On completion of Program: Postgraduate
Certificate/Diploma
Contact
Fanshawe College
1460 Oxford Street East
P.O.BOX 7005
London, On
N5Y 5R6
Phone: 519-452-4277
Fax: 519-452-4420
Or
Deborah King
Phone: 519-452-4430 ext. 4662
Email: dking@fanshawec.ca
Dorothy Gryszcuk

Phone: 519-452-4492

Email; dgryszczuk@fanshawec.ca

<u>Admission requirements</u>

Eligibility

The minimum requirements for the Postgraduate programs is a University degree or College diploma

Each program may have additional admission requirement(s), as such it is advisable that you visit the specific admission requirements section of each program

- FLEMING COLLEGE

<u>Post-graduate Certificate/Diploma</u>

Eco-Tourism and Adventure Tourism Management

Duration of Program: 2 Semesters

Start Date: September

On completion of Program: Postgraduate Certificate/Diploma

Expressive Arts

Duration of Program: 8 weeks

Start Date: April

On completion of Program: Postgraduate Certificate/Diploma

Geographic Information Systems Applications Specialist

Duration of Program: 2 Semesters

Start Date: September and January

On completion of Program: Postgraduate Certificate/Diploma

Geographic Information Systems Cartographic Specialist

Duration of Program: 2 Semesters

Start Date: September

On completion of Program: Postgraduate Certificate/Diploma

Museum Management and Curatorship

Duration of Program: 3 Semesters (1 year)
Start Date: September
On completion of Program: Postgraduate
   Certificate/Diploma
Natural Resources Technology-Law Enforcement
Duration of Program: 2 Semesters
Start Date: September
On completion of Program: Postgraduate
   Certificate/Diploma

Contact:
   Fleming College (Sutherland Campus)
   Brealey Drive
   Peterborough, On
   K9J 7B1
   Phone: 705-749-5530
   Fax: 705-749-5540
   Frost Campus
   Alberta Street South
   Lindsay, On
   K9V 5E6
   Phone: 705-324-9144
   Fax: 705-878-9312
   Or
   Leona Decarlo (recruitment/liaison at
      Sutherland)
   Phone: 705-749-5546
   Email: info@flemingc.on.ca
   Darlene Craig (recruitment/liaison at Frost)
   Phone: 705-878-9301
   Email: info@flemingc.on.ca

Admission requirements
   Eligibility
   The minimum requirements for the Postgraduate
      programs is a University degree or College
      diploma

Each program may have additional admission requirement(s), as such it is advisable that you visit the specific admission requirements section of each program.

- GEORGE BROWN COLLEGE
  Post-graduate Certificate/Diploma Programs
  Advanced Baking and Pastry Arts
  Duration of Program: 1 year
  Start Date: September
  On completion of Program: Postgraduate Certificate/Diploma
  Advanced Digital Design
  Duration of Program: 1 year
  Start Date: September and January
  On completion of Program: Postgraduate Certificate/Diploma
  Advanced Wines and Beverage Management
  Duration of Program: 1 year
  Start Date: September
  On completion of Program: Postgraduate Certificate/Diploma
  Business Management
  Duration of Program: 1 year
  Start Date: September and January
  On completion of Program: Postgraduate Certificate/Diploma
  Business Marketing Analysis
  Duration of Program: 1 year (co-op)
  Start Date: September, January, May
  On completion of Program: Postgraduate Certificate/Diploma
  Costume Studies
  Duration of Program: 1 year (3 Semesters)
  Start Date: January

On completion of Program: Postgraduate
Certificate/Diploma

Database Marketing

Duration of Program: 1 year (co-op)
Start Date: September and January
On completion of Program: Postgraduate
Certificate/Diploma

Design Management

Duration of Program: 1 year
Start Date: September and January
On completion of Program: Postgraduate
Certificate/Diploma

Digital Media

Duration of Program: 1 year
Start Date: September and January
On completion of Program: Postgraduate
Certificate/Diploma

Financial Planning

Duration of Program: 1 year
Start Date: September, January, May
On completion of Program: Postgraduate
Certificate/Diploma

Food and Nutrition Management

Duration of Program: 1 year
Start Date: September
On completion of Program: Postgraduate
Certificate/Diploma

Game Design

Duration of Program: 1 year
Start Date: September
On completion of Program: Postgraduate
Certificate/Diploma

Health Informatics

Duration of Program: 1 year
Start Date: September

On completion of Program: Postgraduate
Certificate/Diploma

Human Resources Management
Duration of Program: 1 year
Start Date: September, January, May
On completion of Program: Postgraduate
Certificate/Diploma

International Fashion Management
Duration of Program: 1 year (co-op)
Start Date: September
On completion of Program: Postgraduate
Certificate/Diploma

Marketing Management-Financial Services
Duration of Program: 1 year (co-op)
Start Date: September, January, May
On completion of Program: Postgraduate
Certificate/Diploma

Registered Nurse-Operating Room
Duration of Program: 16 weeks
Start Date: September, January
On completion of Program: Postgraduate
Certificate/Diploma

Registered Nurse-Perinatal Intensive Care
Duration of Program: 15 weeks
Start Date: September, January
On completion of Program: Postgraduate
Certificate/Diploma

Registered Nurse-Critical Care Nursing
Duration of Program: 16 weeks
Start Date: September, February
On completion of Program: Postgraduate
Certificate/Diploma

Restorative Dental Hygiene
Duration of Program: 1 year
Start Date: September

On completion of Program: Postgraduate
Certificate/Diploma
Sports and Event Marketing
Duration of Program: 1 year
Start Date: September, January, May
On completion of Program: Postgraduate
Certificate/Diploma
Wireless Networking
Duration of Program: 1 year
Start Date: September, January, May
On completion of Program: Postgraduate
Certificate/Diploma
Contact:
George Brown College (St. James Campus)
200 King Street East
Toronto, On
M5A 3W8
Phone: 416-415-2000
Toll Free: 1-800-265-2002
Email: info@gbrownc.on.ca
Website: www.georgebrown.ca
Or
Liaisons
Rosalie Starkey, Manager
Phone: 416-415-5000 ext. 4842
Email: rstarkey@gbrownc.on.ca
Cindy Fong
Phone: 416-415-5000 ext. 2056
Email; cfong@gbrownc.on.ca
Cynthia McDonagh
Phone: 416-415-500 ext. 2267
Email: cmcdonag@gbrownc.on.ca
Sharon Kinasz
Phone: 416-415-5000 ext. 4897
Email: skinasz@gbrownc.on.ca

Admission requirements
Eligibility
The minimum requirements for the
Postgraduate programs is a University degree or
College diploma
Each program may have additional admission
requirement(s), as such it is advisable that you
visit the specific admission requirements section
of each program.

- HUMBER COLLEGE
Post-graduate Certificates/Diploma
3D for Production-Broadcast Design and Animation
Duration of Program: 1 year (3 Semesters)
Start Date: September
On completion of Program: Postgraduate
Certificate/Diploma
3D for Production-Gaming and Interactive Entertainment
Duration of Program: 1 year (3 Semesters)
Start Date: September
On completion of Program: Postgraduate
Certificate/Diploma
Accounting and Information Technology
Duration of Program: 2 Semesters
Start Date: September
On completion of Program: Postgraduate
Certificate/Diploma
Acting for Film and Television (Intensive)
Duration of Program: 1 Semester
Start Date: May
On completion of Program: Postgraduate
Certificate/Diploma
Advertising-Media Sales (Accelerated)
Duration of Program: 2 Semesters
Start Date: September

On completion of Program: Postgraduate
Certificate/Diploma

Art Direction
Duration of Program: 2 Semesters
Start Date: September
On completion of Program: Postgraduate
Certificate/Diploma

Arts Administration-Cultural Management
Duration of Program: 1 year (3 Semesters)
Start Date: September
On completion of Program: Postgraduate
Certificate/Diploma

Broadcasting Radio
Duration of Program: 2 Semesters
Start Date: January
On completion of Program: Postgraduate
Certificate/Diploma

Business Administration-Professional Golf Management
Duration of Program: 2 Semesters
Start Date: September
On completion of Program: Postgraduate
Certificate/Diploma

Child and Youth Worker
Duration of Program: 4 Semesters
Start Date: September
On completion of Program: Postgraduate
Certificate/Diploma

Clinical Research
Duration of Program: 1 year (3 Semesters)
Start Date: September
On completion of Program: Postgraduate
Certificate/Diploma

Comedy-Writing and Performance
Duration of Program: 2 Semesters
Start Date: September

On completion of Program: Postgraduate Certificate/Diploma

Computer Applications Development

Duration of Program: 1 year (3 Semesters)

Start Date: September, January

On completion of Program: Postgraduate Certificate/Diploma

Creative Book Publishing

Duration of Program: 1 Semester

Start Date: May

On completion of Program: Postgraduate Certificate/Diploma

Creative Writing-Comic Script Writing

Duration of Program: 2 Semesters

Start Date: September

On completion of Program: Postgraduate Certificate/Diploma

Creative Writing-Fiction, Creative Non-Fiction, Poetry

Duration of Program: 2 Semesters

Start Date: September

On completion of Program: Postgraduate Certificate/Diploma

Developmental Services Worker

Duration of Program: 3 Semesters

Start Date: September

On completion of Program: Postgraduate Certificate/Diploma

Early Childhood Education-Advanced Studies in Special Needs

Duration of Program: 2 Semesters

Start Date: September

On completion of Program: Postgraduate Certificate/Diploma

Enterprise Content Management

Duration of Program: 1year (3 Semesters)

Start Date: September

On completion of Program: Postgraduate
Certificate/Diploma

*Environmental Systems Engineering
Technology-Energy Management*
Duration of Program: 2 Semesters
Start Date: September
On completion of Program: Postgraduate
Certificate/Diploma

Fundraising and Volunteer Management
Duration of Program: 1 year (3 Semesters)
Start Date: September
On completion of Program: Postgraduate
Certificate/Diploma

Graphic Arts and Prepress Technology
Duration of Program: 2 Semesters
Start Date: September
On completion of Program: Postgraduate
Certificate/Diploma

Home Inspection
Duration of Program: 2 Semesters
Start Date: September
On completion of Program: Postgraduate
Certificate/Diploma

Human Resources Management
Duration of Program: 2 Semesters
Start Date: September
On completion of Program: Postgraduate
Certificate/Diploma

Independent Documentary Production
Duration of Program: 2 Semesters
Start Date: September
On completion of Program: Postgraduate
Certificate/Diploma

Interactive Multimedia
Duration of Program: 3 Semesters

Start Date: September
On completion of Program: Postgraduate
Certificate/Diploma
International Marketing-Asia
Duration of Program: 2 Semesters
Start Date: September
On completion of Program: Postgraduate
Certificate/Diploma
International Marketing-Europe
Duration of Program: 2 Semesters
Start Date: September
On completion of Program: Postgraduate
Certificate/Diploma
International Marketing-Latin America
Duration of Program: 2 Semesters
Start Date: September
On completion of Program: Postgraduate
Certificate/Diploma
International Project Management
Duration of Program: 1year (3 Semesters)
Start Date: September
On completion of Program: Postgraduate
Certificate/Diploma
*Internet Management Advanced Web Development
for E-Business*
Duration of Program: 1 year (3 Semesters)
Start Date: September
On completion of Program: Postgraduate
Certificate/Diploma
Internet Management-Content Management
Duration of Program: 1 year (3 Semesters)
Start Date: September
On completion of Program: Postgraduate
Certificate/Diploma
Internet Software Development-Java Enterprise Solutions

Duration of Program: 2 Semesters
Start Date: September
On completion of Program: Postgraduate
Certificate/Diploma

Internet Software Development-Microsoft.Net Solutions
Duration of Program: 2 Semesters
Start Date: September
On completion of Program: Postgraduate
Certificate/Diploma

Internet Software Development-Oracle Java Solutions
Duration of Program: 2 Semesters
Start Date: September
On completion of Program: Postgraduate
Certificate/Diploma

Journalism (Accelerated)
Duration of Program: 4 Semesters
Start Date: September
On completion of Program: Postgraduate
Certificate/Diploma

Marketing Management-Canadian Securities
Duration of Program: 2 Semesters
Start Date: September
On completion of Program: Postgraduate
Certificate/Diploma

Marketing Management-Regular Profile
Duration of Program: 2 Semesters
Start Date: September
On completion of Program: Postgraduate
Certificate/Diploma

Media Copywriting
Duration of Program: 1 year (3 Semesters)
Start Date: September
On completion of Program: Postgraduate
Certificate/Diploma

Mould and Die Design

Duration of Program: 2 Semesters
Start Date: January
On completion of Program: Postgraduate
Certificate/Diploma

Photography (Advanced)
Duration of Program: 2 Semesters
Start Date: September
On completion of Program: Postgraduate
Certificate/Diploma

Post Production
Duration of Program: 1 year (3 Semesters)
Start Date: September
On completion of Program: Postgraduate
Certificate/Diploma

Project Management
Duration of Program: 1 year (3 Semesters)
Start Date: September
On completion of Program: Postgraduate
Certificate/Diploma

Public Administration
Duration of Program: 1 year (3 Semesters)
Start Date: September
On completion of Program: Postgraduate
Certificate/Diploma

Public Relations
Duration of Program: 2 Semesters
Start Date: September, January
On completion of Program: Postgraduate
Certificate/Diploma

Regulatory Affairs
Duration of Program: 1 year (3 Semesters)
Start Date: September
On completion of Program: Postgraduate
Certificate/Diploma

Sales and Marketing for Health Sector Industries

Duration of Program: 1 year (3 Semesters)
Start Date: January
On completion of Program: Postgraduate
Certificate/Diploma

Supply Chain Management
Duration of Program: 2 Semesters
Start Date: September
On completion of Program: Postgraduate
Certificate/Diploma

Teacher of English as a Foreign Language
Duration of Program: 2 Semesters
Start Date: September
On completion of Program: Postgraduate
Certificate/Diploma

Teacher of English as a Second Language
Duration of Program: 2 Semesters
Start Date: September
On completion of Program: Postgraduate
Certificate/Diploma

Television Production and Writing
Duration of Program: 2 Semesters
Start Date: September
On completion of Program: Postgraduate
Certificate/Diploma

Website Administration with a Specialization in Security
Duration of Program:1 year (3 Semesters)
Start Date: September
On completion of Program: Postgraduate
Certificate/Diploma

Wireless Communications
Duration of Program: 2 Semesters
Start Date: September, January
On completion of Program: Postgraduate
Certificate/Diploma

Contact:

Humber College (North Campus)
205 Humber College Boulevard
Toronto, On
M9W 5L7
Fax: 416-675-2451
Website: www.humber.ca (general)
Prospective Students Website:
www.prospectivestudents.humber.ca
Or
Luisa Macchia
Phone: 416-675-6622 ext.5248
Email: luisa.maccchia@humber.ca
Sarah Jane Brimley
Phone: 416-675-6622 ext. 4746
Email: sarah_jane.Brimley@humber.ca
Lori Ann Beckford
Phone: 416-675-6622 ext.4576
Email: LoriAnn.Beckford@humber.ca

Admission requirements

Eligibility

The minimum requirements for the
Postgraduate programs is a University degree or
College diploma

Each program may have additional admission
requirement(s), as such it is advisable that you
visit the specific admission requirements section
of each program.

- LAMBTON COLLEGE

Post-graduate Certificate/Diploma Programs

Event Management

Duration of Program: 1 year
Start Date: September
On completion of Program: Postgraduate
Certificate/Diploma

Human Resource Management
    Duration of Program: 1 year
    Start Date: September
    On completion of Program: Postgraduate
        Certificate/Diploma
Infant/Toddler Care and Guidance (Part Time)
    Duration of Program: 1 year
    Start Date: September, May
    On completion of Program: Postgraduate
        Certificate/Diploma
Information Technology Professional
    Duration of Program: 1 year
    Start Date: November, May
    On completion of Program: Postgraduate
        Certificate/Diploma
Child Care Administrator (Part time)
    Duration of Program: 16 weeks
    Start Date: September
    On completion of Program: Postgraduate
        Certificate/Diploma
Resource Teacher Program (Part Time)
    Duration of Program: 1 year
    Start Date: September
    On completion of Program: Postgraduate
        Certificate/Diploma
Contact:
    Lambton College
    1457 London Road
    Sarnia, On
    N7S 6K4
    Phone: 519-542-7751
    Fax: 519-541-2446
    Email: info@lambton.on.ca
    Website: www.lambton.on.ca
    Or

Liaison
David Simon (Liaison/recruitment officer)
Phone: 519-541-2403
Email: info@lambton.on.ca
Cathie Holden (Acting Registry)
Phone: 519-542-7751 ext.3310

Admission requirements

Eligibility

The minimum requirements for the Postgraduate programs is a University degree or College diploma

Each program may have additional admission requirement(s), as such it is advisable that you visit the specific admission requirements section of each program.

- LOYALIST COLLEGE
  Post-graduate Certificate/Diploma Programs
  Advertising-Media Marketing and Sales

  Duration of Program: 1 year
  Start Date: September
  On completion of Program: Postgraduate Certificate/Diploma

  Broadcast Journalism

  Duration of Program: 7 weeks
  Start Date: May
  On completion of Program: Postgraduate Certificate/Diploma

  Development Services Worker

  Duration of Program: 1 year
  Start Date: September
  On completion of Program: Postgraduate Certificate/Diploma

  E-Journalism

  Duration of Program: 1 year

Start Date: September
On completion of Program: Postgraduate
Certificate/Diploma
E-Journalism (fast Track)
Duration of Program: 7 weeks
Start Date: May
On completion of Program: Postgraduate
Certificate/Diploma
Photojournalism (fast track)
Duration of Program: 7 weeks
Start Date: May
On completion of Program: Postgraduate
Certificate/Diploma
Print Journalism (fast track)
Duration of Program: 7 weeks
Start Date: May
On completion of Program: Postgraduate
Certificate/Diploma
Social Service Worker
Duration of Program: 1 year
Start Date: September
On completion of Program: Postgraduate
Certificate/Diploma
Contact:
Loyalist College
P.O.Box 4200
Wallbridge-Loyalist Road
Belleville, On
K8N 5B9
Phone: 613-969-1913 ext. 2204
Toll Free: 1-888-569-2547
Fax: 613-969-7905
Email: Liaison@loyalistc.on.ca
Website: www.loyalistcollege.com
Or

Laura Naumann
Phone; 613-969-1913 ext. 2399
Lnaumann@loyalistc.on.ca
Sean Fitzgibbon
Phone: 613-969-1913 ext. 2330
Email: Sfitzgib@loyalistc.ca

Admission requirements

Eligibility

The minimum requirements for the Postgraduate programs is a University degree or College diploma

Each program may have additional admission requirement(s), as such it is advisable that you visit the specific admission requirements section of each program.

- MICHENER INSTITUTE

Diploma Programs

The Michener Institute offers some interesting Short duration Science diploma programs.

Cardiovascular Perfusion Technology

Duration of Program: 16 months (could be less with transfer credits)

Start Date: September

On completion of Program: Diploma

Diagnostic Cytology

Duration of Program: 20 months (could be less with transfer credits)

Start Date: September

On completion of Program: Diploma

Genetics Technology

Duration of Program: 18 months (could be less with transfer credits)

Start Date: September

On completion of Program: Diploma

Ultrasound
>Duration of Program: 16 months (could be less with transfer credits)
>Start Date: September
>On completion of Program: Diploma

Contact:
>Michener Institute
>222 St. Patrick Street
>Toronto, On
>M5T 1V4
>Phone: 416-596-3177
>Phone: 1-800-387-9066
>Fax: 416-596-3180
>Website: www.michener.ca
>Or
>Liaison
>Jennifer Gould
>Phone: 416-596-314
>Email: jgould@michener.ca
>Student Services
>Phone: 416-596-3177
>Email: info@michener.ca
>Admission requirements

Eligibility
>Each program may have additional admission requirement(s), as such it is advisable that you visit the specific admission requirements section of each program.

- MOHAWK COLLEGE
Post-Graduate Certificate/Diploma Programs
>Advanced Network and Security Connectivity
>Duration of Program: 1 year
>Start Date: September
>On completion of Program: Postgraduate

Certificate/Diploma

Convention and Meeting Planning
Duration of Program: 1 year
Start Date: September
On completion of Program: Postgraduate
Certificate/Diploma

Diagnostic Cardiac Sonography
Duration of Program: 1 year
Start Date: September
On completion of Program: Postgraduate
Certificate/Diploma

E-Commerce-Business to Business (B 2 B) Specialist
Duration of Program: 1 year
Start Date: January
On completion of Program: Postgraduate
Certificate/Diploma

Human Resources Management
Duration of Program: 1 year
Start Date: September
On completion of Program: Postgraduate
Certificate/Diploma

Instructor for the Visually impaired-Orientation and Mobility
Duration of Program: 1 year
Start Date: September
On completion of Program: Postgraduate
Certificate/Diploma

Instructor for the Visually impaired-Rehabilitation Teaching
Duration of Program: 1 year
Start Date: September
On completion of Program: Postgraduate
Certificate/Diploma

Interactive and Direct Marketing
Duration of Program: 1 year

Start Date: September
On completion of Program: Postgraduate
Certificate/Diploma
International Business Management
Duration of Program: 1 year
Start Date: September
On completion of Program: Postgraduate
Certificate/Diploma
Public Relations
Duration of Program: 1 year
Start Date: September
On completion of Program: Postgraduate
Certificate/Diploma
Video Journalism
Duration of Program: 1 year
Start Date: September
On completion of Program: Postgraduate
Certificate/Diploma
Contact:
Mohawk College (Fennel Campus)
P.O.BOX 2034
Hamilton, On
L8N 3T2
Phone: 905-575-2000
Toll Free: 1-866-410-4795
Fax: 905-575-2392
Email: admissions@mohawkcollege.ca
International Email:
international.aducation@mohawkcollege.ca
Liaison
Trent Jarvis
Phone: 905-5752411
Email: admissions@mohawkcollege.ca
Sandy Willet
Phone: 905-575-2114

Email: admissions@mohawkcollege.ca

Admission requirements

Eligibility

The minimum requirements for the Postgraduate programs is a University degree or College diploma

Each program may have additional admission requirement(s), as such it is advisable that you visit the specific admission requirements section of each program.

- NIAGARA COLLEGE

Post-graduate Certificate/Diploma Programs

Advanced Care Paramedic

Duration of Program: 1 year

Start Date: September

On completion of Program: Postgraduate Certificate/Diploma

Computer Network Operations

Duration of Program: 1 year

Start Date: September, January

On completion of Program: Postgraduate Certificate/Diploma

Ecosystem Restoration

Duration of Program: 1 year

Start Date: September

On completion of Program: Postgraduate Certificate/Diploma

Environmental Management and Assessment

Duration of Program: 1 year

Start Date: September, January

On completion of Program: Postgraduate Certificate/Diploma

Event Management

Duration of Program: 1 year

Start Date: September

On completion of Program: Postgraduate
Certificate/Diploma

Geographic Information Systems

Duration of Program: 1 year

Start Date: September

On completion of Program: Postgraduate
Certificate/Diploma

Hotel Management Systems

Duration of Program: 1 year

Start Date: September

On completion of Program: Postgraduate
Certificate/Diploma

Human Resources Management

Duration of Program: 1 year

Start Date: September

On completion of Program: Postgraduate
Certificate/Diploma

Interactive Multimedia

Duration of Program: 1 year

Start Date: September

On completion of Program: Postgraduate
Certificate/Diploma

International Business Management

Duration of Program: 1 year

Start Date: September

On completion of Program: Postgraduate
Certificate/Diploma

Public Relations

Duration of Program: 1 year

Start Date: September

On completion of Program: Postgraduate
Certificate/Diploma

Teaching English as a Second Language (TESL)

Duration of Program: 1 year

Start Date: September
On completion of Program: Postgraduate
Certificate/Diploma
Tourism Development
Duration of Program: 1 year
Start Date: September
On completion of Program: Postgraduate
Certificate/Diploma

Contact:
Niagara Campus
Admissions
Phone: 905-735-2211 ext. 7619
Info Center:
Phone: 905-735-2211 ext. 7559
Website: www.niagarac.on.ca

Admission requirements
Eligibility
The minimum requirements for the
Postgraduate programs is a University degree or
College diploma
Each program may have additional admission
requirement(s), as such it is advisable that you
visit the specific admission requirements section
of each program.

- ST. LAWRENCE COLLEGE
Post-graduate Certificate/Diploma Programs
Behavioural Science Technology-for B.A Psychology graduates
Duration of Program: 10 months
Start Date: September
On completion of Program: Postgraduate
Certificate/Diploma
Business Administration-Human Resources
Duration of Program: 1 year
Start Date: September

On completion of Program: Postgraduate
Certificate/Diploma
Communicative Disorders Assistant
Duration of Program: 10 months
Start Date: September
On completion of Program: Postgraduate
Certificate/Diploma
Contact:
St. Lawrence College (Kingston Campus)
King & Portsmouth
Kingston, On
K7L 5A6
Phone: 613-544-5400 ext. 1610 or 1627
Fax: 613-545-3920
Brockville Campus
2288 Parkdale Avenue
Brockville, On
K6V 5X3
Phone: 613-345-0660 ext. 3135
Fax: 613-345-2231
Cornwall Campus
2 Belmont Street
Cornwall, On
K6H 4Z1
Phone: 613-933-6080 ext. 2532
Fax; 613-937-1523
Website: www.sl.on.ca
Liaison Office
Phone: 613—544-5400 ext. 1555
Email: liaison@sl.on.ca
Admission requirements
Eligibility
The minimum requirements for the
Postgraduate programs is a University degree or
College diploma

Each program may have additional admission requirement(s), as such it is advisable that you visit the specific admission requirements section of each program.

- SAULT COLLEGE
  Post-graduate Certificate/Diploma Programs
  Business Management
  Duration of Program: 1 year
  Start Date: September
  On completion of Program: Postgraduate Certificate/Diploma
  Geographic Information Systems-Application Specialist
  Duration of Program: 1 year
  Start Date: September
  On completion of Program: Postgraduate Certificate/Diploma
  Contact:
  Sault College
  P.O.BOX 60
  443 Northern Avenue
  Sault Ste. Marie, On
  P6A 5L3
  Phone: 705-759-6700
  Toll Free: 1-800-461-2260
  Fax: 705-759-3273
  Website: www.saultcollege.ca
  Admissions
  Phone: 705-759-6700
  Toll Free; 1-800-461-2260
  Email: registrar@saultc.on.ca
  Admission requirements
  Eligibility
  The minimum requirements for the Postgraduate programs is a University degree or College diploma

Each program may have additional admission requirement(s), as such it is advisable that you visit the specific admission requirements section of each program.

- SENECA COLLEGE
  Post-graduate Certificate/Diploma Programs
  3D Animation
    Duration of Program: 1 year
    Start Date: September, January
    On completion of Program: Postgraduate Certificate/Diploma
  3D Gaming
    Duration of Program: 1 year
    Start Date: September, January
    On completion of Program: Postgraduate Certificate/Diploma
  Accounting and Information Technology
    Duration of Program: 1 year
    Start Date: September, January
    On completion of Program: Postgraduate Certificate/Diploma
  Applied Electronics Design
    Duration of Program: 1 year
    Start Date: September, January
    On completion of Program: Postgraduate Certificate/Diploma
  Bioinformatics
    Duration of Program: 1 year
    Start Date: September
    On completion of Program: Postgraduate Certificate/Diploma
  Corporate Communications
    Duration of Program: 1 year
    Start Date: September

On completion of Program: Postgraduate
Certificate/Diploma

Corporate Communications
Duration of Program: 1 year (co-op)
Start Date: September, January
On completion of Program: Postgraduate
Certificate/Diploma

Costume Production for Film and Television
Duration of Program: 1 year
Start Date: January
On completion of Program: Postgraduate
Certificate/Diploma

Customer Contact Center Management
Duration of Program: 1 year (co-op)
Start Date: January
On completion of Program: Postgraduate
Certificate/Diploma

Database Application Developer
Duration of Program: 1 year
Start Date: September, January
On completion of Program: Postgraduate
Certificate/Diploma

Electro Mechanical Design
Duration of Program: 1 year
Start Date: September, January
On completion of Program: Postgraduate
Certificate/Diploma

Financial Services Compliance Administration
Duration of Program: 1 year
Start Date: September
On completion of Program: Postgraduate
Certificate/Diploma

Financial Services Underwriting
Duration of Program: 1 year
Start Date: September, January

On completion of Program: Postgraduate
Certificate/Diploma
Forensic Accounting
Duration of Program: 1 year
Start Date: September
On completion of Program: Postgraduate
Certificate/Diploma
Global Logistics and Supply Chain Management
Duration of Program: 1 year
Start Date: September
On completion of Program: Postgraduate
Certificate/Diploma
Human Resources Management
Duration of Program: 1 year
Start Date: September, January
On completion of Program: Postgraduate
Certificate/Diploma
Human Resources Management
Duration of Program: 1 year (co-op)
Start Date: September, January
On completion of Program: Postgraduate
Certificate/Diploma
International Business Management
Duration of Program: 1 year
Start Date: September
On completion of Program: Postgraduate
Certificate/Diploma
International Health Services
Duration of Program: 1 Semester
Start Date: September
On completion of Program: Postgraduate
Certificate/Diploma
Internet Systems Administration
Duration of Program: 1 year
Start Date: September

On completion of Program: Postgraduate
Certificate/Diploma

Legal and Corporate Administration
Duration of Program: 1 year
Start Date: September
On completion of Program: Postgraduate
Certificate/Diploma

Marketing Management
Duration of Program: 1 year
Start Date: September
On completion of Program: Postgraduate
Certificate/Diploma

*Pharmaceutical Regulatory Affairs
and Quality Operations*
Duration of Program: 1 year (co-op)
Start Date: September, January
On completion of Program: Postgraduate
Certificate/Diploma

Private Police and Investigations
Duration of Program: 1 year
Start Date: September, January
On completion of Program: Postgraduate
Certificate/Diploma

Regulatory Law Administration
Duration of Program: 1 year
Start Date: September
On completion of Program: Postgraduate
Certificate/Diploma

Technical Communications
Duration of Program: 1 year (co-op)
Start Date: September
On completion of Program: Postgraduate
Certificate/Diploma

Veterinary Technologist
Duration of Program: 1 year

Start Date: January
On completion of Program: Postgraduate
Certificate/Diploma
Visual Effects for Film and Television
Duration of Program: 1 year
Start Date: September, January
On completion of Program: Postgraduate
Certificate/Diploma
Contact:
Seneca College (Newnham)
Admissions Office
1750 Finch Avenue East
Toronto, On
M2J 2X5
Phone; 416- 491-5050 ext. 2800
Fax: 416-493-3958
Email: admissions@senecac.on.ca
Website: www.senecac.on.ca
Admission requirements
Eligibility
The minimum requirements for the
Postgraduate programs is a University degree or
College diploma
Each program may have additional admission
requirement(s), as such it is advisable that you
visit the specific admission requirements section
of each program.

• SHERIDAN COLLEGE
Post-graduate Certificate/Diploma Programs
Computer Animation
Duration of Program: 1 year
Start Date: September, January
On completion of Program: Postgraduate
Certificate/Diploma

Advanced Illustration
    Duration of Program: 1 year
    Start Date: September
    On completion of Program: Postgraduate
    Certificate/Diploma

Advanced Television and Film
    Duration of Program: 1 year
    Start Date: September
    On completion of Program: Postgraduate
    Certificate/Diploma

Computer Animation-Digital Character Animation
    Duration of Program: 1 year
    Start Date: September
    On completion of Program: Postgraduate
    Certificate/Diploma

Computer Animation-Digital Visual Effects
    Duration of Program: 1 year
    Start Date: September
    On completion of Program: Postgraduate
    Certificate/Diploma

Computer Integrated Manufacturing
    Duration of Program: 1 year
    Start Date: September
    On completion of Program: Postgraduate
    Certificate/Diploma

Corporate Communications
    Duration of Program: 1 year
    Start Date: September
    On completion of Program: Postgraduate
    Certificate/Diploma

Design for an Aging Population
    Duration of Program: 1 year
    Start Date: September
    On completion of Program: Postgraduate
    Certificate/Diploma

Early Childhood Education Intensive
Duration of Program: 1 year
Start Date: September
On completion of Program: Postgraduate
Certificate/Diploma

Educational Assistant
Duration of Program: 1 year
Start Date: September
On completion of Program: Postgraduate
Certificate/Diploma

Enterprise Database Management
Duration of Program: 1 Semester
Start Date: September
On completion of Program: Postgraduate
Certificate/Diploma

Environmental Control
Duration of Program: 1 year
Start Date: January
On completion of Program: Postgraduate
Certificate/Diploma

Financial Planning
Duration of Program: 1 year
Start Date: September
On completion of Program: Postgraduate
Certificate/Diploma

Human Resource Management
Duration of Program: 1 year (co-op)
Start Date: September
On completion of Program: Postgraduate
Certificate/Diploma

Human Resource Management
Duration of Program: 1 year (co-op)
Start Date: September, January
On completion of Program: Postgraduate
Certificate/Diploma

Information Technologies Professional Internship
    Duration of Program: 1 year
    Start Date: September
    On completion of Program: Postgraduate
    Certificate/Diploma
Interactive Media
    Duration of Program: 1 year
    Start Date: September
    On completion of Program: Postgraduate
    Certificate/Diploma
International Business
    Duration of Program: 1 year
    Start Date: September
    On completion of Program: Postgraduate
    Certificate/Diploma
Journalism New Media
    Duration of Program: 1 year
    Start Date: September
    On completion of Program: Postgraduate
    Certificate/Diploma
Manufacturing Management
    Duration of Program: 1 year
    Start Date: September
    On completion of Program: Postgraduate
    Certificate/Diploma
Marketing Management
    Duration of Program: 1 year
    Start Date: September
    On completion of Program: Postgraduate
    Certificate/Diploma
Montessori Early Childhood Teacher Education
    Duration of Program: 1 year
    Start Date: May
    On completion of Program: Postgraduate
    Certificate/Diploma

New Media Design
> Duration of Program: 1 year
> Start Date: September
> On completion of Program: Postgraduate
> Certificate/Diploma

Quality Assurance-Manufacturing and Management
> Duration of Program: 1 year (co-op)
> Start Date: January
> On completion of Program: Postgraduate
> Certificate/Diploma

Solid Modeling
> Duration of Program: 1 year
> Start Date: January
> On completion of Program: Postgraduate
> Certificate/Diploma

Contact:
> Sheridan College (Trafalgar Road)
> 1430 Trafalgar Road
> Oakville, On
> L6H 2L1
> Phone: 905-845-9430
> Fax: 905-815-4148
> Davis Campus
> 7899 Mclaughlin Road,
> Box 7500
> Brampton, On
> L6V 1G6
> Phone: 905-459-7533
> Fax: 905-8744313
> Website: www.sheridaninstitute.ca
> Liaison and Student recruitment
> Simone Birthwright
> Phone: 905-845-9430 ext. 2747
> Email: simone.birthwright@sheridaninstitute.ca
> Angela Wigfield

Phone: 905-459-7533 ext. 5200
Email: angela.wigfield@sheridaninstitute.ca
Sara Rumsey
Phone: 905-845-9430 ext. 2135
Sara.rumsey@sheridaninstitute.ca
Karen Marlatt
Phone: 905-845-9430 ext. 2907
Karen.marlatt@sheridaninstitue.ca
June Cupido
Phone: 905-845-9430 ext. 2084
Email: june.cupido@sheridaninstitute.ca
Inquiry Center, Full Time Studies
Phone: 905-459-7533 or 905-845-9430
To order a program calendar
416-657-2015 or 905-338-2416
Email: Sheridan@data-media-inc.com

Admission requirements

Eligibility

The minimum requirements for the
Postgraduate programs is a University degree or
College diploma
Each program may have additional admission
requirement(s), as such it is advisable that you
visit the specific admission requirements section
of each program.

**Note: The Colleges mentioned above are Public
Colleges. However some registered Private Career Colleges
offer Post-graduate diploma/Certificate Programs.

Generally Tuition for Private Colleges is more expensive
than those of Public Colleges.

And not all of the private Colleges have a good standing
in the academic and employment circles.

REGISTERED PRIVATE CAREER COLLEGES

- ACADEMY OF APPLIED PHARMACEUTICAL
  SCIENCES
  Pharmaceutical Quality Control Laboratory
    Duration of Program: 24 weeks
    Start Date: February, March, May, June, August,
      September November
    On completion of Program: Postgraduate
      Certificate/Diploma
  Professional Regulatory Affairs
    Duration of Program: 18 weeks
    Start Date: February, March, May, June, August,
      September November
    On completion of Program: Postgraduate
      Certificate/Diploma
  Pharmaceutical Quality Control & Quality Assurance
    Duration of Program: 24 weeks
    Start Date: February, March, May, June, August,
      September November
    On completion of Program: Postgraduate
      Certificate/Diploma.
  Contact:
    200 Consumers Road
    Suite 200
    North York, On
    M2J 4R4
    Phone: 416-502-2277
    Fax: 416-502-2278
    Website: www.aaps.ca
  Admission Requirements and Eligibility:
    Contact the College

- TORONTO INSTITUTE OF PHARMACEUTICAL
  TECHNOLOGY

Post-graduate Certificate/Diploma Programs

Manufacturing Technology
Duration of Program: 52weeks
Start Date: January, March, June, and September.
On completion of Program: Postgraduate
Certificate/Diploma

Research and Development
Duration of Program: 52 weeks
Start Date: January, March, June, and September.
On completion of Program: Postgraduate
Certificate/Diploma

Quality Assurance & Quality Control
Duration of Program: 39 weeks
Start Date: January, March, June, and September.
On completion of Program: Postgraduate
Certificate/Diploma

High Performance Liquid Chromatography
Duration of Program: 8 weeks
Start Date: January, March, June, and September.
On completion of Program: Postgraduate
Certificate/Diploma

Contact:
55 Town Center Court
Suite 200
Scarborough, On
M1P 4X4
Canada
Phone: 416-296-8860
Fax: 416-296-7077
Email: admin@tipt.com
Website: www.tipt.com

Admission Requirements and Eligibility:
Contact the College

A List of registered Private Career Colleges in Ontario may be obtained from the Website: www.edu.gov.on.ca/eng/general/list/pvs02.html

British Columbia

Colleges in British Columbia
- Vancouver Community College
- Langara College
- Camosun College
- Capilano College
- Douglas College
- Northern Island College
- Northern Lights College
- College of the Rockies
- Selkirk College
- Okanagan University College
- Northwest Community College
- British Columbia institute of Technology
- The College of New Caledonia
- Kwantlen University College
- University College of the Caribo
- University College of the Fraser Valley
- Open Learning Agency (Online and Correspondence programs)
- Justice institute of British Columbia
- Emily Carr institute of Art and Design
- Malaspina University College

For information on Post-graduate Certificate/Diploma offered by Colleges in Other provinces call the Colleges to inquire.

Universities Where You Can Obtain (MBA) Masters of Business Administration in Canada

Ontario

- UNIVERSITY OF TORONTO

    The University of Toronto's MBA program is coordinated by The Rotman School of Management.

    Duration of Program: 20 months

    Program Type: Full-Time, Part-Time and Executive

    Majors: Various majors including specialization in Law, Nursing and Engineering

    Contact:

    105 St. George Street

    Toronto, On

    Canada, M5S 3E6

    Phone: 416-978-3499

    Fax: 416-978-5812

    Email: mba@rotman.utoronto.ca

    Website: www.rotman.utoronto.ca

- YORK UNIVERSITY (TORONTO)

    The York University MBA program is coordinated by The Schulich School of Business

    Duration of Program: 2 years

    Program Type: Full Time, Weekend courses, Opportunity to study abroad

    Majors: 19 areas of specialization, and students are geared to specialize in more than one area.

    Contact:

    4700 Keele Street

    Toronto, On

    Canada, M3J 1P3

    Phone: 416-736-5060

Fax: 416-650-8174
Email: admissions@schulich.yorku.ca
Website: www.schulich.yorku.ca

- QUEEN'S UNIVERSITY (KINGSTON)
  The Queen's University MBA program is mainly
  for people that already have an undergraduate
  degree in Business in addition to a minimum of
  two years work experience.
  Duration of Program: 12—15 months
  (accelerated)
  Program Type: Full time, Executive
  Majors: Science and Technology (12months),
  Executive Degree (15 months)
  Contact:
  Goodes Hall
  143 Union Street
  Kingston, On
  Canada, K7L 3N6
  Phone: 613-533-2330
  Email: info@business.queensu.ca
  Website: www.mbast.com

- UNIVERSITY OF GUELPH (GUELPH)
  Duration of Program: 1 year
  Program Type: Full Time
  Majors; Agribusiness Management, Hospitality,
  Tourism
  Contact:
  Faculty of Management
  Mcdonald Institute, Room 105
  University of Guelph
  Guelph, On
  N1G 2W1 Canada
  Phone: 519-824-4120 ext. 56607
  Fax: 519-836-0661

Toll free: 1-888-622-2474
Email: plago@uoguelph.ca
Website: www.mba.uoguelph.ca

- **BROCK UNIVERSITY**
  Duration of Program: 2 years
  Program type: Full Time (at St. Catharines
  University), Part Time
  Majors: Accounting, Finance, Marketing, Human
  Resources
Contact:
  500 Glenridge Avenue
  St. Catharines, On
  Canada, L2S 3A1
  Phone: 905-688-555- ext. 3916
  Fax: 905-988-5488
  Email: mba@brocku.ca

- **ROYAL MILITARY COLLEGE (KINGSTON)**
  Duration Of Program: 2 years
  Program Type: Full Time, Part Time
  Majors: Military, Government, Commercial Sector,
Contact:
  P.O.BOX 17000, Station Forces
  Kingston, On
  K7K 7B4 Canada
  RMC Liaison Office
  Phone: 613-541-6000 ext. 6984
  Toll free: 1-866-762-2672

- **UNIVERSITY OF OTTAWA**
  Duration of Program: 12—15 months
  Program Type: Full Time, Part Time
  Majors: Finance, International Marketing,
  International Management, Governance,
  Technology

Contact:

136 Jean-Jacques Lussier
Ottawa, On
Canada, K1N 6N5
Phone: 613-562-5884
Fax: 613-562-5912
Email: mba@management.uottawa.ca

- **UNIVERSITY OF WESTERN ONTARIO (LONDON)**
  Duration of Program: 2 years
  Program Type: Full Time, Part Time
  Majors: Many Majors

Contact:

1151 Richmond Street N
London, On
Canada, N6A 3K7
Phone: 519-661-3206
Fax: 519-661-3485
Email: mba@iney.uwo.ca

- **UNIVERSITY OF WINDSOR (WINDSOR)**
  The University of Windsor's MBA is coordinated by
  The Odette School of Business.
  Duration of Program; 2 years
  Program Type: Full Time, Weekends
  Majors: Many majors including joint degree with law

Contact:

Sunset Avenue 418
Windsor, On
Canada, N9B 3P4
Phone: 519-253-3000 ext. 3097
Fax: 519-973-7073
Email: mba@uwindsor.ca

- LAURENTIAN UNIVERSITY (SUDBURY)
  Duration of Program:
  Program Type: Online
  Majors: Many majors including one that leads to a
    diploma
  Contact:
  Program Manager, CGA/LU Online Programs
  School of Commerce and Administration
  Laurentian University
  Sudbury, On
  P3E 2C6 Canada
  Phone: 705-675-1151 ext. 2136
  Fax: 705-675-6518
  Email: jhenri@laurentian.ca

- WILFRED LAURIER UNIVERSITY
  (WATERLOO)
  Duration of Program: 1—3 years
  Program Type: Full Time, Part Time, Weekends
    (Toronto Campus for the weekend program)
  Majors: Management, Development of Managers
  Contact:
  75 University Avenue West
  Waterloo, On
  Canada, N2L 3C5
  Phone: 519-884-0710 ext. 6220
  Fax: 519-886-6978
  Email: mferraro@wlu.ca

- LAKEHEAD UNIVERSITY (THUNDER BAY)
  Duration of Program: 1 year
  Program type: Full Time, Part Time
  Majors: Leadership, Management, Decision
    Making Skills
  Contact:
  Faculty of Business Administration

955 Oliver Road
Thunderbay, On
P7B 5E1 Canada
Phone: 807-343-8110
Fax: 807-343-8023
Email: business@lakeheadu.ca

- CARLETON UNIVERSITY (OTTAWA)

    The Carleton University's MBA program is coordinated by The Eric Sprott School of Business.

    Duration of program: 12—16 months

    Type of Program: Full Time, Part Time, Students also have an option of studying abroad (in Iran, China)

    Majors: Management, Technology, Productivity and Innovation in seven areas.

Contact:

    1125 Colonel By Drive
    Ottawa, On
    Canada, K1S 5B6
    Phone: 613-520-2388
    Fax: 613-520-4427
    Email: www@sprott.carleton.ca

- MCMASTER UNIVERSITY (HAMILTON)

    The McMaster University's MBA program is coordinated by Michael G. DeGroote School of Business.

    Duration of Program: 2 year

    Program type: Full Time, Part time

    Majors: Health Services Management,

Contact:

    1280 Main Street
    Hamilton, On
    Canada, L8S 4M4

Phone: 905-525-9140 ext. 24105
Fax: 905-521-8995
Email: bizinfo@mcmaster.ca

Quebec

- CONCORDIA UNIVERSITY (MONTREAL)
  The Concordia University's MBA Program is
  coordinated by The John Molson School of
  Business.
  Duration of Program: 1—2 years
  Program Type: Full Time, Part Time
  Majors: Many Majors including Aviation.
  Contact:
  1455 de Maisonneuve Blvd. West
  Montreal, QC
  Canada, H3G 1M8
  Phone: 514-848-2424 ext. 2779
  Fax: 514-848-2424 ext. 4502
  Email: arthur@jmsb.concordia.ca

- HEC MONTREAL
  The HEC Montreal Business School operates in
  affiliation with the University of Montreal
  Duration of Program: 1 year
  Program Type: Full time, Part Time
  Majors: Many majors offered in English and
  French
  Contact:
  3000 Chmin de la Cote-Sainte-Catherine
  Montreal, Quebec
  H3T 2A7
  Phone: 514-340-6151 or 514-340-6136
  Fax: 514-340-5640
  Email: info@hec.ca
  Website: www.hec.ca

- LAVAL UNIVERSITY (QUEBEC CITY)
    Duration of Program: 2 years
    Program type: Full Time, Part Time
    Majors: International Financial Markets, Financial
    Management of International Companies
  Contact:

- MCGILL UNIVERSITY (MONTREAL)
    Duration of Program: 2 years, 1 year (covers study
    in Japan), 2—5 years (for majors in Medicine,
    Dentistry and law)
    Program Type: Full Time, Part Time
    Majors: Various including Law, Dentistry and
    Medicine
  Contact:
    1001 Sherbrooke Street West
    Montreal, QC
    Canada, H3A 1G5
    Phone: 514-398-4066
    Fax: 514-398-2499
    Email: mba.mgmt@mcgill.ca

- UNIVERSITY OF QUEBEC (TRAINING IN
  CAMPUSES THROUGHOUT QUEBEC)
    Duration of Program: Varies
    Program type: Weekends, Once a month,
    Distance Learning
    Majors: Many including Financial Management,
    Certification, Taxation
  Contact:
    Service de l'admission UQAM
    Case Postale 6190, Succursale Centreville
    Montreal, Quebec
    H3C 4N6
    Phone: 514-987-3132
    Or 514-987-4448

514-987-7704
Fax: 514-987-3084
Or 514-987-3084

British Columbia

- MALASPINA UNIVERSITY COLLEGE
(VANCOUVER ISLAND)
     Duration of Program: 12 months
     Program Type: Full Time, Part Time,
       Students have the option to study abroad (at
       Hertfordshire University, England)
     Majors: Various
  Contact:
     Masalpina University College
     900 Fifth Street
     Nanaimo, BC
     V9R 5S5 Canada
     Phone: 250-740-6316 or 250-740-6178
     Email: Kelly@mala.bc.ca
     Or saurazasj@mala.bc.ca

- SIMON FRASER UNIVERSITY
(BURNABY—VANCOUVER)
     Duration of Program: 12—24 months
     Program Type: Full Time, Part time, Executive
     Majors; International Business, Leadership,
       Marketing, Market Intelligence, Technology
       Management, Global Asset Management,
       Wealth Management
  Contact:
     SFU MBA Program
     Faculty of Business Administration
     Burnaby, BC
     Canada, V5A 1S6
     Phone: 604-291-3047

Fax: 604-291-3404
Email: mba@sfu.ca

- UNIVERSITY OF BRITISH COLUMBIA (VANCOUVER)

    The University of British Columbia MBA program is coordinated by The Sauder School of Business.

    Duration of program; 15 months

    Program Type: Full time, Part time (with Internships, Projects)

    Majors: Various International Business courses

Contact:

    2053 Main Mall
    Vancouver, BC
    Canada, V6T 1Z2
    Phone: 604-822-8500
    Fax: 604-822-8521
    Email: mba@sauder.ubc.ca

- UNIVERSITY OF VICTORIA

    Duration of Program: 17 months

    Program Type: Full time, Part Time

    Majors: Entrepreneurship, Management, Law

Contact:

    Faculty of Business
    P.O.BOX 1700 STN CSC
    Victoria, BC
    Canada, V8W 2Y2
    Phone: 250-472-4728
    Fax: 250-721-7066
    Email: mba@business.uvic.ca

- ROYAL ROADS UNIVERSITY (VICTORIA)

    Duration of Program: Varies

    Program Type: Full Time, Part Time, Internet

based distance learning
Majors: Global Aviation, Public Relations
<u>Contact:</u>
Office of the Registrar
Royal Roads University
2005 Sooke Road
Victoria, BC
V9B 5Y2 Canada
Phone: 250-391-2600 ext. 4157
Toll free: 1-877-775-7272
Email: mehgan.Summerville@royalroads.ca
Or MBA@royalroads.ca

Nova Scotia

• DALHOUSIE UNIVERSITY (HALIFAX)
Duration of Program: 16 months
Program Type: Full Time, Part Time
Majors: Many Majors with a particular aim at
gearing students to become managers of small
and big organizations.
<u>Contact:</u>
6152 Coburg Road
Halifax, NS
Canada, B3H 3J5
Phone: 902-494-7080
Fax: 902-494-1107
Email: Amita.MacInnis@dal.ca

• MOUNT ST. VINCENT UNIVERSITY (HALIFAX)
The Mount St. Vincent University is coordinated
in conjunction with Heriot Watt University.
Duration of Program: Varies
Program Type: Distance learning
Majors: Tourism
<u>Contact:</u>

166 Bedford Highway
Halifax, Nova Scotia
B3M 2J6 Canada
Phone: 902-457-6117 Or 902-457-6511
Toll free: 1-800-665-3838
Email: admissions@msvu.ca
Or rgistrar@msvu.ca

- ST. MARY'S UNIVERSITY (HALIFAX)
    The St. Mary's University MBA program is
      coordinated by The Sobey School of Business
    Duration of Program: 2 years
    Program Type: Full Time, Part Time
    Majors: Multinational Corporations,
      Entrepreneurs
  Contact:
    Saint Mary's University
    Halifax, NS
    Canada, B3H 3C3
    Phone: 902-420-5002
    Fax: 902-420-5119
    Email: mba@stmarys.ca

- UNIVERSITY COLLEGE OF CAPE BRETON
    Duration of Program: Varies
    Program Type: Full Time, Part Time
  Contact:
    1250 Grand Lake Road
    Sydney, NS
    Canada, B1M 1A2
    Phone: 902-563-1467
    Fax: 902-562-0075
    Email: gmacinty@uccb.ns.ca

New Brunswick

- LANSBRIDGE UNIVERSITY (NEW BRUNSWICK)
    Duration of Program: Varies
    Program Type: Online/Internet based, Executive
      MBA
    Majors: Many
  Contact:
    10 Knowledge Park Drive
    Suite 120
    Fredericton, New Brunswick
    E3C 2M7 Canada
    Phone: 1-506-443-078
    1-800-839-5602
    Fax: 1-506-459-2909
    Email: admissions@lansbridge.com

- UNIVERSITY OF NEW BRUNSWICK (ST. JOHN'S CAMPUS)
    Duration of Program: 4 years
    Program Type: Full Time, Part Time
    Majors: Joint Law/MBA
  Contact:
    UNB Saint John
    P.O.BOX 5050
    Saint John, NB
    Canada, E2L 4L5
    Phone: 506-648-5746
    Fax: 506-648-5574
    Email: mba@unbsj.ca
    OR
    P.O.BOX 4400
    Fredericton, NB
    Canada, E3B 5A3

Phone: 506-453-4869
Fax: 506-453-3561
Email: fadmin@unb.ca

Alberta

- UNIVERSITY OF CALGARY
    The MBA program of the University of Calgary is
    coordinated by Haskayne School of Business.
    Duration of Program: 2—5 years
    Program Type: Full Time, Part Time
    Majors: Energy, Management, Human Resources,
    combine degrees with Law, Medicine, Social
    work
Contact:
    2500 University Drive NW
    Calgary, AB
    Canada, T2N 1N4
    Phone: 403-220-5685
    Fax: 403-282-0095
    Email: webmaster@haskayne.ucalgary.ca

- ATHABASCA UNIVERSITY (ATHABASCA,
    WITH SATELLITE CAMPUSES IN CALGARY
    AND EDMONTON)
    Duration of Program: 2—3 years
    Program Type: Full Time, Part Time, Internet
    based distance learning
    Majors: Accountancy/Accounting, Defense
    (military)
Contact:
    1 University Drive
    Athabasca, AB
    T9S 3A3 Canada
    Phone: 780-459-1144
    Toll free: 1-800-561-4650

Fax: 780-459-2093
Toll free fax: 1-800-561-4660
Email: liaison@mba.athabascau.ca

- UNIVERSITY OF ALBERTA (EDMONTON)
  Duration of Program: 2 years
  Program Type: Full Time, Part Time
  Majors: Natural Resources, Sports Management,
    Law, Engineering, Agriculture, Forestry
Contact:
  Office of MBA Programs
  2-30 Business Building
  Edmonton, AB
  Canada, T6G 2R6
  Phone: 780-492-3946
  Fax: 780-492-7825
  Email: mba.programs@ualberta.ca

Newfoundland

- MEMORIAL UNIVERSITY OF
  NEWFOUNDLAND (ST. JOHN)
  Duration of Program: 1—2 years
  Program Type: Full Time, Part Time, students has
    the option to study in Europe
  Majors: Many Majors
Contact:
  Faculty of Business Administration
  St. John's, NF
  Canada, A1B 3X5
  Phone: 709-737-8522
  Fax: 709-737-7680
  Email: business@mun.ca

Saskatchewan

- UNIVERSITY OF SASKATCHEWAN (SASKATOON)
  Duration of Program: 1—2 years
  Program Type: Full Time, Part Time
  Majors: Management
  Contact:
  College of Commerce
  25 Campus Drive
  Saskatoon, SK
  Canada, S7N 5A7
  Phone: 306-966-8678
  Fax: 306-966-2515
  Email: hanson@commerce.usask.ca

- UNIVERSITY OF REGINA (REGINA)
  Duration of Program: Varies
  Program Type: Part Time, Executive
  Majors: Management
  Contact:
  Faculty of Administration
  Education Building 517
  University of Regina
  Regina, SK
  S4S 0A2 Canada
  Phone: 306-585-4724
  Fax: 306-585-5361
  Email: admin.grad@uregina.ca

- FIRST NATIONS UNIVERSITY OF CANADA (REGINA, SASKATOON, PRINCE ALBERT)
  Duration of Program: Varies
  Program Type: Full Time, Part Time, in conjunction with the University of Saskatchewan
  Majors: Indigenous Management

- UNIVERSITY OF LETHBRIDGE
  Duration of Program: Varies
  Program Type: Full Time, Part point in time
  Majors: Accounting, First Nations Governance
  Contact:
  Phone: 403-329-2148
  Or 403-381-0140/403-382-7173

Manitoba

- UNIVERSITY OF MANITOBA (WINNIPEG)
  Duration of Program: 11 months
  Program Type: Full Time, Part Time
  Majors: Many majors
  Contact:
  324 Drake Centre
  Room 268 Drake Centre
  Winnipeg, MB
  Canada, R3T 2N2
  Phone: 204-474-8488
  Fax: 204-474-7529
  Email: Asper_Grad@Umanitoba.ca

** Note: It is advisable that you start as soon as possible to undertake any of the programs discussed in this edition. A common mistake Foreign Trained Professionals make on arriving in Canada is thinking that they can get a job as easily and as good as Canadian groomed Professionals within the Canadian job market. Well, they could, but not in most cases. Some Foreign Trained Professionals also think that it is a waste of time and resources going back to school for the sole purpose of becoming employable. They may be right considering the fact that they have the expertise it takes to do the job. But history has proved it time and again that no time spent acquiring knowledge and expertise is a waste. Some Foreign Trained Professionals spend years doing 'survival jobs' while sending out resumes and going from one interview to another. The months and in some cases years spent on 'survival jobs', sending resumes and attending unproductive interview sessions is enough to complete any of the academic bridge programs and or co-op placement programs.

STUDENT FINANCE IN CANADA

Financial support may be available for your education and training. Visit the following websites to find out your eligibility for financial support and scholarship:

- Ontario Student Assistance Plan (OSAP)
  Website: www.osap.gov.on.ca
- CanLearn Interactive
  www.canlearn.ca
- Students Awards
  www.studentsawards.com

The following is an alphabetical list of Students Assistance Offices in different Provinces and Territories:

Alberta

Alberta Learning
Students Finance
Edmonton
Phone: 780-427-3722
Toll Free: 1-800-222-6485
Website: www.alis.gov.ab.ca

British Columbia

Student Services Branch
Ministry of Advanced Education
Phone: 250-387-6100 (Victoria region)
604-660-2610 (lower mainland)
Toll Free: 1-800-561-1818
(anywhere in Canada/USA)
TTY: 250-952-6832

Website: www.bcsap.bc.ca

Manitoba

Student Aid Branch
Department of Advanced Education and Training
Phone: 204-945-6321
204-945-2313 (from outside Manitoba)
Toll Free: 1-800-204-1685 (within Manitoba)
TTY: 1-866-209-0696(within North America)
Website: www.studentaid.gov.mb.ca

New Brunswick

Student Financial Services
Department of Education
Phone: 506-453-2577(Fredericton region)
Toll Free: 1-800-667-5626
Website: www.studentaid.gnb.ca

Newfoundland and Labrador

Student Aid Division
Department of Youth Services
and Post secondary Education
Phone: 709-729-5849
Toll Free: 1-888-657-0800
Website: www.edu.gov.nf.ca/studentaid/

Nova Scotia

Student Assistance Office
Department of Education
Phone: 902-424-8420
Toll Free: 1-800-565-8420 (within Nova Scotia)
TDD: 902-424-2058
Website: www.studentloans.ednet.ns.ca

Ontario

Student Support Branch
Ministry of Training, Colleges and Universities
(Students attending a post-secondary institution in
Ontario must contact the financial aid office at their
post-secondary institution for assistance)
Phone: 807-343-7260 (outside Ontario)
TDD: 1-800-465-3958
Website: www.osap.gov.on.ca

Prince Edward Island

Student Financial Services
Department of Education
Phone: 902-368-4640
Website: www.studentloan.pe.ca

Saskatchewan

Student Financial Assistance Branch
Saskatchewan Learning
Phone: 306-787-5620 (Regina region0
Toll Free: 1-800-597-8278
Website: www.student-loans.sk.ca

Yukon

Student Financial Assistance
Advanced Education Branch
Department of Education
Phone: 867-667-5929
Toll Free: 1-800-661-0408 or
1-800-661-5929 (within Yukon)
Website: www.education.gov.yk.ca

If you are residing in any of the following Provinces/
Territories:
• Quebec

- Northwest Territory
- Nunavut.

It is noteworthy at this point to know that the above listed Provinces/Territories by choice do not participate in the Canada Student Loans Program, but have their Provincial/Territorial Student Financial Assistance programs in place. Their programs have the same underlying principles as those in other provinces.

Consult the Provincial/Territorial Student Financial Assistance Office, Website and or the Financial Aid Office of your institution of choice for further information.

If you are designated as a Protected Person or Convention Refugee in Canada, it is also noteworthy to know that you are now eligible for student financial assistance from the Government of Canada. The Government of Canada recognized in the 2003 Federal Budget the need to amend the Canadian Student Financial Assistance Act to include Protected Persons and Convention Refugees as recipients of the Canadian Student Loan Program (CSLP) for Full-time and Part-time students.

Students Assistance in Canada includes:
a. Full-time students
Full-time students are offered assistance on the basis of need
b. Part-time students
Part-time students are given aid on the basis of income.

In theory, all Canadian Citizens including Permanent Residents are free to apply for the Student Assistance Program. But the lone factor of Canadian Citizenship and Permanent Residency does not guarantee eligibility for the Student Financial Assistance. To obtain student financial assistance in Canada, one must be eligible. The eligibility criteria are put in place as a check to who can apply, and to ward off abuses and misuse of the publicly subsidized loans.

To obtain the Student Financial Assistance you must apply and qualify for the assistance program in your province of residence.

However if you do not qualify for the mainly need-based government student loan/assistance, there are other avenues for student assistance in Canada.

Other Forms of Student Assistance and Student Credit in Canada

Non-governmental Student Financial Assistance

Educational Institutions

Canadian post-secondary institutions—Colleges and Universities spend over $220m annually in student financial assistance.

The assistance is divided into

a. Need-based Awards
b. Merit-based Awards
c. Need-Merit (Hybrid) Awards
d. Institutional Work-Study Awards

Canadian Universities are the third largest provider of Students Financial Assistance in Canada. First is the provincial government of Quebec and second is the Canada Millennium Scholarship Foundation.

Banks

Canadian Banks offer student loans in the form of a line of credit. In offering students loans, the banks have at the back of their minds the future income prospects of students on graduation. The basis of Banks student loans quite unlike the government's (publicly funded) is not Need-based. Government students loan program does not require students to make any form of repayment while they are still in school, but the Banks require the student to make monthly interest payment on the borrowed amount while they are still in school. Though after graduation, most banks give a longer grace period for the graduates before they start paying both the interest and the principal. The Banks grace period is usually 12 months while the government's grace period is usually 6 months. Like the government student financial assistance, the student has to be eligible to obtain the banks line of credit.

<u>Eligibility</u>

a.   Proof of full or part time enrollment at a recognized Canadian University or College

b.   Canadian Citizen or Landed Immigrant/ Permanent Resident

For international students who could provide a Canadian co-signer, a line of credit may be obtained

c.   A Canadian co-signer who is financially independent and able to pay the interest in question

In the opinion of most people, students do not have a steady means of income, as such a co-signer is need to guarantee that the monthly interest on the loan is paid. If the student can provide a guaranteed means of paying the monthly interest, the bank will drop the co-signer requirement.

d.   The past borrowing habit and credit history of the student and the co-signer are checked and must score a relatively good standing.

In offering the line of credit to students, Banks do not usually consider the field of study. But nonetheless some Banks have individual arrangements for some programs.

<u>Example</u>

Royal Bank

Royal Bank in all provinces offers a negotiable annual maximum credit limit, an annual minimum credit limit of $5,000, and a negotiable total maximum credit limit for all graduate programs.

Bank of Montreal

Bank of Montreal in all provinces offers a program-dependent and negotiable annual maximum credit limit, and total maximum credit limit of $65,000—$100,000 for the following programs:

a. Medicine
b. Dentistry
c. Veterinary Medicine
c. Optometry
d. Pharmacy
e. Chiropractic
f. Accounting
g. Law

Canadian Imperial Bank of Commerce (CIBC)

CIBC in all provinces offers an annual maximum credit limit of $15,000, and a total maximum credit limit of $80,000 for the following programs.

a. Medicine
b. Dentistry
c. Veterinary Medicine
c. Optometry
d. Law
e. Master's of Business administration (MBA)

TD Canada Trust

TD Canada Trust Bank in all provinces offer a program-dependent and negotiable annual maximum credit limit, and a total maximum credit limit of $6,000—$60,000 for the following programs.

a. Medicine
b. Dentistry
c. Veterinary Medicine

    c.   Graduate programs

    d.   Law

    e.   Master's of Business administration (MBA)

The data given above is according to the survey made in 2001 by the Canadian Millennium Scholarship Foundation. Changes may occur at any time.

Another form of Assistance to students comes in the form of Student Employment Programs

The different kinds of Student Employment Programs are as follows:

a.   Wage subsidy

This is a kind of job support where by the company (public/private) pays only a percentage of the wage and the government subsidizes the rest of the Students wage.

b.   Mentoring

In this program students receive guidance, support and exposure in the work environment.

c.   Job placements

In this program the students are provided with referrals, consultations and job market information

d. Entrepreneur programs

This program is specially designed to encourage students to start their own small business that is somewhat related to their field of study. The program provides the students with financial and technical support.

For more information on Student Financial Assistance Program see the *books:*

- The Price of Knowledge: Access and student Finance in Canada.
  Millennium Research Series 2002

By Sean Junor and Alexander Usher
- Students Loans in Canada: past, present and future
  By Ross Finnie and Saul Schwartz
- Your Guide To Scholarships and Bursaries:
  Funding for Colleges and Universities: Province by
  Province and Canada-wide lists
  By Darlene Kidd
- Scholarships Canada.com Entrance Awards
  Directory.
- Comprehensive Information on Canadian
  Scholarships and Awards.
  Published by Edge Interactive
  ISBN: 0-9731678-0-7

PART 5

9

YOU CAN GIVE YOURSELF A JOB
AND BE YOUR OWN BOSS

START YOUR OWN BUSINESS

There are boundless opportunities to start your own business in Canada.

The following is an excerpt from the factual fiction book entitled *Overqualified Labourer*.

"I applied for a line of credit to finance a business and luckily the bank approved it and the business was born," said Mr. Prat.

"You like it? Being a businessman?" asked Goodwill

"Although I'd never been a businessman, but I didn't allow the lack of knowledge of the business world to be a barrier. I'm feeling so empowered now. More empowered than I'd ever been as an Engineer. My birth country made me an Engineer, an employee, but Canada my adopted country hewn an entrepreneur out of me. An employer." said Mr. Prat.

"I never knew I am a great Entrepreneur. It takes coming to Canada and the ambush of the bully—'No Canadian

Experience' to sprout the Entrepreneurial genius in me. God bless Canada," he added

"You see when you come into this territory. As a new comer in a new environment, one is squeezed, eased and squeezed, It is one's responsibility to remain eased" said Mr. Prat pausing

"The winner's creed" thought Goodwill

"And how do you do this? Remaining eased" continued Mr. Prat

"By thinking of what you do for yourself, Canada and Canadian employment procedure rather than waiting on Canada and the employment procedure to do things for you. Like that you will escape the spell and toll of 'No Canadian Experience'..."

"Be a winner," thought Goodwill

"Will you be going back to your country any time soon?" asked Goodwill.

"About five of my friends went back sad and dejected, but me, never, I love Canada" said Mr Prat

"Don't quit" thought Goodwill

"It's a wonderful place here. How can I go home now that I'm an employer? And I employ only Foreign Trained Professionals. I have two in my team now. I don't employ Canadian groomed professionals. It's my own little way of contributing to ease it for the new arrivals" said Mr. Prat

"Only Foreign Trained Professionals eh?" asked Goodwill

"Yes, I hire whom I deem right," said Mr. Prat

"It's discrimination you know," said Goodwill

"Yes, and I feel comfortable with it" said Mr. Prat

"Do you forgive those who snubbed you during your search for an employment opportunity?" asked Goodwill

"It isn't so much as forgiving as recognising that I practise a bigoted selection of employees as my own little way of helping Foreign Trained Professionals find jobs and live their dreams in this great land, " said Mr. Prat.

"And you know what?

Foreign trained folks are not only a little less expensive to hire. They are in addition, very hard working, ready to accept a junior position. They know their stuff and very ready to learn and learn fast. They are very enterprising and never take anything for granted.

They are good.

Hire Foreign Trained Professionals anywhere you see them" added Mr. Prat

Goodwill nodded approvingly.

Back home, Goodwill the South African trained Chemist recounted Mr Prat's story and juxtaposing it with his own ordeal, Mr. Befod the Jamaican Business Analyst, the Romanian Electrical Engineer, Brito the Nigerian Sociologist, the Pakistani Medical Doctor and a host of others.

"Mr. Prat's is a success story, a winner. But there are thousands who are not as lucky. It's like a race, some survive, others quit and some hang on battling just to keep the dream alive." thought Goodwill as he posed to pen the compelling factual fiction prose—"Overqualified Labourer: No Canadian Experience".—A sure entertainer

Before thinking of starting your own business, make sure you have discovered yourself. Business ownership is not for everybody. You need an entrepreneurial trait and skills to be able to run a successful business. Just like finding and holding a good job, you need skills to start and run a successful business. Lots of people can start and run a business into bankruptcy and themselves into dissatisfaction, stress and depression, but not everybody can start and run a business from shoestring to a multi- thousand/million dollar success, personal satisfaction and probably happiness.

Before thinking of starting your own business, answer the following questions honestly.

1. **Why do I want to start my own business?**
   Probable answers may include:

a. Because I like being my own boss
    The lure of power and freedom, of being
    completely independent could be overwhelming
    sometimes. Power and freedom are two very good
    things that every human being craves, but not all
    could handle on their own. However it is good
    to be not just a boss but also a good and capable
    boss.

b. To make lots of money and take control of my
    financial life
    It is extremely good to make lots of money and
    enjoy all that money could buy. But remember that
    if you love abundance, you will never be satisfied
    with increase—good for business.

c. To escape the spell and toll of the bully—'No
    Canadian Experience'
    Your fear is rational and the trauma not
    unfounded. However get ready for this escape
    route, it could be rocky as well.

d. Because I like taking risks
    Business in itself is really a risk. And risk taking is
    part of going through life. The ability to take risks
    is a good quality of an entrepreneur.

e. To do something different, to make a change
    Change is inherent to the human nature and
    human environment. We live in a dynamic world
    and life itself is dynamic. But change of this nature
    is better done when it is reasonable/necessary.

f. I want to start my own business because I can't
    find and hold a good job anywhere else
    In life, when desirable is unattainable, you make
    your attainable your desirable. But make the best
    out of this attainable.

g. Because I have the drive/enthusiasm
    Although drive and enthusiasm are good traits of

an entrepreneur, but the two alone may not carry you through. You also need a functional plan. Like a warrior for success, your drive and enthusiasm will guide you through long hours working on your laid down business plan.

h. I want to start my own business because I have a business idea/plan.
A good business idea, a good plan, drive and enthusiasm will carry you through to success.

i. I am People smart
People smartness in addition to being extremely useful in business is also required for success in most things in life.

j. Because I have lots of common sense
Common sense is the basis of good sense. Most seemingly difficult and wondrous things in life were achieved using common sense. Rocket science and the science of cloning require lots of common sense. But unfortunately good sense is not always common. Common sense will play a huge factor in running a successful business.

k. I have trouble and liability shooting abilities
Both are good entrepreneurial traits that will help you resolve issues in your business as they arise.

l. I want my own business because I am very decisive and deliberate
The daily running of a business involves planning, making decisions, and executing plans and decisions. If you are decisive and deliberate, your business has scored a vital point on its match to success.

m. Because I am creative, original and tactful
Creativity, originality and tactfulness are known winners. This is another huge point for running a successful business.

2. Why won't I Start My Own Business?

Probable answers may include:

a. I am afraid of uncertainties and risks involved in business

It is very good to be honest in identifying one's weaknesses, provided you do not misrepresent your weaknesses. Coming to Canada is somewhat stepping into uncertainties, and as such, it is a risk in itself. Uprooting from home, from the comfort of well established social structure and protection—abandoning family, friends, a cherished knowledge of how the mechanics of things work in your native home to make a leap of faith into a strange land is sheer bravery, courage and adventure. It also takes flexibility, hard work, determination, money, time and emotional upheaval to relocate. So? You are already a risk taker, an adventurer. Well, only you and you alone know how much you are afraid of risks and uncertainties in general and as it relates to business. Probably you are yet to figure out how to undertake this particular 'risk and uncertainty', this book will teach you.

b. I am afraid of taking complete charge and responsibility

Yes, starting your own business means taking total charge and total responsibility. It means taking the final decision all the way, all the time. Some people may not be comfortable with such a charge and responsibility. But yet taking complete charge and responsibility of your professional and financial life is having complete freedom over your professional and financial affairs. And every human being craves freedom. So? You are yet to figure out what is holding you back. Do you know how and where to start?

c. I don't want to start my own business because I have no pre-Knowledge of the business world

This looks like one of the weakest reasons not to start your own business. In starting your own business, the most necessary experience is the experience in the type of business you want to start and not necessarily the general experience of the business world.

d. Because I do not want to forgo my profession
You can start a business that is related to your profession.

e. Because I am not a businessman/Entrepreneur
It has never been a good idea for one to try being what he/she is not.

But nobody was born a businessman. People learn to become businessmen.

And remember, you failed in all the things you didn't try out, but stand the chance to fail and or succeed if you try. Well, you know yourself better. However, remember the following quotes by Mr Prat, the character in the factual fiction—Overqualified Labourer:

"Although I'd never been a businessman, but I didn't allow the lack of knowledge of the business world to be a barrier.

"I never knew I am a great Entrepreneur. It takes coming to Canada and the ambush of the bully—'No Canadian Experience' to sprout the Entrepreneurial genius in me. God bless Canada"

Advantages of Owning Your Own Business

Most of the advantages of being self employed tilt towards **freedom**:

a. Freedom is one of the greatest cravings of all human endeavours. Starting and running your own business gives you the freedom to become

the Commander-in-Chief, the Supreme Disciple of
your professional and financial being.

b. Starting and running your own business offers you
the freedom to set and work at your own pace.

c. Managing your own business allows you the
freedom to make your decisions as you deem fit.

d. Owning a business means there will be no Boss
breathing down your neck all the time.

e. The glory of success in the business is all yours.

f. If you build an empire out of the shoestring
business, it's all yours.

g. You don't work your heart out to build someone
else an empire.

Disadvantages of owning your own Business

Most of the disadvantages of owning a business tilts towards
the price of freedom:

Freedom like most things in life has it's own price

a. Being your own Commander-in-Chief also means
being liable for all failures in the business.

b. Taking all the glory for success also means taking
all the blames for failure.

c. You work long hours for all profits and losses.

d. Being a boss may be more stressful than being an
employee.

**However, the primary things you need to start and
run a successful business include:**

1. **A business idea**

It always starts with an idea, a brilliant and viable
idea. As a professional and or a skilled immigrant
in a relatively new/foreign country who needs to
be in control of his/her professional and financial
destiny, your idea needs to tilt towards your
profession, skills and for a particular audience.

Conduct all the necessary research on this idea as it relates to this economy and market. The next step will be to develop your plan based on the results from the research on this idea. In conducting your research, use the resources available including the Library, Bookstores, Yellow pages and Directories, Trend Books, Magazines and Newspapers, Research Studies, Internet, interviewing people and cold calls.

Have a look at the Book:
Look Before You Leap:
Market Research Made Easy
Published By Self-Counsel Press
Author: Don Doman, Dell Dennison
& Magaret Doman
ISBN: 0-88905-292-8

2. Expertise, Experience and Knowledge in the business venture you are about to undertake

If your business idea tilts towards your profession, skill or trade, then you already have the expertise, the experience and knowledge of the business venture you are undertaking. It makes things easier than going into an area where you are a novice.

3. A business plan

Remember the advantages of planning as discussed in chapter 3 of this book.

Your business plan will dissect, ensemble, structure and direct your business idea. Depending on how you want to finance your business, potential investors will vet your business plan before investing. It is therefore necessary to have a detailed business plan.

The following are the features of a business plan:

a. A business name
b. Business/Company Objectives
c. Business Overview
d. Ownership
e. Workers hierarchical Structure
f. Management
g. Mission Statement
h. Product and Services
i. Operations
j. Location of Business Premise
k. Capital equipment
l. Competitors/Competition
m. Risks
n. Success Strategy
o. Marketing/Advertising and Publicity Strategy
p. Financial Plan

For help on how to write a business plan, use the following resources:

a. The library
b. Websites:
   www.planmaker.com
   www.pasware.com
   www.sba.gov/shareware/starfile.html
   www.jianusa.com
   www.planet-corp.com
   www.brs-inc.com
   www.smartonline.com
c. Books:
   • Preparing a Successful Business Plan
     By Rodger D. Touchie
     Self-Counsel Press
     ISBN: 1-55180177-9
   • Rules Book of Business Plans For Start-Up: Create a Winning Plan That You Can Take To The Bank

Published by Entrepreneur Press
Author: Roger Rule
ISBN: 1-932531-05-X
- Business Plan For Dummies
Published by Wiley Publishing Inc.,
Author: Tiffany Paul
ISBN: 1-56884-868-4
- The Business Planning Guide
Published by Dearborn Trade Publishing
Author: David H. Bangs, Jr
ISBN: 079315409-X
- Business Plans Kit For Dummies
Published by Wiley Publishing Inc.,
Author: Steven Peterson
ISBN: 076455365-8

Small Business Self-Help Centres

Toronto

North York
North York Civic Centre (main floor)
5100 Yonge Street
North York, On
M2N 5V7
Phone: 416- 395-7434
Fax: 416-395-7444

Downtown
City Hall (main floor east)
Toronto, On
M5H 2N2
Phone: 416-394-6646
Fax: 416-394-0675

Etobicoke
Etobicoke Civic Centre (main floor, north block)

399 The West Mall
Etobicoke, On
M9C 2Y2
Phone: 416-394-8949
Fax: 416-394-5537

Scarborough
150 Borough Drive (first floor)
Scarborough, On
M1P 4N7
Phone: 416-396-7169
Fax: 416-396-5088

Missisauga

Central Library 4th Floor
301 Burnhamthorpe Road West
Mississauga, On
L5B 3Y3
Phone: 905-615-3275
Fax: 905-615-4447

Brampton

33 Queen Street West (1st floor)
Brampton, On
L6Y 1L9
Phone: 905-874-2650
Fax: 905-874-2670

Hamilton

2 King Street West
L.D. Jackson Square
Hamilton, On
L8P 1A1
Phone: 905-540-6400
Fax: 905-540-6411

Kingston

67 Brock Street
The Carriage Way
Kingston, On
K7L 1R8
Phone: 613-544-2725 ext. 229
Fax: 613-546-2882

London

1764 Oxford Street East
London, ON
N5V 3R6
Phone: 519-659-2882
Fax: 519-7050

Niagara Falls

City Hall
4310 Queen Street
P.O.BOX 1023
Niagara Falls, On
L2E 6X5
Phone: 905-356-7521 ext. 5000
Fax: 905-357-9293

Ottawa

110 Laurier Avenue West (Ground floor)
Ottawa, On
K1P 1J1
Phone: 613-560-6081
Fax: 613-560-2102

The above centres offers advice and guidance to people starting their own business, and people who already have their business up and running. The advice, information and guidance they offer includes: writing a business plan, financing a business, business management, and general assistance.

Start-Up Capital

Sometimes entrepreneurs with good business idea and an excellent business plan do not have enough funds to start up their business. As such, they have to depend on other people's money to start up their business. When approaching a financial institution for a start up loan, the bait you need is a good business plan and an excellent loan proposal.

Sources of Funding

a. **Equity**

This is the term used to represent the money that you and probably your partner(s)/associate(s) put into the business.

b. **Home Equity**

The equity in your home is the difference between the appraised value of your home and your current mortgage balance. You can use your home equity as collateral security if you need to borrow money.

c. **Banks**

d. **Small Business Administration Act**

All Chartered Banks and Alberta Treasury branches are authorized to advance loans under the Small Business Administration Loans Act.

e. **Private Individuals**

f. **Institutional Term Lenders**

Term lending is available from:
Most Chartered Banks
Credit Unions
Business Development of Canada (BDC)

g. **Credit Unions**

h. **Leasing**

i. **Accounts Receivables (Factoring)**

j. **Venture Capital**
For more information on Venture Capital and
Venture Capitalists of Canada contact:
> Canada Venture Capital Association
> 234 Eglinton Avenue East
> Suite 200
> Toronto, On
> M4P 1K5
> Phone: 416-487-0519
> Website: www.cvca.ca

k. **Franchising**
For more information on Franchising Contact:
> Canadian Franchising Association
> 2585 Skymark Avenue, Suite 300
> Mississauga, On
> L4W 4L5
> Phone: 905-625-2896
> Toll Free: 1-800-665-4232
> Fax: 905-625-9076
> Website: www.cfa.ca
> Or
> International Franchise Association
> 1350 New York Avenue N.W., Suite 900
> Washington, D.C. 20005-4709
> Phone: 202-628-8000
> Website: www.franchise.org

Books on Franchising
  - Franchising in Canada
    Published by Self-Counsel Press

Author: Michael Coltman
ISBN: 1-55180-094-2

- A Guide for Franchisors and Franchisees,
  Business, Taxation and Accounting Issues
  Published by: CCH Canada limited
  Author: Taylor Gilbert, David Thompson
  and Peter Dabbikeh
  ISBN: 1-55141-755-3
- Franchising: A Complete Guide for
  Canadian Buyers and Sellers
  Published by: Key Porter Books
  Author: Bev Cline
  ISBN: 1-55013-113-3

1. **Government Funding**

   Government financial assistance for Small Business
   in Canada is an unsentimental, unbiased form of
   business funding. It may be very time consuming,
   involves lots of paper work, but it is a good source
   of financial assistance to start up a Small business,
   and businesses that are already in operation.

   Types of Government funding
   i.   Cash grants
   ii. Management Assistance
   iii. Loan guarantees
   iv. Reduced interest rates
   v.   Subsidies

   For more information about Government funding,
   programs and services see the following:

   - Business Development of Canada (BDC)
     Phone: 1-800-INFO-BDC
     (1-800-4636-232)
     Website: www.bdc.ca
   - Reference Canada
     They provide information about all

Federal Government Programs and
Services for Small Business.
Phone 1-800-667-3355

- Export Development of Canada
Corporate Communications Department
Export Development of Canada
151 O'Connor Street
Ottawa, On
K1A 1K3
Phone: 613-598-2500
Toll Free: 1-800-575-4422
Website: www.edc.ca

Books on Government Funding
- Handbook of Grants and Subsidies
Published by Canadian Research and
Publication Centre
Author: Canadian Research and
publication centre
ISBN: 2892120519
- Government Programs and services
Published by Employment and
Immigration Canada
Author: Canada Employment and
Immigration (Commission)
ISBN: 0662591194
- Your Guide To Government Of Canada
Services And Support For Small Business
Published by Government of Canada
ISSN: 1209-0069
- Your Guide To Government Of Canada
Services And Support For Small Business
Published by Industry Canada
Author: Industry Canada
ISBN: 0662251539

- Your Guide To Government Of Canada Services And Support For Small Business
  Published by Government of Canada
  Author: Entrepreneurship and Small Business Office
  ISBN: 0662251539
- Sources of Small Business Funding in Canada
  Published by Entrepreneurial Business Consultants of Canada
  Author: Entrepreneurial Business consultants of Canada
- Government Assistance for Canadian Business
  Published by Carswell
  Author: Prudhomme Donna, Singer Ronald, and Roy Robert
  ISBN: 0459573462
- The Canadian Reference Directory on Business Planning and Financing
  Published by The Canadian Sources of Funds Index
  Author: The Canadian Sources of Funds Index
- The Canadian Business Assistance Handbook
  Published by The Canadian Institute of Chartered Accountants (CICA)
  Author: CICA
- Your Guide To Government Financial Assistance For Business in Ontario
  The latest details of all Federal, Provincial and other Assistance Programs that relate to enterprise in Ontario
  Published by Productive Publications

Author: Iain Williamson
ISBN: 1-55270-133-6
ISSN: 1198-0524

- Canadian Industrial Incentives Legislation
  Published by Butterworths
- Industrial Assistance Programs in Canada
  Published by CCH Canada Ltd.
  Author: Horsley David, David Bramwell
  ISBN: 0887965628
- Government Assistance Programs in
  Canada: Practical Handbook
  Published by CCH Canada
  Author: Huras Lorraine, Miller Peter,
  Peat Marwick Thorne
  ISBN: 0887968228
- Your Guide to Government Financial
  Assistance in Ontario
  Published by: Productive Publications
  Author: Iain Williamson
  ISSN: 1198-0524
- Your Guide to Government Financial
  Assistance in Quebec
  Published by: Productive Publications
  Author: Iain Williamson
  ISSN: 11980540
- Your Guide to Start Up Financing in
  Canada
  Published by: Productive Publications
  Author: Iain Williamson
  ISBN: 0920847080 V1
  0920847099 V2
  0920847102 V3
  0920847072 V3.set

OR
You can visit any of the following Centres

Canadian Business Service Centres (CBSC)

CBSC is found in every province. In the province of Quebec, it is called Info Entrepreneurs. The centres provide information on:

a. Financial Assistance Program
b. Starting a Business
c. Regulatory Requirements
d. Taxation
e. Trade and Export Opportunities

Contact

> Website: www.net-inst.com/cbsc
> Email: cobsc@cbsc.ic.gc.ca
> Addresses of Canada Business Service Centres by Province

Ontario

> Canada—Ontario Business Call Centre
> Toronto Ontario
> M5V 3E5
> Phone: 416-954-INFO (4636)
> Toll Free: 1-800-240-4192
> Website: www.cbsc.org/ontario/index.html
> Email: cobcc@cbsc.ic.gc.ca

British Columbia

> Canada/British Columbia Business Service Centre
> 601 West Cordova Street
> Vancouver, BC
> V6B 1G1
> Phone: 604-775-5525
> Toll Free: 1-800-667-2272
> Fax; 604-775-5515
> Toll Free Fax: 1-800-667-2272
> Email: olson.dave@cbsc.ic.gc.ca (For Business Start Up)
> marcarenhas.carm@cbsc.ic.gc.ca

(For Trade and Markets/Export-Import)
Website: www.sb.gov.bc.ca/small-bus/sbhome.html

Alberta

The Business Link
Business Service Centre
Ste. 100, 10237-104 Street
Edmonton, Alberta
T5J 1B1
Phone: 403-422-7722
Toll Free: 1-800-272-9675
Fax: 403-422-0055
Info-Fax: 403-427-7971
Toll Free Fax: 1-800-563-9926
Website: www.cbsc.org/alberta/index.html
Email: buslink@cbsc.ic.gc.ca

Nova Scotia

Canada/Nova Scotia Business Service Centre
1575 Brunswick Street
Halifax, Nova Scotia
B3J 2G1
Phone: 902-426-8604
Toll Free: 1-800-668-1010
Fax: 902-426-65-30
Info-Fax: 902-426-3201
Info-Fax: 1-800-401-3201
TTY: 1-800-797-4188
Email: halifax@cbsc.ic.gc.ca
Website: www.cbsc.org/ns/index.html

Quebec

Info Entrepreneurs
5 Place Ville Marie
Niveau Plaza, Suite 12500, Plaza Level

Montreal, Quebec
H3B 4Y2
Phone: 514-496-4636
Toll Free: 1-800-322-4636
Fax; 514-496-5934
Info Fax: 514-496-4010
Info Fax: 1-800-401-3201
TTY: 1-800-887-6550
Email: info-entrepreneurs@bfdrq-fordg.gc.ca
Website: www.cbsc.org/org/quebec/index.html

Manitoba

Canada Business Service Centre
330 Portage Avenue, 8th Floor
P.O.BOX 2609
Winnipeg, Manitoba
R3C 4B3
Phone: 204-984-2272
Tool Free: 1-800-665-2019
Fax: 204-983-3852
Info Fax: 204-984-5527
Info Fax: 1-800-665-9386
Email: manitoba@cbsc.ic.gc.ca
Website: www.cbsc.ic.gc.ca

New Brunswick

Canada/New Brunswick Business Service Centre
570 Queen Street
Fredericton, New Brunswick
E3B 6Z6
Phone: 506-444-6140
Tool Free: 1-800-668-1010
Fax: 506-444-6172
Info Fax: 506-444-6169
Info Fax: 1-800-401-3201

TTY: 1-800-887-6550
Email: cbscnb@cbsc.ic.gc.ca
Website: www.cbsc.org/nb/index.html

Newfoundland

Canada Business Service Centre
90 O'Leary Avenue
P.O.BOX 8687
St. John's, Newfoundland
A1B 3T1
Phone: 709-772-6022
Toll Free: 1-800-668-1010
Fax: 709-772-6090
Info Fax: 1-888-772-6030
Email: St.johns@cbsc.ic.gc.ca
Website: www.cbsc.org/nfld/index.html

Northwest Territories

Canada/Northwest Territories Business Service Centre
P.O.BOX 1320
8th Floor Scotia Centre
Yellowknife, Northwest Territories
X1A 2L9
Phone: 867-873-7958
Toll Free: 1-800-661-0599
Fax: 867-873-0575
Info Fax: 1-800-661-0825
Email: yel@cbsc.ic.gc.ca
Website: www.cbsc.org/nwt/index.html

Saskatchewan

Canada/Saskatchewan Business Service Centre
122-3rd Avenue, North
Saskatoon, Saskatchewan
S7K 2H6

Phone: 306-956-2323
Toll Free: 1-800-667-4374
Fax: 306-956-2328
Info Fax: 306-956-2310
Info Fax: 1-800667-9433
Email: saskatooncsbsc@cbsc.ic.gc.ca
Website: www.cbsc.org/sask/index.html

Prince Edward Island

Canada/Prince Edward Island Business Service Centre
75 Fitzroy Street
P.O.BOX 40
Charlettown, Prince Edward Island
C1A 7K2
Phone: 902-368-0771
Toll Free: 1-800-668-1010
Fax: 902-566-7377
Info Fax: 902-368-0776
Info Fax: 1-800-401-3201
TTY: 902-368-0724
Email: pei@cbsc.ic,gc.ca
Website: www.cbsc.org/pei/index.html

Yukon

Canada/Yukon Business Service Centre
201-208 Main Street
Whitehorse, Yukon
Y1A 2A9
Phone: 867-633-6257
Toll Free: 1-800-661-0543
Fax: 867-667-2001
Info Fax: 867-633-2533
Info fax: 1-800-841-4320
Email: perry.debbie@cbsc.ic.gc.ca

For information on how to Finance Your Small Business in Canada see the Books:

- Where To Go When The Bank Says No
  Financing your Small Business in Canada
  Published by McGraw-Hill Ryerson Limited
  Author: Gary Fitchett
  With John Alton
  Kathleen Aldridge
  ISBN: 0-07-560225-3
- When The Banks Says No
  Creative Financing for Closely Held Business
  Published by Liberty Hall Press
  Author: Lawrence W. Tuller
  ISBN: 0-8306-3590-4
- Starting A Successful Business in Canada
  16th Edition
  Published by Self-Counsel Press
  Author: Jack D. James
  ISBN: 1-55180-573-1
- Your Guide To Government Financial Assistance
  For Business in Ontario
  The latest details of all Federal, Provincial and
  other Assistance Programs that relate to enterprise
  in Ontario
  Published by Productive Publications
  Author: Iain Williamson
  ISBN: 1-55270-133-6
  ISSN: 1198-0524

Be a Businessman/Entrepreneur

Being a Businessman/Entrepreneur is quite different from being an employee. As a businessman, you have to breathe, eat, drink, sleep and dream your business. You have to be prepared for it.

MAKING A BUSINESS CHOICE

In choosing a business, you must choose a business that has to do with what you enjoy doing. As a professional and or a skilled tradesperson, it is assumed that you enjoy your chosen profession and as such it is advisable that you choose a business that is somewhat related to your chosen profession.

Examples:

A chiropodist is used to, and enjoys examining and treating foot injuries and diseases. He/She may want to start a business that has to do with comfortable and healthy foot wears and accessories.

A Biochemist, Chemist, Pharmacists, Medical doctors and professionals in life Science knows much about Laboratory Reagents, Biochemicals/Chemicals, Laboratory Equipments, Pharmaceuticals, Hospital Equipments etc., they may like to start a business that has links to these things they know so much about.

A lawyer knows much about the Law and may not want to deviate from the legal profession, and when he/she wants to go into business he/she might choose to become a Legal Research Lawyer/Associate. They comb through all branches of the Law chasing and tracking down some specific legal information that other lawyers may need in the courts.

An Agriculturist, an Agronomist, a Botanist, all know so much about agriculture, Agronomy, Plants, Horticulture that when thinking about starting a business, they may think along that line.

A Computer Programmer, An Internet Specialist, A Computer Scientist all know many things about computers, computer parts, computer chips, software, online business, e-commerce that when they think business, they may choose to think computers, software business, online business, e-commerce.

An Engineer knows so much about Engineering that when thinking of business, he/she remembers so much in the Engineering business world.

A Business Analyst and an Accountant are both respected professionals in the accounting world and in dissecting businesses. It is assumed that they will be excellent Business Consultants.

Skilled Tradespersons including a Carpenter, Welder, Toolist, Mechanic, General Machinist and Die Maker will be excellent in establishing a business related to their trades.

A Massage Therapist will undoubtedly be at home in establishing a business related to this his/her chosen profession.

But the above suggestions do not mean that people do not make a career change or establish businesses in a field entirely different from what they have been doing for a long time. Whatever type of business you choose to establish, it is advisable to establish a business in what you enjoy doing. Imagine making money doing what you most enjoy doing. Fun eh? Real fun.

Will you go for a Traditional Business or an Online Business?

Traditional business means non-virtual business, non-internet-based business. Online Business means businesses conducted on the Internet/World Wide Web.

One good thing about the online business is that depending on how your Website is designed nobody knows how big or small you business is. You can be whatever you want to be on the Internet.

The process of establishing an online business and a traditional business is almost the same except for some few steps that sets starting an online business apart from a traditional business.

Steps For Establishing A Business Online

a. Establish a relationship with a courier company who will be responsible for delivering your products to your customers.

Courier Companies like:

Canada Post

UPS

TNT

DHL

FEDEX

For local (within the city) deliveries, you may arrange with local efficient dispatchers to be more cost effective.

b. Find an Internet Service provider (ISP) for your Internet services

c. Create a website and employ the services of Internet/computer programmers, writers, graphic artists, and photographers.

d. Obtain a merchant account to be able to accept credit card payment online.

Ensure that your Website can undertake a secure financial transaction online. Secure transaction is the greatest concern of people who do business online.

Merchant Account could be obtained from Banks and Financial institutions.

For examples of where to obtain a merchant account see the websites:

- Merchant Account Company
  www.merchantaccount.com
- USB Merchant Services
- Merchant Express
  www.merchantexpress.com
- Keycorp Merchant Services
  www.keybank.com
- Secure-Bank.Com
  www.secure-bank.com

- Electronic Transfer, Inc.
  www.paymentmall.com
- Harris Bankcard Centre
  www.harrisbank.com/smallbusiness/merchant/
  cihome.html
- Credit Merchant Account Services
  www.merchantaccount.net
- EPD Credit Card Services
  www.apc.net/edp/cc.html
- First American Card Services
  www.1stamericancardservice.com/basefold.html

For more information on how to start an online business see the books:

- The Unofficial Guide to Starting a Business Online
  Published by Wiley Publishing, Inc.
  Author: Jason R. Rich
  ISBN: 0-02-863340-7
- Doing Big Business on the Internet
  Published by Self-Counsel Press
  Author: Hurley & Birkwood
  ISBN: 1-55180-119-1
- Selling On The Web
  Author: Paul Galloway
  ISBN: 1563824876
- Start an eBay Business
  Published by Alpha Books
  Author: Barbara Weltman
  ISBN: 159257-333-9
- Small Business Online
  A Strategic Guide for Canada Entrepreneurs
  Published by Prentice Hall Canada Inc.,
  Author: Jim Carroll with Rich Broadhead
  ISBN: 0-13-976895-5
- 101 Ways To Promote your Website

Published by Maximum Press
Author: Susan Sweeney
ISBN: 1931644217

- Start Your Own Business On eBay: Your Step by Step Guide To Success
Published by Entrepreneur Press
Author: Jacquelyn Lynn
ISBN: 1932531122

- Start Your Own E-Business
Published by Entrepreneur Press
Author: Entrepreneur Press
ISBN: 1932156747

- Selling On The Net: The Complete Guide
Published by NTC Business Books
Author: Lewis, Herschell Gordon
ISBN: 0844232343

- Selling On The Internet: How To Open An Electronic Storefront And Have Millions Of Customers Come To You
Published by McGraw-Hill
Author: James C. Gonyea, Wayne M. Gonyea
ISBN: 0070241872

- The Online Business Book
Published by Adam Media Corporation
Author: Rob Liflander
ISBN: 158062-3204

- Guerrilla Marketing Online
Published by Houghton Mifflin
Author: Jay Conrad Levinson and Charles Rubin
ISBN: 0-395-86061-X

- Internet Marketing For Dummies
Published by Wiley Publishing Inc.,
ISBN: 0-7645-0778-8

- Low-Cost Website Promotion
Published by Adam Media Corporation

- Author: Barry Feig
  ISBN: 1-58062-501-0
- Online Business Resources
  Published by Made E-Z
  Author: Paul Galloway
  ISBN: 1-56382-510-4
- Generating Trust in Online Business:
  From Theory To Practice
  Published by IQ
  Author: Magda Fusaro
  ISBN: 2-922417-28-X
- Absolute Beginners Guide To Launching an eBay
  Business
  Published by Que
  Author: Michael Miller
  ISBN: 0-7897-3058-8
- Starting an eBay Business For Dummies
  Published by Wiley Publishing Inc.,
  Author: Marsha Collier
  ISBN: 0-7645-6924-4
- Online Business Planning
  Published by Career Press
  Author: Robert T. Gorman
  ISBN: 1-56414-369-4

Your Business Structure

In Canada, businesses are differentiated into structures using the Terms:

a. A Proprietorship
    This form of business structure involves only
    one person. It is the simplest and easiest form of
    business to start. In this form of business, the
    assets of the business owner and the assets of the
    business are inseparable. It is a one-in-all, all-in-
    one type of thing. The actions of the proprietor

while conducting business binds the business
and the actions/activities of the business bind
the proprietor. You and your assets are liable to
everything that goes wrong—taxes, debts, lawsuits,
etc in the business. The business dies with the
death of the proprietor.

b. Partnership
This form of business structure is one step ahead
of the proprietorship structure of business. It
involves two or more persons who out of free will
enter into an agreement/partnership to undertake
a business venture for the purpose of generating
profit, with each partner(s) entitled to a certain
capital contribution and share of profit.
There is a Provincial Partnership Act in every
province in Canada that governs the Partnership
Business.
All Partners are liable to the losses, taxes, debt and
lawsuits that may be incurred by the business. In
other words Partnership is about the same thing
with Proprietorship except that in Partnership you
have more than one person sharing the profits and
or liabilities of the business. And the business does
not die with the death of one Partner. But with the
death of all the Partners, the business also dies.
In Partnership, a lot of trust, confidence and
faith are required amongst the partners, because
the excesses of one Partner in the conduct of the
business binds the other partners of the business.

c. Corporation
This type of business structure involves two
or more people bound by Memorandum of
Association/Articles of Incorporation. It is a
limited liability company—meaning that the
business is a separate legal entity from the

owners of the business. As such, the owners—
shareholders of the company are not liable for the
company's debt, losses, and lawsuits above their
capital contributions for share ownership in the
company. The company often outlives the owners
(shareholders).

There are three types of Corporation

    i.   C- Corporation
    ii. S-Corporation
    iii. Limited Liability

See your Lawyer/Accountant for tax advantages of each
type of corporation and incorporation processes/procedures.
Your lawyer will also clarify you on issues about licenses,
permits, insurance, laws and regulations as regards you and
your business.

For more information on incorporation of a company,
how to start a business in Canada see the **books**

- Start A Successful Business in Canada
  Published by self-Counsel Press
  Author: Jack D. James
  ISBN: 1-55180-573-1
- Incorporation and Business Guide
  Published by Self-Counsel Press
  Author: M. Stephen Georgas
  ISBN: 1-55180-219-8
- Starting a Business: A complete Guide to Starting
  and Managing Your own company
  Published by Key Porter Books Limited
  Author: Gordon Brockhouse
- Start Your Own Business: The Canadian
  Entrepreneur's Guide
- Published by Stoddart Publishing Company
  Limited
  Author: Peter D. Cook
- The Complete Canadian Small Business Guide

Published by McGraw-Hill Ryerson
Author: Douglas A. Gray and Diana Lynn Gray
ISBN: 0-07-086495-0
• Small Business Success: A Practical Guide for the
  Entrepreneur
  Published by CCH Canadian Limited
  Author: Tony Fattal
• Vault Reports Guide To Starting Your Own Business
Published by Houghton Mifflin Company
  Author: Jonathan Reed. Aspatore with H. S.
  Hamadeh, Samer Hamadeh & Mark Oldman
  ISBN: 0-395-86170-5
• Building a Dream
  A Canadian Guide To Starting Your Own Business
  Published by Mcgraw-Hill Ryerson
  Author: Walter S. Good
  ISBN: 0-07-086271-0
• Starting on a Shoestring
  Building a Business Without a Bankroll
  Published by John Wiley & Sons, Inc.
  Author: Arnold S. Goldstein
  ISBN: 0-471-23288-2
• The Complete Canadian Small Business Guide
  Published by McGraw Hill
  Author: Douglas Gray and Diana Gray
  ISBN: 007086495-0

You may also like to visit the following offices:
• Ministry of Industry, Trade and Technology
  Hearst Block
  900 Bay Street (7th Floor)
  Toronto, On
  M7A 2E1
  Phone: 416-965-5494
  Toll Free: 1-800-387-6142

- Small Business Development Corporation
  Ministry of Revenue
  33 King Street West
  Oshawa, On
  L1H 8H9
  Phone: 416-434 7232

Your Business Image

Your image on paper and or in person must be business—clean and simple.

Do it to impress, make no mistakes about it. Your image in person and on paper is part of your business product and it must be packaged excellently well.

In person, you need a briefcase and a business suit. You need to be people smart—smile, pay attention and listen to people, and address people by their names.

On paper, you need a letterhead, logo, good business card, a brochure and mailing labels. All go a long way to make you appear like the professional you are.

The Office

As a new business owner, depending on your type of business, you must choose an office according to the resources at your disposal. You may like to have a commercial space, an executive office suite, a shared space, a subleased space or you may choose to run your business from your home. Running a business from home is the most cost effective.

In your office you must have:
a. Computer
b. Printer
c. Photocopy machine
d. Fax machine
e. Scanner
f. Phone

Or you can just have a computer with Internet connection,

a phone line and then an all-in-one machine that has fax, copier, scanner, and printer.

Your Computer

Use a desktop or a laptop computer with a 56k modem. Install the following software in the computer:

Word processor (MS Office)—Use this to write letters, create mailing labels, address envelopes. In the MS office you've got MS word, Excel, Access, Outlook, and Powerpoint.

Spreadsheet—You can create charts and do your finances with spreadsheet program. Use MS Excel for your spreadsheet needs.

QuickBooks Pro—With this you can create custom invoices, compute sales, and do electronic banking, bill payments, control inventory and payroll. Use it for all accounting and bookkeeping.

Database—Use the Database program to keep record of clients, sellers, vendors and all your business contacts/links. With the database program you can keep record of phone calls, faxes, meeting, conferences, seminars time and dates of events and incidents. You may want to use Dbase or Fox Pro for your database needs.

Graphic—Use this to create flyers, announcements newsletters and advertisements. You may want to use PageMaker, QuarkXpress and Clarisworks for your graphic exploits.

Schedular—Use this to manage your schedules.

Your Phone

Look, Sound Big and Professional Using Phone System Tricks. Call Bell Canada and or Sprint Canada to inquire about calling packages.

You must have the following features to operate smoothly:

- Voice Mail

Choose a group voice mail where the callers/clients will select from a list of names, hierarchy and departments in the company by pressing the appropriate numbers on their touch tone phone as will be directed by your outgoing message.

Use a good and professional voice to record your outgoing message. You may employ the services of a friend who has a good and professional voice or you can employ the services of a professional.

An example of a professional out going message is:

Hello, you have reached the administrative office of The BIZ Company. We are sorry that we are unable to take your call at this moment. We are either on another line or assisting other clients. If you leave your name and your phone number and a brief message, someone will get back to you as soon as possible.

As could be seen in the above message, always use 'we' when addressing your company. Never use 'I' though you may be running the company alone. By using the plural 'we', you give the impression that the company is a big company with many employees, that you are not running the company alone.

- Caller Display/Caller ID with name

This feature allows you to see the telephone number of the caller and probably know who is calling before answering the phone.

- Call Waiting

This feature allows you while on a line with a person, to keep this person on one line, and check who is on the incoming call. But if you identify the incoming caller using the caller display, you may choose to ignore him/her if need be, and your voice mail will answer the phone.

- Ring Mate/Ring Tones

Ring-mate/Ring-tone allows you the freedom of using two phone numbers (Home/Business) on one line thereby saving you the extra cost of paying for another line. In using the ring mate feature, your two phone numbers ring on the same phone line but with different tones. The different ring tones allow you to know which phone number is being called and how to answer it.

- Call Transfer/Forwarding Feature

If you are not home and or in the office, but must attend to a particular call, the call transfer feature allows you to transfer the call to your office phone and or to your cell phone. But this doesn't need to happen often.

- Fax Switch Box

With a fax switch box, you can connect your fax machine to your phone line and when a call comes in, the switch box differentiates and directs the call to the right section.

- Three-way Calling

For furniture, Home office equipment and other office basics, visit the office supply superstore in your area:

- Staples
- Home depot
- Wal-Mart.

10

A Dozen and One Businesses You Can Run From Your Home With Less Than $20,000

CONSULTING

The field of consulting is as wide as the oceans. It is growing even wider and will never stop growing. Consultants have sprang up in fields ranging from Rocket Science, through Gene Therapy, Cloning, Engineering, Business, Military, to Dating, People Smartness, Marital Harmony, Hair Styling and Nail Polishing. There is no aspect of human endeavour where consultants have not pitched their flags.

As a consultant, you need the following skills:
a.　Problem solving
b.　People smartness
c.　Cross examination
d.　Imagination, Instinct and intuition of a Psychologist
e.　Instincts to develop leads
f.　Trendy
g.　Pro-active

h.   Specificity
i.   Research oriented
j.   Ability to read extensively including magazines,
      journals, publications and newsletters

But above all you need: Knowledge, Expertise and Experience.

Your consultancy firm is like an oracle, and you the consultant, the supreme priest. As a consultant you dispense advice, clarification, and lasting solutions to the problems, confusions, and difficulties of your clients, be them Governments, Companies, Organizations and or individuals.

The usefulness of knowledge, expertise and experience is not knowledge, expertise and or experience in themselves, but their application to resolve issues and achieve success. As a consultant, you need to know how to apply specific knowledge, expertise and experience to a specific problem to achieve a specific solution.

You are a professional with knowledge, expertise and years of experience. Having spent years in formal training, years of work experience and invariably practical application of your knowledge and expertise, you have the core things it takes to be a consultant in your field. What are you waiting for? Rise to the bait and join the razzle.

Be a consultant in your own field!

What You need To Start-Up

a.   A Computer (with Internet connection)
      Use a desktop or a laptop computer with a 56k
      modem. Install the following software:
      Word processor (MS Office)—Use this to write
      letters, create mailing labels, address envelops. In
      the MS office you've got MS word, Excel, Access,
      Outlook, and Powerpoint.
      Spreadsheet—You can create charts and do your

finances with spreadsheet program. Use MS Excel for your spreadsheet needs.

QuickBooks Pro—With this you can create custom invoices, compute sales, and do electronic banking, bill payments, control inventory and payroll. Use it for all accounting and bookkeeping.

Database—Use the Database program to keep record of clients, sellers, vendors and all your business contacts/links. With the database program you can keep record of phone calls, faxes, meeting, conferences, seminars time and dates of events and incidents. You may want to use Dbase or Fox Pro for your database needs.

Graphic—Use this to create flyers, announcements newsletters and advertisements. You may want to use PageMaker, QuarkXpress and Clarisworks for your graphic exploits.

Scheduler—Use this to manage your schedules.

b. Phone, Fax, Printer, Scanner, Copier (can buy all-in-one)

c. Office Furniture (including office supplies and office accessories)

d. Insurance

e. Fees payable to become a member in professional and or trade associations.

f. Books

g. Marketing/advertising cost.

h. Business suits, ties, shoes, briefcase (all for personal image improvement) and other miscellaneous expenses

The total cost of your start-up needs will not exceed $20,000 Canadian.

Professional/Trade Associations You May Like To Join

- Canadian Association of Management Consultants

BCE Place
181 Bay Street
P.O.BOX 835
Toronto, Ontario
M5J 2T3
Phone: 416-860-1515
Website: www.camc.com

Books You May Need To Buy

- Start and Run a Profitable Consulting Business
  Published by Self-Counsel Press
  Author: Douglas A. Gray
  ISBN: 1-55180-106-X
- How to Become a Successful Consultant in Your
  Own Field
  Published by Prima Publishing
  Author: Hubert Bermont
  ISBN: 0761511008
- The Complete Guide To Consulting Success
  Published byUpstart Publishing
  Author: Ted Nicholas, Howard L. Shenson, and
  Paul Franklin
  ISBN: 1574100556
- Consulting For Dummies
  Published by IDG Books Worldwide
  Author: Bob Nelson and Peter Economy
  ISBN: 0764550349
- Marketing Your Consulting and Professional
  Services
  Published in New York by John Wiley & Sons
  Author: Dick Connor, Jeffrey P. Davidson, and
  Richard A. Connor
  ISBN: 0471133922
- Consultant & Independent Contractor Agreements
  Published by Nolo Press

Author: Stephen Fishman
ISBN: 0873374576
- How To Be Your Own Publicist
Published by McGraw-Hill
Author: Jessica Hatchigan
ISBN:0-07-138332-8
- 6 Steps To Free Publicity
Published by Career Press Inc
Author: Marcia Yudkin
ISBN: 1-56414-675-8
- Guerrilla Publicity
Published by Adams Media Corporation
Author: Jay Conrad Levinson, Rich Frishman and Jill Lublin
ISBN: 1-58062-682-3
- Marketing Without Advertising
Author: Michael Phillips, Salli Rasberry
ISBN: 0873376080

Other sources of information include:

- Seminars
- Magazines
- Journals
- Newsletters
- Trade Publications
- Websites

Marketing/How To Get Business

Hunting for business for your consultancy firm is about the same thing as searching for a job in your field. As such, you have to apply all the job search skills discussed in the early chapters of this book, customizing them to suit your present need and position.

a. Cold calls (for information interview)
b. Networking

    c.   Resumes

    d.   Brochure/Flyers

    e.   Business Cards

    f.   Create a Website

    g.   Join Associations/social clubs

    h.   Trade fairs

Good luck!

Export/import Agent

Many Canadian companies both big and small are in constant need of the knowledge and connections of an independent export/import agent to sell/buy their goods—raw materials, semi-finished and or finished products and components abroad.

As a Professional/Skilled Immigrant, you can fill this niche and undertake the exportation/importation of goods and or services from your country/global region of origin to and from Canada. You can become a commissioned agent, in which case you make a commission on any sale you make for the company/manufacturer. On the other hand, you can become a retainer agent, and be paid a fixed amount of money to work for a company/manufacturer for a particular product in a particular period of time.

As an Export/Import agent, you need to know:

    a.   Export/Import procedures and documentation

    b.   You must be conversant with the government procedures (Canadian /your home government and the countries you will be doing business in)

    c.   Knowledge of goods that require export/import license

    d.   Methods of guaranteeing payments

    e.   Knowledge of letters of credit (revocable, irrevocable, transferable and non-transferable letters of credit)

f.   Knowledge of custom procedures

g.   Knowledge of Export/Import Financing

h.   Knowledge of cultural/language

Having come from the country or a global region where you will be doing business, you do not have the problem of cultural/language barriers.

What You Need To Start-Up

a.   A Computer (with Internet connection)
Use a desktop or a laptop computer with a 56k modem. Install the following software:
Word processor (MS Office)—Use this to write letters, create mailing labels, address envelopes. In the MS office you've got MS word, Excel, Access, Outlook, and Powerpoint.
Spreadsheet—You can create charts and do your finances with spreadsheet program. Use MS Excel for your spreadsheet needs.
QuickBooks Pro—With this you can create custom invoices, compute sales, and do electronic banking, bill payments, control inventory and payroll. Use it for all accounting and bookkeeping.
Database—Use the Database program to keep record of clients, sellers, vendors and all your business contacts/links. With the database program you can keep record of phone calls, faxes, meeting, conferences, seminars time and dates of events and incidents. You may want to use Dbase or Fox Pro for your database needs.
Graphic—Use this to create flyers, announcements newsletters and advertisements. You may want to use PageMaker, QuarkXpress and Clarisworks for your graphic exploits.
Scheduler—Use this to manage your schedules.

b.   Phone, Fax, Printer, Scanner, Copier (can buy all-

in-one)
c.   Office Furniture (including office supplies and office accessories)
d.   Insurance
e.   Fees payable to become a member in professional and or trade associations.
f.   Books
g.   Marketing/advertising cost.
h.   Business suits, ties, shoes, briefcase (all for personal image improvement) and other miscellaneous expenses

The total cost of your start-up needs will not exceed $20,000 Canadian.

Professional/Trade Associations You May Like To Join/Know

- Canadian Exporters Association
  99 Bank Street,
  Suite 250
  Ottawa, On
  K1P 6B9
  This body has Regional Offices across Canada
- Canadian Importers Association
  438 University Avenue
  Suite 1618
  P.O.BOX 60
  Toronto, On
  M5G 2K8
  Phone: 416-595-5333
  Website: www.importers.ca
  This Association offers seminars for their new members—'Import Canada'
- The Alliance of Manufacturers and Exporters Canada
  1 Nicholas Street,

Suite 1500
Ottawa, On
K1N 7B7
Phone: 613-238-8888
Website: www.the-alliance.org

5995 Avesbury Road
Suite 900
Mississauga On,
L5R 3P9
Phone: 905-568-8300

75 International Boulevard,
Suite 400
Toronto, On
M9W 6L9
Phone: 416-798-8000
Fax: 416-798-8050

- Ontario Association of Trading Houses
  Website: www.oath.on.ca
- Quebec Association of Export Trading Houses
  Website: www.amceq.org
- Canada Custom and Revenue Agency
  This agency delivers a useful information service
  for would-be importers/exporters.
  Contact them at:
  Ontario
      Great Toronto Area (GTA)
      Phone: 416-952-0114
      ACIS: 1-800-461-2096
      English: 1-800-461-9000
      French: 1-800-952-2036
  Ottawa
      Phone: 613-991-0537
  Windsor
      Phone: 519-257-6355

> Hamilton: 905-308-8605
> London: 519-645-5843

- Team Canada Inc.
  Phone (Toll Free): 1-888-811-1119

Books You May Need To Buy

- Exporting from Canada
  Published by Self-Counsel Press
  Author: Gerhard W. Kautz
  ISBN: 1-55180-342-9
- Your Guide To Canadian Export Financing
  Author: Iain Williamson
  Export-Import Financing
  Author: M. Venedikian
- Documentary Letters of Credit
  Published by The International trade Services of
  Bank of Nova Scotia. It is also available through
  their Website: www.scotiabank.ca/trade/index.
  html
- Export Manager
  Guide to Export marketing and Management
  Published by XPO International
  Author: Morris NG
  ISBN: 0-9698593-0-9
- A Basic Guide to Exporting
  Published by World Trade Press
  Author: Woznick Alexander
  ISBN: 1885073844
  1885073836(pbk)
- A Basic Guide to Importing
  Published by Lincolnwood, 111, USA: NTC
  Business Books
  Author: US Customs Service
  ISBN: 0844234036 (pbk)
- Export/Import Procedures and Documentation

Published by AMACON
Author: Thomas E. Johnson
ISBN: 0814403506 or 081440734

- Profitable Exporting
  A Complete Guide To Marketing your Product Abroad
  Published by Willey
  Author: John S. Gordon, J.R. Arnold
  ISBN: 0-471-61334-7
- The Export Directory of Canada
  Published by Government Printing Bureau
  Author: Canada Department of Trade and Commerce
- Techniques of Exporting
  Published by Frye Publishing
  Author: J R. Arnold
  ISBN: 0-919741-56-8
- Step by Step Guide To Exporting
  Published by Team Canada
  Author: Team Canada
  ISBN: 066234104X
- The Export Marketing Imperative
  Published by Thomson
  Author: Michael R. Czinkota, Iikka A. Ronkainen, and Maria Ortiz-Bounofina
  ISBN: 0-324-22258-0
- Multinational Distribution Channel
  Tax and Legal Strategies
  Author: R. Dudane Hall, Ralph J. Gilbert
  ISBN: 0275901157
- Successful Cold Call Selling
  Published by American Management Association
  Author: Lee Boyan
  ISBN: 0-8144-7718-6
- How To Be Your Own Publicist

Published hill-Hill
Author: Jessica Hatchigan
ISBN:0-07-138332-8

- Guerrilla Publicity
  Published by Avon, MA: Adams Media Corporation
  Author: Jay Conrad Levinson, Rich Frishman and Jill Lublin
  ISBN: 1-58062-682-3
- Marketing Without Advertising
  Author: Michael Phillips, Salli Rasberry
  ISBN: 0781726824
- The Export Institute of USA
  Website: www.exportinstitute.com
  Books From the export Institute includes:
  The Export Sales and Marketing Manual
  (Often referred to as 'The Bible of Exporting')
  Step-by-Step Analysis of Exporting, locating foreign Markets and Sales Reps., Pricing, Contracts, Shipping and Payment
  1,200 URLS to export websites worldwide
- Foreign Importers and Exporters Sales Leads
  Complete Contact Information on 150,000 Active Import Distributors, Wholesalers and Agents in 137 countries. Data is classified by geographical regions and by the 50,000 types of products they have purchased.
- Become a Successful Export Agent
  - Covers basic requirements in education, knowledge, foreign languages, computer skills and finances. Includes errors to avoid and 10 steps action plan.
- International Market Research and Business intelligence Reports:
  Comprehensive Market research studies and industry trade activity reports covering 200

Countries, 2,000 categories of products and 16,000 international trading companies.
- Export classroom package for Educators: Based upon the export sales and marketing manual, instruction is provided with the most current export information, 100 stimulating topics for classroom discussion and 200 examination question and answers.

Order the above books and publications from Export institute of USA by visiting their website www.exportinstitute. com

Additional sources of Information

- Canada Export Development Corporation
  "Road to Exporting: Guide to Federal government Services"
  Website: www.infoexport.gc.ca/businesswomen/ menu-e.asp
- Forum for International Trade Training (FITT)
  This body provides training in International Business
  Toll Free Phone: 1-800-561-3488
  Website: www.fitt.ca
- PEMD
  Website: www.infoexport.gc.ca
- Royal Bank of Canada
  Website: www.royalbank.ca
- Export Development Corporation
  Website: www.edc.ca
- Bank of Nova Scotia
  Website: www.scotiabank.ca
- Team Canada Inc
  Toll Free Phone: 1-888-811-1119
  Fax: 1-888-449-5444

Website: www.exportsource.gc.ca
- Agriculture and Agri-Food Canada For Canada Agri-Food exporters
  Toll Free Phone: 1-888-811-1119
  Website: www.ats.agr.ca
- Atlantic Canada Opportunities Agency
  Website: www.acoa.ca
- Canada Economic Development for Quebec Regions
  Website: www.dec-ced.gc.ca
- Business Development Bank
  Toll Free Phone: 1-888-463-6232
  Website: www.bdc.ca
- British Columbia Trade and Investment Office
  Website: www.cse.gov.bc.ca
- Win Exports
  Website: www.dfait-maneci.gc.ca
  Toll Free Phone: 1-800-551-4946
- Nova Scotia Export Development Corporation
  Website: www.novascotiabusiness.com
- Ontario Exports Inc.,
  Website: www.ontario-canada.com/export

Marketing/How To Get Business

Hunting for business for your Export/Import firm is about the same thing as searching for job in your field. As such, you have to apply all the job search skills discussed in early chapters of this book, customizing them to suit your present need and position.

i. Cold calls to manufacturers for information interviews about who wants to export/import what.

j. Make contact with the trade division of Embassies and Consulates of foreign Countries for export/import leads in their countries.

k.   Visit Chambers of Commerce
l.   Networking
m. Resumes
n.   Brochure/Flyers
o.   Business Cards
p.   Create a Website
q.   Join Associations/social clubs
r.   Trade fairs
Good luck!

Manufacturer's/Independent Sales Representative

Manufacturers/sales representatives are paid commissions on sales of goods/services they made for manufacturers/service companies. Such sales may be realised nationally and or internationally. A manufacturers/sales representative may choose to deal in a particular industry or line of product. The products may range from raw material through semi-finished to finished products, and services may range from repair through maintenance to entertainment, education and health services. The sales may be to retailers, wholesalers, to a manufacturer or from one service provider to another.

A manufacturer's /Independent Sales Representative has a duty to:

i.   Employ the best of efforts to sell and promote the product/services of the company/industry he/she is representing
ii.   Meet sales quota requirements
iii. Represent the product/services at trade fairs and trade shows.
iv.   Be able to report and forecast sales within a reasonable margin of error
v.   Have and maintain a comprehensive list of clients
vi.   The responsibility to protect intellectual and or industrial property rights
vii. Respond to all sales inquiries

As a Manufacturer's/Independent Sales Representative, you need:

a.   To be peoples smart

Possessing charm—being accessible, listening to people, addressing people by their names, being generally warm, good appearance and knowing how to talk to people, how to explain things to people, are extremely required in selling, and invariably to be a good salesperson.

b.   Good Knowledge of the product/services you are
       selling

A chemist selling chemical reagents and laboratory equipments already have good background knowledge of the product he/she is selling. Having the knowledge of the product/services you are selling makes it easier for you as a salesperson.

Some manufacturer's/sales representatives represent a number of companies and or products round the globe. If you will work in that capacity then you will need to learn foreign languages and cultures.

What You Need To Start-Up

a.   A Computer (with Internet connection)

Use a desktop or a laptop computer with a 56k modem. Install the following software:

Word processor (MS Office)—Use this to write letters, create mailing labels, address envelopes. In the MS office you've got MS word, Excel, Access, Outlook, and Powerpoint.

Spreadsheet—You can create charts and do your finances with spreadsheet program. Use MS Excel for your spreadsheet needs.

QuickBooks Pro—With this you can create custom invoices, compute sales, and do electronic banking, bill payments, control inventory and payroll. Use it for all accounting and bookkeeping.

Database—Use the Database program to keep record of

clients, sellers, vendors and all your business contacts/links. With the database program you can keep record of phone calls, faxes, meeting, conferences, seminars time and dates of events and incidents. You may want to use Dbase or Fox Pro for your database needs.

Graphic—Use this to create flyers, announcements newsletters and advertisements. You may want to use PageMaker, QuarkXpress and Clarisworks for your graphic exploits.

Scheduler—Use this to manage your schedules.

The following software are especially for you the Manufacturer's/Independent Sales Representative

- Representative Profit management System (RPMS)
  Website: www.rpms.com
- Manufacturers Agents Computer System (MACS)
- Website; www.macsworld.com
  WinRep Software
  Website: www.winrep.com
- Reps for Windows
  Website: www.repworld.com

b. Phone, Fax, Printer, Scanner, Copier (can buy all-in-one)

c. Office Furniture (including office supplies and office accessories)

d. Insurance

e. Fees payable to become a member in professional and or trade associations.

f. Books

g. Marketing/advertising cost.

h. Business suits, ties, shoes, briefcase (all for personal image improvement) and other miscellaneous expenses

The total cost of your start-up needs will not exceed

$20,000 Canadian.

Professional/Trade Associations You May Like To Join/Know

- Canadian Association of Manufacturers Representatives
- Canadian Association of Independent Sales Representatives
- The Alliance of Manufacturers and Exporters Canada
  1 Nicholas Street,
  Suite 1500
  Ottawa, On
  K1N 7B7
  Phone: 613-238-8888
  Website: www.the-alliance.org

  5995 Avesbury Road
  Suite 900
  Mississauga On,
  L5R 3P9
  Phone: 905-568-8300

  75 International Boulevard,
  Suite 400
  Toronto, On
  M9W 6L9
  Phone: 416-798-8000
  Fax: 416-798-8050
- Automotive Parts Manufacturers Association
  195 The West Mall, Suite 516
  Toronto, On
  M9C 5K1
  Phone: 416-620-4220
  Fax: 417-620-9730
  Website: www.apma@interware.net
- Canadian Chemical Producers Association

Phone: 1-800-267-6666
Fax: 613-237-40-61
- Canadian Sanitation Supply Association
  300 Mill Road, Suite G-10
  Etobicoke, On
  M9C 4W7
  Phone: 416-620-9320
  Fax: 416-620-7199
  Email: info@cssa.com
- Machinery and Equipment Manufacturers
  Association of Canada
  116 Albert Street, Suite 701
  Ottawa, On
  K1P 5G3
  Phone: 613-232-7213
- Canadian Plastic Industry Association
  5925 airport road, Suite 500
  Mississauga, On
  L4V 1W1
  Phone: 905-678-7748
  Fax: 905-678-0774
- Non-prescription Drug Manufacturers Association
  of Canada
  1111 Prince of Wales Drive, Suite 406
  Ottawa, On
  K2C 3T2
  Phone: 613-723-0777
  Fax: 613-723-0779
  Email: ndmac@ndmac.ca
- Automotive Industries Association of Canada
  1272 Wellington Street
  Ottawa, On
  K1Y 3A7
  Phone: 613-728-5821
  Fax: 613-728-6021

Email: aia@aiacanada.com
Website: www.aftmkt.com/associations
- Aerospace Industries Association of Canada
  60 Queen Street, Suite 1200
  Ottawa, On
  K1P 5Y7
  Phone: 613-232-4297
  Fax: 613-232-1142
  Website: www.aiac.ca
- Canadian Association of Mining Equipment and
  Services for Export
  345 Renfrew Drive, Suite 101
  Markham, On
  L3R 9S9
  Phone: 1-905-513-1834
  Email: minesupply@camese.org
- North American Industries Representatives
  Association (NIRA)
  Website: www.nira.org
- Ontario Motor Vehicle Industry Council
  36 York Mills Road, Suite 110
  North York, Ontario
  M2P 2E9
  Phone: 416-226-4500
  Toll Free: 1-800-943-6002
  Website: www.omvic.on.ca

Books You May Need To Buy

- Selling Through Independent Representatives
  Published by AMACON
  Author: Harold J. Novick
  ISBN: 0-8144-0522-3
  Thomas Register of Manufacturers
  Website: www.thomasregister.com
- The export Directory of Canada

Contains a List of Canadian Manufacturers, Procedures and Export
- A list of Manufacturing Firms in British Columbia
  Segregated in size, groups according to employment
  Published by Victoria, British Columbia
  Author: BC Bureau of Economics and Statistics
- Your Guide to statistics Canada's New Census of Manufacturers Publication
- Selling to Government
  A Guide to Government Procurement in Canada
  Multinational Distribution Channel
  Tax and legal strategies
  Author: R. Dudane Hall, Ralph J. Gilbert
  ISBN: 0275901157
- Successful Cold Call Selling
  Published by American Management Association
  Author: Lee Boyan
  ISBN: 0-8144-7718-6
- How To Be Your Own Publicist
  Published hill-Hill
  Author: Jessica Hatchigan
  ISBN:0-07-138332-8
- Guerrilla Publicity
  Published by Adams Media Corporation
  Author: Jay Conrad Levinson, Rich Frishman and Jill Lublin
  ISBN: 1-58062-682-3
- Marketing without Advertising
  Author: Michael Phillips, Salli Rasberry
  ISBN: 0873376080

Other Sources of Information

- The Canadian chamber of Commerce
  BCE Place
  181 Bay Street

P.O.BOX 818
Toronto, On
M5J 2T3
Phone: 416-868-6415
Fax: 416-868-0189
Website: www.chamber.ca

- Ontario Chamber of Commerce
2345 Yonge Street, Suite 808
Toronto, On
M4P 2E5
Phone: 416-482-5222
Website: www.occ.on.ca

Chambers of Commerce may provide list of Manufacturers, Service Firms and Government agencies

Trade fairs

You may also want to have a look at the books and sources of information for the Export/Import Agent.

Marketing/How To Get Business

Hunting for business for your Manufacturer's/Independent sales Reps firm is about the same thing as searching for a job in your field. As such, you have to apply all the job search skills discussed in the early chapters of this book, customizing them to suit your present need and position.

a.   Cold calls to manufacturers/Service industries for information interviews about who wants the services of a Sales Representative.

b.   Make contact with the trade division of Embassies and Consulates of foreign Countries for Representation leads in their countries.

c.   Visit Chambers of Commerce

d.   Networking

e.   Resumes

f.   Brochure/Flyers

g. Business Cards
h. Create a Website
i. Join Associations/social clubs
j. Trade fairs
Good luck!

Marketing/Advertising Agency

As an Advertising/Marketing Agency, your agency will be employing attractive packages, designs and or appealing information to bring a product(s) and or service(s) to the attention of the public, with the sole purpose of getting the public to buy the product(s) or use the service(s).

The marketing/advertising agency reaches the audience through:

- Television
- Radio
- Online (internet)
- Newspapers
- Magazines
- Seminars
- Conferences
- Door-to-Door

The Agency may choose to specialize in a particular industry, product, line of products, and or services.

The agency may also choose to market/advertise using a specific channel: Television, Radio, Online, Newspapers, Magazines, Seminars, Conferences, or Door-to-Door.

It is advisable that your agency markets/advertises for the industry, products, and services related to your profession, where you already know the literature, trends, approach, where and when conferences and seminars are held.

As a marketing/advertising agent, you need:

a. To understand marketing/advertising as an industry/trade
b. Knowledge of the products/services you are

advertising

c. Knowledge of how to use your chosen medium effectively

What You Need To Start-Up

a. A Computer (with Internet connection)

Use a desktop or a laptop computer with a 56k modem. Install the following software

Word processor (MS Office)—Use this to write letters, create mailing labels, address envelopes. In the MS office you've got MS word, Excel, Access, Outlook, and Powerpoint.

Spreadsheet—You can create charts and do your finances with spreadsheet program. Use MS Excel for your spreadsheet needs.

QuickBooks Pro—With this you can create custom invoices, compute sales, and do electronic banking, bill payments, control inventory and payroll. Use it for all accounting and bookkeeping.

Database—Use the Database program to keep record of clients, sellers, vendors and all your business contacts/links. With the database program you can keep record of phone calls, faxes, meeting, conferences, seminars time and dates of events and incidents. You may want to use Dbase or Fox Pro for your database needs.

Graphic—Use this to create flyers, announcements newsletters and advertisements. You may want to use PageMaker, QuarkXpress and Clarisworks for your graphic exploits.

Scheduler—Use this to manage your schedules.

b. Phone, Fax, Printer, Scanner, Copier (can buy all-in-one)

c. Digital Photo Camera

d. Office Furniture (including office supplies and office accessories)

e. Insurance
f. Fees payable to become a member in professional and or trade associations.
g. Books
h. Marketing/advertising cost.
i. Business suits, ties, shoes, briefcase (all for personal image improvement) and other miscellaneous expenses

The total cost of your start-up needs will not exceed $20,000 Canadian.

Books You May Need To Buy
- How to Open and Run a Home-Based Communication Business
  Published by Globe Pequot Press
  Author: Louann Nagy and Werksman
  ISBN: 1564406318
- The 22 Irrefutable Laws of Advertising and when to violate them
  Published by John Wiley & Sons Asia Pte Ltd.
  Author: Micheal Newman
  ISBN: 0470-82106-X
- The 22 Immutable Laws of Marketing
  Published by Harper Business
  Author: Al Ries and Jack Trout
  ISBN: 0887306667
- How To Start And Run Your Own Advertising Agency
  Published by McGraw-Hill
  Author: Allan Krieff
  ISBN: 0070352194
- 6 Steps To Free Publicity
  Published by Career Press Inc
  Author: Marcia Yudkin
  ISBN: 1-56414-675-8
- Public Relations: Strategies And Tactics

       Published by Addison Wesley Publishing
       Author: Dennis L. Wilcox
       ISBN: 0321015479

- The Practice of Public Relations
  Published by Princetice Hall
  Author: Fraser Seitel
  ISBN: 0131020250
- Guerrilla Publicity
  Published by Adams Media Corporation
  Author: Jay Conrad Levinson, Rich Frishman and Jill Lublin
  ISBN: 1-58062-682-3
- How To Be Your Own Publicist
  Published byMcGraw-Hill
  Author: Jessica Hatchigan
  ISBN:0-07-138332-8
- Marketing Without Advertising
  Author: Michael Phillips, Salli Rasberry
  ISBN: 0873376080

Marketing/How To Get Business

Hunting for business for your Marketing/Advertising Agency is about the same thing as searching for job in your field. As such, you have to apply all the job search skills discussed in the early chapters of this book, customizing them to suit your present need and position.

    k.   Cold calls to Companies and Businesses for information interviews about who may need the services, and provide them with reasons why they may need the services of your agency.

    l.   Networking

    m. Resumes

    n.   Brochure/Flyers

    o.   Business Cards

    p.   Create a Website

q.   Join Associations/social clubs

r.   Trade fairs

Good luck!

Maintenance and Repair Services

There are vast number of things that require maintenance and repair including:

- Computers (including monitors and printers)
- Small engines
- Medical equipments
- Hospital equipments
- Dental equipments
- Laboratory equipments
- Engineering equipments
- And other less sophisticated things like:
  Watch, Clock, Television, VCR, DVD Player, Fax Machine, Scanner, Copier, CD Player, Fridges, Radio, Coffee machines, Expresso coffee machine, Cash register machines, Lawn mower, Projector, Vacuum cleaner, Telephones, Home/Kitchen appliances, Hair dryer etc.

Some of the maintenance and repair services require:

- Training
- Certification
- License

To be in the business of Maintenance and Repair services, you need:

a.   Technical aptitude

b.   Certification, where necessary

c.   Training

d.   License, where necessary

e.   A Vehicle (in some cases)

f.   Replacement parts

What You Need To Start-Up

a.   A Computer (with Internet connection)

Use a desktop or a laptop computer with a 56k modem. Install the following software:

Word processor (MS Office)—Use this to write letters, create mailing labels, address envelopes. In the MS office you've got MS word, Excel, Access, Outlook, and Powerpoint.

Spreadsheet—You can create charts and do your finances with spreadsheet program. Use MS Excel for your spreadsheet needs.

QuickBooks Pro—With this you can create custom invoices, compute sales, and do electronic banking, bill payments, control inventory and payroll. Use it for all accounting and bookkeeping.

Database—Use the Database program to keep record of clients, sellers, vendors and all your business contacts/links. With the database program you can keep record of phone calls, faxes, meeting, conferences, seminars time and dates of events and incidents. You may want to use Dbase or Fox Pro for your database needs.

Graphic—Use this to create flyers, announcements newsletters and advertisements. You may want to use PageMaker, QuarkXpress and Clarisworks for your graphic exploits.

Scheduler—Use this to manage your schedules.

b.   Phone, Fax, Printer, Scanner, Copier (can buy all-in-one)

c.   Digital Photo Camera

d.   Office Furniture (including office supplies and office accessories)

e.   Insurance

f.   Fees payable to become a member in professional and or trade associations (if any).

g.   Books

h.   Marketing/advertising cost and other miscellaneous expenses.

The total cost of your start-up needs will not exceed $20,000 Canadian.

Books You May Need To Buy

- Start your own computer Repair Business
  Published by McGraw-Hill
  Author: Linda Rohrbough, Michael F. Hordeski
  ISBN: 0079119018
- The Computer and Network Professionals Certification Guide
  Published by Sybex Publishing
  Author: J Scott Christianson with Lee Fajen
  ISBN: 0782122604
  Website: www.certification-upgrade.com
- How To Start Your Own Appliance Repair Business from Home Without Capital or Experience: For major Appliances
  Author: Loughurst Rey D
  ISBN: 1563021102
- Opportunities in Installation and Repair Careers
  Published by Vgm Career Horizons
  Author: Mark Rowh
  ISBN: 0844241369
- How to start and Manage a Farm Equipment Repair Service Business
  ISBN: 1887005269
- Upgrading and Repairing PCs Quick Reference
  Author: Scott Mueller
  ISBN: 0789716690
- Marketing Without Advertising
  Author: Michael Phillips, Salli Rasberry
  ISBN: 0873376080
- Guerrilla Publicity

Published by Adams Media Corporation
Author: Jay Conrad Levinson, Rich Frishman, Jill Lublin
ISBN: 1-58062-682-3

Marketing/How To Get Business

Hunting for business for your Maintenance and Repair firm is about the same thing as searching for a job in your field. As such, you have to apply all the job search skills discussed in the early chapters of this book, customizing them to suit your present need and position.

    a.   Cold calls to companies and businesses for information interviews about who may need the services, and provide them with reasons why they may need the maintenance and repair services of your Firm.

    b.   Networking

    c.   Yellow pages advertisement

    d.   Brochure/Flyers

    e.   Business Cards

    f.   Create a Website

    g.   Join Associations/social clubs

    h.   Trade fairs

Good luck!

Translator/Interpreter

Do you remember how much money you paid to have your academic and professional credentials translated from the language in which it was issued to English?

Yes you do.

Good!

Every year, hundreds of thousands of Foreign Trained Professionals and Skilled Immigrants like you pay the same amount of money or more to have their documents translated into English and or French language. Many more companies and organisations spend even more dollars to have documents and texts translated into languages other than English language.

Some Foreign Trained Professionals come from non-English/non-French speaking countries and or countries that speak English/French and other language(s):

Portuguese, Spanish, Russian language, Hindi, Punjabi, Urdu, Igbo language, Afghan language, Chinese, Swahili language, Japanese, Vietnamese language, Bosnian language, Romanian language, Czech language, Zulu language, Ukrainian language, Arabic language, Pakistani language, Polish language, Korean language, Taiwanese language, Thai language, etc.

The ability to speak one and or more of these languages in addition to speaking English/French language is an automatic qualification to the foremost requirement in becoming a translator/interpreter

Possible areas for Translation work

a. Documents (official and unofficial)
b. Films/Videos
c. Books—prose/poetry
d. Technical texts
e. Website text content

As a translator, you must be clear and concise, using the exact meaning of words in translating.

Possible Places for Interpretation work

a. Seminars
b. Law courts
c. Conferences
e. Churches
f. Rallies
g. Airports/Seaports/Land borders

Translating and Interpreting in some areas may need Certification and or License.

As a translator/interpreter, you need to have a good

knowledge of the two languages in question. You may also subcontract other translators. In technical text translating, it is always advisable to have a technical knowledge in the field of the text.

What You Need To Start-Up

a. A Computer (with Internet connection)

Use a desktop or a laptop computer with a 56k modem. Install the following software:

Word processor (MS Office)—Use this to write letters, create mailing labels, address envelopes. In the MS office you've got MS word, Excel, Access, Outlook, and Powerpoint.

Spreadsheet—You can create charts and do your finances with spreadsheet program. Use MS Excel for your spreadsheet needs.

QuickBooks Pro—With this you can create custom invoices, compute sales, do electronic banking, bill payments, control inventory and payroll. Use it for all accounting and bookkeeping.

Database—Use the Database program to keep record of clients, sellers, vendors and all your business contacts/links. With the database program you can keep record of phone calls, faxes, meeting, conferences, seminars time and dates of events and incidents. You may want to use Dbase or Fox Pro for your database needs.

Graphic—Use this to create flyers, announcements newsletters and advertisements. You may want to use PageMaker, QuarkXpress and Clarisworks for your graphic exploits.

Scheduler—Use this to manage your schedules.

b. Phone, Fax, Printer, Scanner, Copier (can buy all-in-one)

d. Office Furniture (including office supplies and office accessories)

e. Insurance
f. Fees payable to become a member in professional and or trade associations (if any).
g. Books (trans-language dictionary)
h. Marketing/advertising cost and other miscellaneous expenses.

You may also want to have your Translation firm Online. In that case you may need to implement the steps for establishing a business Online as explained in the 'Steps for Establishing a Business Online' section of this book.

The total cost of your start-up needs will not exceed $20,000 Canadian.

Professional/Trade Associations/Organizations You May Like To Join/Know

- Canadian Translators and Interpreters Council (CTIC)
  This is an umbrella organization for the provincial and territorial associations of British Columbia, Alberta, New Brunswick, Nova Scotia, Newfoundland and Labrador, Northwest Territories, Nunavut, Manitoba, Ontario, Quebec, Saskatchewan, Yukon.
- Association of Translators and Interpreters of Ontario (ATIO)
  Phone: 613-241-2846
  Toll free: 1-800-234-5030
  Website: www.atio.on.ca
- Association of Translators and Interpreters of Manitoba (ATIM)
  200 Ave de la Cathedrale, BOX 83
  Winnipeg, Manitoba
  R2H 0H7
  Phone: 204-797-3247
  Email: info@atim.mb.ca

Website: www.atim.mb.ca
- Association of Translators and Interpreters of Alberta (ATIA)
  P.O.BOX 546
  Main Post Office
  Edmonton AB
  T5J 2K8
  Phone: 780-434-8384
  Website: www.atia.ab.ca
- Society of Translators and Interpreters of British Columbia (STIBC)
  Website: www.stibc.org
- Translators and Interpreters association of Quebec Ordre des Traducteurs et Interpretes Agrees du Quebec (OTIAQ)
  Website: www.otiaq.org
- Association of Visual Language Interpreters of Canada
  Website: www.avlic.ca
- Association of Translators and Interpreters of Saskatchewan (ATISK)
  Website: www.atis-sk.ca
- Canadian Translators, Terminologists and Interpreters Council
  Website: www.cttic.org
- Corporation of Translators, Terminologists and Interpreters of New Brunswick
  Website: www.ctinb.nb.ca
- Literary Translators Association of Canada
  Website: www.geocities.com
- Network of Translators in Education
  Website: www.rte-net.ca
- The Nunavut Interpreters and Translators Society
  Website: www.nunanet.com
- American Translators Association

Website: www.atanet.org
In this site you may learn one or two things about translation and interpretation profession.
- Institute of Translation and Interpreting
  Website: www.iti.org.uk
  In this site you may find some basic start-up information for interpreters and Translators.
- Foreign Language Forum on Compuserve
  Website: www.go.compuserve.com/foreignlanguage
- International Association of Conference Interpreters
  10 Avenue de Secheron--Ch,
  1202 Geneva, Switzerland.
  Website: www.aiic.net

Marketing/How To Get Business

Hunting for business for your Translation/Interpreter firm is about the same thing as searching for a job in your field. As such, you have to apply all the job search skills discussed in the early chapters of this book, customizing them to suit your present need and position.

- a. Cold calls to Companies, Businesses that engage in international transactions, Organisations, Law firms, Immigration office, Seminar/Conference/Rally Organizers, churches for information interviews about who may need the services, and provide them with reasons why they may need the services of your Firm.
- b. Networking
- c. Yellow pages advertisement
- d. Brochure/Flyers
- e. Business Cards
- f. Create a Website
- g. Join Associations/social clubs
- h. Trade fairs

Good luck!

Online Florist/Gift Shop

Emotion is indigenous to man. Emotion, manifestation of emotion and tangible exchange of emotion has been as old as mankind. Ferrying the tangible expression of peoples lovely emotion could be a lovely and interesting business.

Online business has been described by lots of people as, "the gold rush of the present century". And joining this razzle of 'gold rush' by transporting the tangible expression of people's lovely emotions and passion couldn't be more dazzling.

As an online florist/gift shop owner, you do not handle, take care of, stock flowers, plants and gift items. You arrange with traditional florists (flower shop owners) and gift shop owners for supply. But nevertheless, you need to have a good knowledge of flowers and gift items.

For setting up your flower/gift shop online, see the section of this book that explains the 'Steps For Establishing a Business Online'. In addition, you will need:

a. Phone, Fax, Printer, Scanner, Copier (can buy all-in-one)
b. Office Furniture (including office supplies and office accessories)
c. Insurance
d. Fees payable to become a member in professional and or trade associations (if any).
e. Books
f. Marketing/advertising cost and other miscellaneous expenses.
h. Digital photo Camera

The total cost of your start-up needs will not exceed $20,000 Canadian.

Books You May Need To Buy

• The Unofficial Guide to Starting a Business Online
Published by Wiley Publishing, Inc.

Author: Jason R. Rich
ISBN0-02-863340-7
- Doing Big Business on the Internet
  Published by Self-Counsel Press
  Author: Hurley & Birkwood
  ISBN: 1-55180-119-1
- Selling On The Web
  Author: Paul Galloway
  ISBN: 1563824876
- Start an eBay Business
  Published by Alpha Books
  Author: Barbara Weltman
  ISBN: 159257-333-9
- Small Business Online
  A Strategic Guide for Canada Entrepreneurs
  Published by Prentice Hall Canada Inc.,
  Author: Jim Carroll with Rich Broadhead
  ISBN: 0-13-976895-5
- 101 Ways To Promote your Website
  Published by Maximum Press
  Author: Susan Sweeney
  ISBN: 1931644217
- Start Your Own Business On eBay: Your Step by
  Step Guide To Success
  Published by Entrepreneur Press
  Author: Jacquelyn Lynn
  ISBN: 1932531122
- Start Your Own E-Business
  Published by Entrepreneur Press
  Author: Entrepreneur Press
  ISBN: 1932156747
- Selling On The Net: The Complete Guide
  Published by NTC Business Books
  Author: Lewis, Herschell Gordon
  ISBN: 0844232343

- Selling On The Internet: How To Open An
  Electronic Storefront And Have Millions Of
  Customers Come To You
  Published by McGraw-Hill
  Author: James C. Gonyea, Wayne M. Gonyea
  ISBN: 0070241872
- The Online Business Book
  Published by Adam Media Corporation
  Author: Rob Liflander
  ISBN: 158062-3204
- Guerrilla Marketing Online
  Published by Houghton Mifflin
  Author: Jay Conrad Levinson and Charles Rubin
  ISBN: 0-395-86061-X
- Internet Marketing For Dummies
  Published by Wiley Publishing Inc.,
  ISBN: 0-7645-0778-8
- Low-Cost Website Promotion
  Published by Adam Media Corporation
  Author: Barry Feig
  ISBN: 1-58062-501-0
- Online Business Resources
  Published by Made E-Z
  Author: Paul Galloway
  ISBN: 1-56382-510-4
- Generating Trust in Online Business: From Theory
  To Practice
  Published by IQ
  Author: Magda Fusaro
  ISBN: 2-922417-28-X
- Absolute Beginners Guide To Launching an eBay
  Business
  Published by Que
  Author: Micheal Miller
  ISBN: 0-7897-3058-8

- Starting an eBay Business For Dummies
  Published by Wiley Publishing Inc.,
  Author: Marsha Collier
  ISBN: 0-7645-6924-4
- Online Business Planning
  Published by Career Press
  Author: Robert T. Gorman
  ISBN: 1-56414-369-4
- Marketing without Advertising
  Author: Michael Phillips, Salli Rasberry
  ISBN: 0873376080
- Guerrilla Publicity
  Published by Adams Media Corporation
  Author: Jay Conrad Levinson, Rich Frishman, Jill Lublin
  ISBN: 1-58062-682-3

Visit the following websites to have an idea of what you own site may look like:

- www.1800flowers.com
- www.proflowers.com
- www.ftd.com
- www.floristconnection.com
- www.flowersshope.com
- www.fromyouflowers.com
- www.800flowerdelivery.com
- www.coasttocoastflorist.com
- www.flowerdelivery.com
- www.secure.strawberrynet.com
- www.londonflowernet.com

Although the traditional florists with whom you made arrangement for the supplies will handle everything from floral designs and arrangements, floral design techniques, to proper care and handling of fresh cut flowers, you may need to know/take lessons in:

316 ◆ A Complete Guide to Overcome No Canadian Experience

a. Design Forms

In floral design forms, you will learn design forms including Symmetrical triangle, Circular, Asymmetrical triangle, Vertical, Oval, Fan shape, Crescent & Hogarth curve, European tied Bouquets

b. Design Techniques

In design techniques, you will learn Basing, Focal Area, Terracing, Grouping, Clustering, Zoning, Banding, Binding, Shadowing, Framing & Parallelism, Colour harmony and new experimental design styles.

c. Proper Care and Handling of Fresh Cut Flowers

In Care and Handling, you will learn the processing of freshly cut flowers, merchandising, flower & plant identification, the availability of flowers and plants in the Canadian market.

d. Wedding Etiquette

In wedding etiquette, you will learn wedding order procedures, wiring and taping techniques, preparing a Brides Bouquet, Bridesmaids, Maid of Honour, flower gifts, set up flowers for a wedding ceremony and reception, Corsages and Boutonnieres.

e. Funerals and Sympathy Tributes

In Funeral and Sympathy Tributes, you will learn step-by-step construction of Funeral basket, Casket spray, Standing spray, Vase arrangement, Wreaths, Hearts and Crosses, rightful pricing and delivery.

f. Supply Channels

In this study, you will visit wholesale florists, where you will see large selection of fresh, silk and dried flowers. You will see all sorts of flowers including Orchids, tropical flowers and plants, hybrids, gift baskets, Vases etc.

This program will last a maximum total duration of three weeks.

Possible places to obtain this training includes:

Canadian Institute of Floral Design

2794A Lakeshore Blvd. W.
Unit #3
Toronto, On
M8V 1H5
Phone: 416-733-2387
Toll Free: 1-877-285-1931
Fax: 416-733-2387
Website: www.proflorists.net/

Outside Toronto and Ontario, look around for a floral design school in your area.

Marketing/How to Get Business

a. Promote your website to increase the number of visitors to the website
b. Advertise your website in the Yellow pages, newspapers and magazines
c. Create brochures and flyers
d. Business cards
e. Look for corporate contracts in offices, schools, establishments, Churches—a good source for knowing up coming weddings
f. Organize/join a flower club
g. Organize/join a birthday club
h. Reach for Funeral houses, Hospitals, and for event organizers

Good luck!

Dating Club

This is the business of facilitating the meeting of people with mutual attraction and emotional needs, making it possible for them to explore the depths of their mutual attraction and needs.

As a dating club operator, your business is practically linking people with people. As such, you need to be people smart, have knowledge of horoscope, horoscopic signs and harmony, outgoing and warm.

As a dating club operator, you may undertake:

a. Live Speed Dating
b. Online Speed Dating
c. Personal Introduction Service
d. Matchmaking
e. Organize Parties/Social events
f. Dance Classes
g. Singles Dance Parties
h. Garden Parties

How Live Speed Dating works

The dating club, through its marketing channel or membership pool invites about 40 or more people (20 males and 20 females) for a price of say $40 or more each. The meeting takes place in a hotel, bar, pub, restaurant and or banquet room. Each invitee will be given a card, pen or pencil to mark the tag number of each person he/she meets. Each and every female/male invitee will be given an opportunity to sit with each and every male/female invitee for a maximum period of say ten minutes. If he/she likes the person, she/he marks his/her tag number on the card. The whole thing will be going on amidst music, entertainment, refreshment, side attraction etc. At the end of the day, every body turns in his/her card, and the people are free to mingle normally. The dating club will then sort out the cards to find out who and who have a mutual chemistry, and will immediately notify them through email, phone, fax, or in writing. The club may give a follow through help by inviting them to dance classes for a price, inviting them to singles dance parties until they make a total nuptial take off.

Online Dating

People pay their membership dues and help themselves online. The dating club also help in finding matches for members.

What You Need To Start-up

To set up your dating club, you will need to visit the section of this book that explains the 'Steps for setting your business Online'. In addition, you need:

a. Phone, fax, printer, Scanner, Copier (can buy all-in-one)
b. Office furniture (including office supplies and office accessories)
c. Insurance
d. Digital photo Camera
e. Marketing/Advertising cost and other miscellaneous expenses

The total cost of your start-up need will not exceed $20,000 Canadian

Books You may need

- Doing Big Business on the Internet
  Published by Self-Counsel Press
  Author: Hurley & Birkwood
  ISBN: 1-55180-119-1
- Selling On The Web
  Author: Paul Galloway
  ISBN: 1563824876
- Start an eBay Business
  Published by Alpha Books
  Author: Barbara Weltman
  ISBN: 159257-333-9
- Small Business Online
  A Strategic Guide for Canada Entrepreneurs
  Published by Prentice Hall Canada Inc.,
  Author: Jim Carroll with Rich Broadhead
  ISBN: 0-13-976895-5
- 101 Ways To Promote your Website
  Published by Maximum Press
  Author: Susan Sweeney

ISBN: 1931644217
- Start Your Own Business On eBay: Your Step by Step Guide To Success
  Published by Entrepreneur Press
  Author: Jacquelyn Lynn
  ISBN: 1932531122
- Start Your Own E-Business
  Published by Entrepreneur Press
  Author: Entrepreneur Press
  ISBN: 1932156747
- Selling On The Net: The Complete Guide
  Published by NTC Business Books
  Author: Lewis, Herschell Gordon
  ISBN: 0844232343
- Selling On The Internet: How To Open An Electronic Storefront And Have Millions Of Customers Come To You
  Published by McGraw-Hill
  Author: James C. Gonyea, Wayne M. Gonyea
  ISBN: 0070241872
- The Online Business Book
  Published by Adam Media Corporation
  Author: Rob Liflander
  ISBN: 158062-3204
- Guerrilla Marketing Online
  Published by Houghton Mifflin
  Author: Jay Conrad Levinson and Charles Rubin
  ISBN: 0-395-86061-X
- Internet Marketing For Dummies
  Published by Wiley Publishing Inc.,
  ISBN: 0-7645-0778-8
- Low-Cost Website Promotion
  Published by Adam Media Corporation
  Author: Barry Feig
  ISBN: 1-58062-501-0

- Online Business Resources
  Published by Made E-Z
  Author: Paul Galloway
  ISBN: 1-56382-510-4
- Generating Trust in Online Business: From Theory
  To Practice
  Published by IQ
  Author: Magda Fusaro
  ISBN: 2-922417-28-X
- Absolute Beginners Guide To Launching an eBay
  Business
  Published by Que
  Author: Micheal Miller
  ISBN: 0-7897-3058-8
- Starting an eBay Business For Dummies
  Published by Wiley Publishing Inc.,
  Author: Marsha Collier
  ISBN: 0-7645-6924-4
- Online Business Planning
  Published by Career Press
  Author: Robert T. Gorman
  ISBN: 1-56414-369-4
- Guerrilla Publicity
  Published by Adams Media Corporation
  Author: Jay Conrad Levinson, Rich Frishman, Jill
  Lublin
  ISBN: 1-58062-682-3
- Marketing Without Advertising
  Author: Michael Phillips, Salli Rasberry
  ISBN: 0873376080
- The 22 Immutable Laws of Marketing
  Published by Harper Business
  Author: Al Ries and Jack Trout
  ISBN: 0887306667
- 6 Steps To Free Publicity

Published by Career Press Inc
Author: Marcia Yudkin
ISBN: 1-56414-675-8

- Endless Referrals: Network Your Everyday
Contacts into Sales (New and Updated Edition)
Author: Bob Burg
ISBN: 0070089973

Marketing/How to get business

a. Promote your website to increase the number of visitors to the website
b. Advertise in the yellow pages, newspapers, magazines, billboards
c. Create brochures and flyers
d. Business cards

Good luck!

Massage Therapy

No other ailment afflicts the human community as much as Pain, Aches, Anxiety and Stress. They have been around as much as mankind, and so have been the endeavour to treat, cure and or manage them—Relaxation/Touch Therapy.

The oldest known documented historical evidence of massage therapy dates as far back as 3000BC. The first school of massage therapy sprung up in China, Asia in the early AD's. In the 19th century, precisely in 1895, Sigmund Freud used massage therapy to treat hysteria. And in the 20th century, in 1991, the Touch Research Institute was established. In 1992, Registration, Certification and Licensing became an issue for the massage therapy profession/trade. The Massage Registration Act was enacted in 1949 and the First Massage Act was passed in 1943 in the USA. North American students who came back from Europe where they went to study, introduced massage therapy in North America in the 1850's. The history of this profession/trade is so vast that people have been sent to jail for using the Touch Therapy, as in the case of William Reich—an Austrian Psychoanalyst and one time student of Sigmund Freud. Mr Reich used Somato Technique massage therapy in his attempt to cure Neuroses.

There are various forms of Massage Therapy including: Acupressure, Aromatherapy massage, Ayurvedic massage, Berry Work massage, Breast massage, Bowen therapy, Chi Nei Tsang massage, Equine massage, Esalen massage, Connective Tissue massage, Geriatric massage, Hawaiian massage, Hermopathy massage, Hot Stone massage, Infant massage, Iridiology massage, Medical massage, Myofascial release, Myotherapy massage, Naprapathy massage, Neuromuscular therapy, Chair massage, Orthopaedic massage, Pregnancy massage, Radiance Breathwork, Radiance Technique, Reflexology, Rosen method, Shiatsu massage, Soft Tissue Release massage, Sports massage, Swedish massage, Thai massage, Therapeutic Touch, Visceral Manipulation, Zero Balancing massage.

You can choose from any of these fields/types of massage to establish your practice/business.

What You Need To Start-up

a. A Computer (with Internet connection)

Use a desktop or a laptop computer with a 56k modem. Install the following software:

Word processor (MS Office)—Use this to write letters, create mailing labels, address envelopes. In the MS office you've got MS word, Excel, Access, Outlook, and Powerpoint.

Spreadsheet—You can create charts and do your finances with spreadsheet program. Use MS Excel for your spreadsheet needs.

QuickBooks Pro—With this you can create custom invoices, compute sales, do electronic banking, bill payments, control inventory and payroll. Use it for all accounting and bookkeeping.

Database—Use the Database program to keep record of clients, sellers, vendors and all your business contacts/links. With the database program you can keep record of phone calls, faxes, meeting, conferences, seminars time and dates of events and incidents. You may want to use Dbase or Fox Pro for your database needs.

Graphic—Use this to create flyers, announcements newsletters and advertisements. You may want to use PageMaker, QuarkXpress and Clarisworks for your graphic exploits.

Scheduler—Use this to manage your schedules.

b. Phone, Fax, Printer, Scanner, Copier (can buy all-in-one)

c. Office Furniture (including office supplies and office accessories)

d. Insurance

e. Fees payable to become a member in professional and or trade associations.

f. Books

g. Marketing/advertising cost and other miscellaneous expenses.

You will need some professional massage supply materials that may include: Massage tables, Table accessories, Table packages, Massage chairs, Massage Oils, Lotions, Creams, Essential oils, Books, Massage charts, Activetics, Sheets and linens, Massage mats, T-shirts, Cold and hot packs, Massage tools, Anatomical chairs, Skeleton models, Body cushions, Cleaners, Hydrocollator, Paraffin bath, Videos and DVDs, Music, Pilates, Yoga supplies.

The occupation specific materials above mentioned could be gotten from:

● Massage Therapy Supply Outlet
    #203, 8815-92 Street
    Edmonton, Alberta

T6C 3P9
Phone: 780-440-1818
Toll Free: 1-800-875-9706
Fax: 780-440-4585
Website: www.mtso.ab.ca
Or visit the following websites:
- www.accupunctureshop.com
- www.bodyworkmall.com
- www.promedproducts.com
- www.massagewarehouse.com
- www.sitincomfort.com
- www.stronglite.com
- www.massageproducts.com
- www.mohawkmedicalmall.com
- www.chinow.com
- www.massage-table-direct.com
- www.totalbodywork.com
- www.massage-chairs-direct.com
- www.aromanotes.com

The total cost of your start-up need may not exceed $20,000.

Professional/Trade Associations or Organizations you may need to join/know

- Canadian Massage Therapist Alliance (CMTA)
  344 Lakeshore Road East, Suite B
  Oakville, On
  L6J 1J6
  Phone: 905-849-7606
  Fax: 905-849-8606
  Email: info@cmta.ca
  Website: www.cmta.ca
- Massage Therapists Association of Alberta
  Box 2403, RPO Plaza Centre
  Red Deer, AB

T4N 6X6
Phone: 403-340-1913
Fax: 403-346-2269
Email: mtaa@telusplanet.net
Website: www.mtaaberta.com
- Massage Therapists' Association of British Columbia (MTABC)
  #205—640 West Broadway
  Vancouver, BC
  V5V 1G4
  Email: mta@smart.com
  Website: www.massagetherapy.bc.ca
- Massage Therapy Association of Manitoba, Inc. (NTAM)
  BOX 65026 Elmwood,
  355 Henderson Highway
  Winnipeg MB
  R2L 1M0
  Phone: 204-254-0406
  Fax: 204-661-1230
  Email: mtam01@shaw.ca
  Website: www.mtam.mb.ca
- New Brunswick Massotherapy Association (NBMA)
  P.O.BOX 20071
  Fredericton NB
  E3B 6Y8
  Phone: 506-459-5788
  Fax: 506-459-5581
  Website: www.nbma-amnb.ca
- Massage Therapists' Association of Nova Scotia (MTANS)
  P.O.BOX 33103, Quinpool Post Office
  Halifax, NS
  B3L 4T6

Phone: 902-429-2190
- East Coast Massage Therapists Association Of Nova Scotia
  Website: www.eastmassage.org
- Ontario Massage Therapist Association (OMTA)
  365 Bloor Street East, Suite 1807
  Toronto, On
  M4W 3L4
  Phone: 416-968-648Toll Free: 1-800-668-2022
  Fax: 416-968-6818
  Email: omta@colliscan.com
- Prince Edwards Island Massage Therapy Association (PEIMTA)
  P.O.BOX 1882
  Charlottetown, PE
  C1A 7N5
  Phone: 902-368-8140
  Fax: 902-368-6524
- Federation Quebecoise Des Massotherapeutes (FQM)
  1265, Mont-Royal est, bureau 204
  Montreal, QC
  H2J 1Y4
  Phone: 514-597-0505
  Toll Free: 1-800-363-9609
  Fax: 514-597-0141
  Email: administration@fqm.qc.ca
  Website: www.fqm.qc.ca
- Massage Therapist Association of Saskatchewan (MTAS)
  230 Ave, R south, Room 327, Old Nurses Residence
  Saskatoon, SK
  S7M 0Z9
  Phone: 306-384-7077

Fax: 306-384-7175
Email: mtas@sasktel.net
- Canadian Sport Massage Therapists Association (CSMTA)
National Office at
1849 Yonge Street, Suite 814
Toronto, On
M4S 1Y2
Phone: 416-488-4414
Fax: 416-488-3079
Email: natoffice@csmta.ca
Website: www.csmta.ca
The sport association has provincial offices in
Ontario- www.csmta.ca/on
Alberta—www.csmta.ca/alberta
British Columbia—www.csmta.ca/bc
Saskatchewan—www.csmta.ca/sask

Books you may Need To Buy

- Building Your Ideal Private Practice: A Guide for Therapists and other Healing Professionals
Author: Lynn Grodzki
ISBN: 0393703312
- Business Mastery: A Guide for Creating a fulfilling, Thriving Business and Keeping it successful.
Author: Cherie Sohnen-Moe
ISBN: 0962126543
- Hands Heal: Communication, Documentation and Insurance Billing for Manual Therapists
Author: Diana L. Thompson
ISBN: 0781726824
- Educated Heart: Professional Guidelines for Massage Therapists, Bodyworkers and Movement Teachers

Author: Nina M. Mclntosh
ISBN: 096741220X

- Myofascial & Deep Tissue Massage
  Author: Alfred Hartemink
- Deep Tissue massage: A Visual Guide To
  Techniques
  Author: Art Riggs
- Deep Tissue Massage andMyofascial Release: A
  Video guide To Techniques
  Author: Art Riggs
- The Massage Connection: Anatomy and
  Physiology
  Author: Kalyani Premkumar
- Mosby's Pathology for Massage Therapists
  Author: Susan G. Salvo
- Pathology A to Z: A Handbook for Massage
  Therapists
  Author: Kalyani Preskumar
- Mosby's Fundamentals of Therapeutic Massage
  Author: Sandy Fritz
- Basic Clinical Massage Therapy: Integrating
  Anatomy and Treatment
  Author: James H. Clay
- A Massage Therapist's Guide to Pathology
  Author: Ruth Werner
- Trial Guide To the Body: How to Locate Muscles,
  Bones & More
  Author: Andrew R. Biel
- The Anatomy Coloring Book
  Author: Wynn Kapit
- Know How To Strengthen, Stretch and Make Your
  Body Flexible
  Author: Alexis Wright
- Review For Therapeutic Massage and Bodywork
  Certification

330 ♦ A Complete Guide to Overcome No Canadian Experience

Author: Joseph Ashton

- Have A Look At the Alternative World
  Author: Gregg Strand
- Guerrilla Publicity
  Published by Adams Media Corporation
  Author: Jay Conrad Levinson, Rich Frishman, Jill Lublin
  ISBN: 1-58062-682-3
- Marketing Without Advertising
  Author: Michael Phillips, Salli Rasberry
  ISBN: 0873376080
- Endless Referrals: Network Your Everyday Contacts into Sales (New and Updated Edition)
  Author: Bob Burg
  ISBN: 0070089973

Marking/How To Get Business

Hunting for business for your Massage Therapy Firm is about the same thing as searching for a job in your field. As such, you have to apply all the job search skills discussed in the early chapters of this book, customizing them to suit your present need and position.

a. Cold calls to Health Clinics, Health Spas, Hospitals, Nursing Homes, Rehabilitation Centres, Companies, Businesses and offices for information interviews about who may need the services, and provide them with reasons why they may need the services of your Massage Therapy Firm.
b. Networking
c. Yellow pages advertisement
d. Brochure/Flyers
e. Business Cards
f. Create a Website
g. Join Associations/social clubs
h. Distribute gift certificates and discounted

treatment packages to your clients, to give to their friends

i.   Send out massage therapy package offers for special days and seasons like Christmas, New Year, Easter, Canada Day, Valentine day etc.

j.   Keep in touch with your clients and call the clients who have not visited your/use your services for some time and remind them of your good services and new discounted offers available.

k.   Find out and incorporate the marketing methods and approaches of other professionals in your field into your own method and approach.

l.   Call your clients, new/old/regulars, a day or two after they use your services to thank them for using the services of your firm, but above all, to ask them how they are feeling.

m.   Offer discounts to your regular clients and offer them one free treatment session if they bring in four or more new clients.

n.   Send out a discounted Massage package offer for students, seniors, couples, singles, teenagers, and some specific professions/professionals like lawyers, truck drivers, factory workers, teachers etc.

o.   Massage of all forms and types help to reduce stress and increase circulation. Develop a weekly newsletter, write in the local newspaper and or magazine giving tips on how to manage stress and use massage to increase circulation. Act like the professional you are.

Good luck!

Research And Information Broker/ Professional

Information is the strategic resource with which companies, businesses, organizations, professionals, and people work. The access to information has led to increased productivity, better service and general efficiency and more direct approach to problems and difficulties. Many more companies, businesses, organizations, professionals and individuals are employing the services of research and information brokers/ professionals to track down information they may need to increase productivity, better service and general efficiency in the workplace, to resolve a specific problem, to stage a viable competition, to elaborate an idea, to vet an innovation etc.

Various names have been employed by the public in an attempt to describe this profession, names like information retriever, information merchant, information finder, information expert, information agent, information researcher, desktop Internet researcher, information professional, information broker. No matter what name whoever chooses to call the trade, it all points to trading on information, to chasing down and retrieving specific information for a price.

As a Research and Information Broker/Professional, you will be in the business of chasing down and retrieving specific information as desired by your client for a price. Your clients may include Companies, Businesses, Banks, Organizations, Professionals and Individuals. The information your clients may be looking for may range from historical, social, public records, commercial, sports, literary, legal, to scientific, technological, architecture, medical, financial and abstract information. For quicker and easier access to information, you may need to subscribe to online subscription databases.

As a Research and Information Broker/Professional you need to:

a. Be research oriented
b. Be curious

c. Have interviewing skills
d. Able to use the library extensively
e. Attention to detail
f. Analytical
g. Able to meet deadlines
h. Able to use questioning and interviewing to develop leads.

As a professional and or skilled person, you may like to specialize in your field and areas related to your field of expertise

What You Need To Start-Up

a. A Computer (with Internet connection)

Use a desktop or a laptop computer with a 56k modem. Install the following software:

Word processor (MS Office)—Use this to write letters, create mailing labels, address envelopes. In the MS office you've got MS word, Excel, Access, Outlook, and Powerpoint.

Spreadsheet—You can create charts and do your finances with spreadsheet program. Use MS Excel for your spreadsheet needs.

QuickBooks Pro—With this you can create custom invoices, compute sales, do electronic banking, bill payments, control inventory and payroll. Use it for all accounting and bookkeeping.

Database—Use the Database program to keep record of clients, sellers, vendors and all your business contacts/links. With the database program you can keep record of phone calls, faxes, meeting, conferences, seminars time and dates of events and incidents. You may want to use Dbase or Fox Pro for your database needs.

Graphic—Use this to create flyers, announcements newsletters and advertisements. You may want to use PageMaker, QuarkXpress and Clarisworks for your graphic exploits.

Scheduler—Use this to manage your schedules.

b. Phone, Fax, Printer, Scanner, Copier (can buy all-in-one)

c. Office Furniture (including office supplies and office accessories)

d. Insurance

e. Fees payable to become a member in professional and or trade associations.

f. Subscription databases

g. Books

h. Marketing/advertising cost.

i. Business suits, ties, shoes, briefcase (all for personal image improvement) and other miscellaneous expenses

The total cost of your start-up needs will not exceed $20,000 Canadian.

Books You May Need To Buy

- Building and Running a Successful Research Business: A Guide for The Independent Information Professional
  Author: Mary Ellen Bates
- Find IT Online: The Complete Guide To Online Research (Third Edition)
  Author: Alan M. Schlein
- The Invisible Web: Uncovering Information Sources Search Engines Can't See
  Author: Chris Sherman
- Super Searchers Make It On Their Own: Top Independent Information Professionals Share their Secrets For Starting and Running A Research Business
  Author: Suzanne Sabroski
- Find It Fast: How to Uncover Expert Information

on Any Subject
Author: Robert I. Berkman
- Naked in Cyberspace: How To Find Personal Information Online
Author: Carole A. Lane, Helen Burwell, Hellen P. Burwell, Owen Davies
- Researching Public Records: How To Get Anything on Anybody
Author: Vincent Parco
- The Online 100: Online Magazines Field Guide To The 100 Most Important Online Databases
Published by Cyberage Books
Author: Mick O'Leary
ISBN: 0910965145
- Information Brokering: A How-To-Do-It Manual (How-To-Do-It Manual for Libraries, No 86)
Author: Florence Mason
- Super Searchers Go To The Source: The Interviewing and Hands-on Information Strategies For Primary Researchers-Online, on the Phone, and in Person (Super Searchers, V.7)
Author: Risa Sacks
- The Extreme Searcher's Internet Handbook: A Guide for the Serious Searcher
Author: Gary Price
- Super Searchers on Competitive Intelligence: The Online and Offline Secrets of Top CI Researchers
Author: Jan Herring
- Encyclopaedia of Investigative Information Sources
Author: J. Michael Ball
- Researching Online for Dummies
Published by IDG Books
Author: Reva Basch
ISBN: 0764503820
- The Online Deskbook: Online Magazine's

Essential Desk Reference for online and Internet
Searchers
Published by Independent Publishing Group
Author: Mary Ellen Bates and Reva Basch
ISBN: 0910965196

- The Investigators Little Black Book 2
  Author: Robert Scott
- The Information Brokers Handbook
  Published by McGraw-Hill
  Author: Sue Rugge and Alfred Glossbrenner
  ISBN: 0070578710
- Find public records Fast: The Complete State,
  County and Courthouse Locator
  Published by Facts on Demand Press
  ISBN: 1889150045
- Start Your Own Information Consultant Business
  Published by Entrepreneur Media
  Author: Walsh George
  ISBN: 1932156739
- Guerrilla Publicity
  Published by Adams Media Corporation
  Author: Jay Conrad Levinson, Rich Frishman, Jill
  Lublin
  ISBN: 1-58062-682-3
- Marketing Without Advertising
  Author: Michael Phillips, Salli Rasberry
  ISBN: 0873376080
- The 22 Immutable Laws of Marketing
  Published by Harper Business
  Author: Al Ries and Jack Trout
  ISBN: 0887306667
- 6 Steps To Free Publicity
  Published by Career Press Inc
  Author: Marcia Yudkin
  ISBN: 1-56414-675-8

- How To Become Your Own Publicist
  Published by McGraw-Hill
  Author: Jessica Hatchigan
  ISBN:0-07-138332-8
- Endless Referrals: Network Your Everyday
  Contacts into Sales (New and Updated Edition)
  Author: Bob Burg
  ISBN: 0070089973

Marketing/How To Get Business

Hunting for business for your Information Brokerage firm is about the same thing as searching for a job in your field. As such, you have to apply all the job search skills discussed in the early chapters of this book, customizing them to suit your present need and position.

a. Cold calls to Manufacturers, Companies, Businesses, Offices, and Organizations for information interviews about who wants what information, and provide them with your profile.

b. Make contact with the trade division of Embassies and Consulates of foreign Countries for information brokerage leads in their countries.

c. Visit Chambers of Commerce

d. Networking

e. Brochure/Flyers

f. Business Cards

g. Create a Website

h. Join Associations/social clubs

i. Trade fairs

Good luck!

Headhunter/Executive Recruiter

Did you as a Foreign Trained Professional and or Skilled Immigrant use the services of a headhunting firm in your endeavour to secure an employment opportunity in your field of expertise? Before you brave up to say goodbye to job search and paid employment and choose to buy yourself a job by becoming self employed and owning your own business.

Yes?

No?

Well, whatever your response is, it is always interesting to watch a scene where the beggar for whatever reason rises to become the giver. By choosing headhunting as a business you do not only own your business, become your own boss and take control of your financial and professional being, you also rise to give to others what you may have asked for, but did not receive.

Headhunting is the business of employment brokerage. As a headhunter, you match job seeking qualified professionals and or skilled persons with employers and employment opportunities. You will be tracking down specific talents/professionals as desired by your clients for a price. You are practically a matchmaker. Your clients may range from Companies, Businesses, Organizations, Governments, offices, other professionals, and Individuals.

Up to two-thirds of hiring in Canada is done through networking. Companies often ask employees within for help in filling a job vacancy in the company. Companies also turn to Headhunters for help. The reason being:

a. It is far cheaper for the companies to use headhunters and or the effort of their employees to fill a vacancy, than to pay for advertisement in the newspaper.

b. It saves the Human Resources Department the time of going through heaps of resumes from prospective job seekers.

c.   The prospective employee will have a reference known to the company/employer.

When a Headhunter fills a job vacancy for an employer, the employer pays to the Headhunter a certain percentage of the employee's agreed monthly or annual wage—an amount of money that may equal the employee's one-week, two weeks, one-month, two months or one year wage depending on the contract. But this amount is not deductible from the employee's wage. A headhunter may not bargain for an employee's wage, but may suggest to the employer the wage expectations of the professionals he/she will present.

Headhunters may offer a guarantee of 3 months, 6 months, one year depending on the nature of the job and or the contract. If the employee for any reason doesn't stay past the period covered in the guarantee, the Headhunter makes a replacement at no extra cost to the employer.

You may choose to specialize in a particular Industry, Field, Trade, and or Profession. As a professional, you may choose to specialize in your own field of expertise. This gives you an edge because you know the field, the profession, and the needed skills. As such, you will be able to vet the quality/calibre of professionals you send to your clients and vice versa.

As a Headhunter, you need to be:

a.   People Smart
b.   Trendy
c.   Pro-active
d.   Analytical
e.   Able to meet deadlines
f.   Maintain list of clients
g.   Knowledge of the company(s) to which you send your clients
h.   Know the job description
i.   Have marketing/advertising skills

j.　Have interviewing skills

k.　Have a Matchmaker's instinct

l.　Be research oriented.

What You Need To Start-Up

a.　A Computer (with Internet connection)

Use a desktop or a laptop computer with a 56k modem. Install the following software:

Word processor (MS Office)—Use this to write letters, create mailing labels, address envelopes. In the MS office you've got MS word, Excel, Access, Outlook, and Powerpoint.

Spreadsheet—You can create charts and do your finances with spreadsheet program. Use MS Excel for your spreadsheet needs.

QuickBooks Pro—With this you can create custom invoices, compute sales, do electronic banking, bill payments, control inventory and payroll. Use it for all accounting and bookkeeping.

Database—Use the Database program to keep record of clients, sellers, vendors and all your business contacts/links. With the database program you can keep record of phone calls, faxes, meeting, conferences, seminars time and dates of events and incidents. You may want to use Dbase or Fox Pro for your database needs.

Graphic—Use this to create flyers, announcements newsletters and advertisements. You may want to use PageMaker, QuarkXpress and Clarisworks for your graphic exploits.

Scheduler—Use this to manage your schedules.

b.　Phone, Fax, Printer, Scanner, Copier (can buy all-in-one)

c.　Office Furniture (including office supplies and office accessories)

d.　Insurance

e. Fees payable to become a member in professional and or trade associations.
f. Subscription databases
g. Books
h. Marketing/advertising cost.
i. Business suits, ties, shoes, briefcase (all for personal image improvement) and other miscellaneous expenses

The total cost of your start-up needs will not exceed $20,000 Canadian.

Professional/Trade Associations You May Like To Join/Know

- Association of Professional Recruiters of Canada
  IPM
  Ste. 2210-1081 Ambleside Drive,
  Ottawa, On
  K2B 8C8
  Phone: 613-721-5957
  Toll Free: 1-888-441-0000
  Fax: 613-721-5850
  Email: info@workplace.ca
  Website: www.workplace.ca
- Canadian Network of Recruiters, Headhunters, Executive Search Firms, Employment Agencies and Management Consultants
  1200 Markham Road, Suite 107
  Toronto, On
  M1H 3C3
  Phone: 416-438-3606
  Fax: 416-438-1849
  Email: info@recruiterwebsites.com
  Website: www.recruiterwebsites.com
- National Association of Executive Search Recruiters

Books You May Need To Buy

- Headhunters: Matchmaking in The Labour Market
  Published by ILR Press
  Author: William Finlay, James E. Coverdill
  ISBN: 0801439272
- The Headhunters Edge
  Published by Random House
  Author: Jefferey E. Christian
  ISBN: 0375505431
- Start Your Own Executive Recruiting Business
  Published by Entrepreneur Press
  Author: Entrepreneur Press, Erickson Mandy
  ISBN: 189198490X
- The Complete Guide to Owning and Operating a
  House-Based Recruiting Business: A Step-by-Step
  business Plan For Entrepreneur
  Published by Writers Club Press
  Author; Charrissa D. Cawley
  ISBN: 0595163955
- How To Market and Sell Your Recruiting Services
  Published by Innovative Consulting
  Author: Bill Radin
  ISBN: 1929836007
- Advanced Strategies For Recruiters
  Published by Innovative consulting
  Author: Bill Radin
  ISBN: 1929836104
- The Recruiters research Blue Book
  Published by Kennedy information
  Author: Andrea A. Jupina
  ISBN: 1885922612
- Recruiting on the Web: Smart Strategies For
  Finding The Perfect Candidate
  Published by McGraw-Hill
  Author: Michael Foster

ISBN: 0071384855
- Effective Recruiting Strategies: Taking a
  Marketing Approach
  Published by Crisp Publications
  Author: Ron Visconti
  ISBN: 1560521279
- The Keys To Successful Recruiting and staffing
  Published by Weddle's
  Author: Barry Siegel
  ISBN: 1928734170
- Guerrilla Publicity
  Published by Adams Media Corporation
  Author: Jay Conrad Levinson, Rich Frishman, Jill
  Lublin
  ISBN: 1-58062-682-3
- Marketing Without Advertising
  Author: Michael Phillips, Salli Rasberry
  ISBN: 0873376080
- The 22 Immutable Laws of Marketing
  Published by Harper Business
  Author: Al Ries and Jack Trout
  ISBN: 0887306667
- 6 Steps To Free Publicity
  Published by Career Press Inc
  Author: Marcia Yudkin
  ISBN: 1-56414-675-8
- How To Become Your Own Publicist
  Published by McGraw-Hill
  Author: Jessica Hatchigan
  ISBN:0-07-138332-8
- Endless Referrals: Network Your Everyday
  Contacts into Sales (New and Updated Edition)
  Author: Bob Burg
  ISBN: 0070089973

Marketing/How To Get Business

Hunting for business for your Headhunting firm is about the same thing as searching for a job in your field. As such, you have to apply all the job search skills discussed in the early chapters of this book, customizing them to suit your present need and position.

a. Cold calls to Manufacturers, Companies, Businesses, Offices, and Organizations for information interviews about who wants to employ a professional, and provide them with your profile.

b. Advertise in the local/national newspapers, offering employment opportunities and job placements. On the other hand, place another advertisement offering Businesses, Companies, and Organizations, Offices, Qualified Professional and Skilled Employees.

c. Find out and incorporate the marketing methods and approaches of other professionals in your field into your own method and approach.

d. Networking

e. Brochure/Flyers

f. Business Cards

g. Create a Website

h. Join Associations/social clubs

i. Trade fairs

Good luck!

Tour Operator/Tourist Guide

Tour operating depends largely on environmental and cultural resources. As a tour operator, you must not only love travelling, sight seeing, culture, and the environment, but you must have a good knowledge of memorable and pleasurable places and tourist sites.

According to the definition by the European Committee

for Standardisation (CEN), a tourist guide is a person who guides visitors in the language of their choice and interprets the cultural and natural heritage of an area. This person normally possesses an area-specific qualification usually issued and or recognised by the appropriate authority.

A tour manager is a person who manages the itinerary on behalf of the tour operator, ensuring the programme is carried out as described in the tour operator's literature, and sold to the traveller/consumer. A tour manager also gives local practical information.

As a tour operator/tourist guide, you must be conversant with the code of guiding practice adopted by the World Federation of Tourist Guides Association (WFTGA) as follows:

a. Promote a professional service to visitors, professional in care and commitment and professional in providing an objective understanding of the place(s) visited, free from prejudice or propaganda.

b. Ensure that as far as possible, what is presented as fact is true, and that a clear distinction is made between this truth and stories, legends, tradition or opinions.

c. Act fairly and reasonably in dealing with all those who engage the services of guides, and with colleagues working in all aspects of tourism.

d. Protect the reputation of tourism in the country by making every endeavour to ensure that guided groups, treat with respect, the environment, wildlife, sights and monuments and also local customs and sensitivities.

e. As representatives of the host country, to welcome visitors, and promote the country as a tourist destination.

The WFTGA aims to establish contact with tourist

guide associations throughout the world, and to reinforce their professional ties. It strives to represent professional tourist guides internationally, and to promote and protect their interests. The association aims to enhance the image of the profession, and to promote a universal code of ethics and skills. To raise, encourage and establish the highest standards of professionalism. The WFTGA aims to develop international training and improving the quality of guiding through education.

When organizing a tour, you have to put in consideration: environmental, social, and economic aspects. In general, tours can be organized around various interests and hobbies, sports or adventures including:

Picnicking, Mountain climbing, Cave exploration, Parachuting tours, Sea diving tours, Bicycle tours, Walking tours, River-rafting tours, Rock climbing tours, Kayaking tours, Cross country tours, Downhill ski tours, Ski resorts tours, Golf course tours, Forest tours, Camping.

Tours could be organized for special niche clients including: Seniors, Students, Couples, Children, Tours for families and Business executives on conferences, Sports teams and clubs.

You may choose to specialize on any of the different kind of tours.

For an effective tour operating business, you need the tour operator's software. Some of these software systems cover the A to Z, the all aspect of inbound and outbound tour operating business. Visit the website: www.caterra.com/tour-operating-software

You will have a list of over 45 Tour Operating software.

What You Need To Start-UP

a.   A Computer (with Internet connection)

Use a desktop or a laptop computer with a 56k modem. Install the following software:

Word processor (MS Office)—Use this to write letters, create mailing labels, address envelopes. In the MS office you've got MS word, Excel, Access, Outlook, and Powerpoint.

Spreadsheet—You can create charts and do your finances with spreadsheet program. Use MS Excel for your spreadsheet needs.

QuickBooks Pro—With this you can create custom invoices, compute sales, do electronic banking, bill payments, control inventory and payroll. Use it for all accounting and bookkeeping.

Database—Use the Database program to keep record of clients, sellers, vendors and all your business contacts/links. With the database program you can keep record of phone calls, faxes, meeting, conferences, seminars time and dates of events and incidents. You may want to use Dbase or Fox Pro for your database needs.

Graphic—Use this to create flyers, announcements newsletters and advertisements. You may want to use PageMaker, QuarkXpress and Clarisworks for your graphic exploits.

Scheduler—Use this to manage your schedules.

b. Phone, Fax, Printer, Scanner, Copier (can buy all-in-one)
c. Office Furniture (including office supplies and office accessories)
d. Insurance
e. Fees payable to become a member in professional and or trade associations (if any).
f. Tour Operators Software systems
g. Video Camera (Digital preferably)
h. Photo Camera (Digital preferably)
i. Books
j. Marketing/advertising cost.
k. Music

l.   Personal image improvement cost and other
     miscellaneous expenses

The total cost of your start-up needs will not exceed
$20,000 Canadian.

Professional/Trade Associations You May Like To Join/Know

- World Federation of Tourist Guide Association
  Head Office
  The WFTGA Administrator,
  Wirtschaftskammer Wien
  FG Freizeitbetriebe
  Judenplats 3—4
  1010 Wien
  Austria
  Phone: 43 1 51450 4211
  Fax: 43 1 51450 4216
  Email: info@wftga.org
  Website: www.wftga.org
- Representative of the Federation in Canada
  Houri Nazaretian
  1363 wecker Drive
  Oshawa, On
  L1J 3P8
  Phone: 905-721-0783
  Fax; 905-721-9062
  Email; knazaretia@aol.com
- Canadian Tour Guide Association of Toronto
  122-250, The Eastmall, Suite 1705
  Toronto, On
  M9B 6L3
  Phone: 416-410-8621
  Fax: 416-410-8621
  Email; info@ctgaoftoronto,org
  Website: www.ctgaoftoronto.org
- Association des Guides Touristiques des Quebec

Inc.
College Merici
Case Postale 79
755, Chemin St.-Louis
Quebec City, QC
G1S 1C1

- The Alberta Tour Directors Association
  Box 8044
  Canmore, AB
  T1W 2T8
  Phone: 403-678-2833
  Email: ctconsultants@monarc.net
  Contact: Alison Day
- Association Professionalle des Guides Touristiques
  Chapitre de Montreal (APGT)
  C.P. 982, Succursale Place d'Armes
  Montreal, QC
  H2Y 3J4
  Phone: 514-990-9849
  Email: renelemieuxguide@hotmail.com
  Contact: Rene Lemieux
  Website: www.apgtmontreal.org
- Canadian Tour Guides Association of British
  Columbia
  BOX 2440
  Vancouver, BC
  V6B 3W7
  Phone: 604-876-2576
  Fax: 604-872-2640
  Email: jeff@ctgaofbc.com
  Contact: Jeff Veniot
  Website: www.ctgaofbc.com
- Capital Tour Guide Association
  496 Parkdale Ave.
  Ottawa, On

K1Y 0A3
Phone: 613-722-5939
Fax: 613-722-5743
Contact: Lenore Leon

Books you May Need to Buy

- Conducting Tours: A Practical Guide
  Published by Thomas Delmar learning
  Author: Marc Mancini, Terri Gaylord
  ISBN: 076681419X
- Start Your Own Specialty Travel & Tour Business
  Published by Self-Counsel Press
  Author: Barbara Braidwood
  ISBN: 1551802848
- Successful International Tour Director: How To
  Become an International Tour Director
  Published by Authors Choice Press
  Author: Geralde Mitchell
  ISBN: 0595167020
- Internet Marketing For Your Tourism Business:
  Proven Techniques For Promoting Tourist Based
  Business Over The Internet
  Published by Maximum Press
  Author: Susan Sweeney
  ISBN: 1885068476
- Becoming A Tour Guide: The Principles of
  Guiding and Site Interpretation
  Published by Int. Thomson Business Press
  Author: Verite Reily Collins
  ISBN: 0826447880
- The Professional Guide: Dynamics of Tour Guiding
  Published by Wiley
  Author: Kathleen Lingle Pond
  ISBN: 047128386X
- Essentials of Tour Management

Published by Prentice hall
Author: Betsy Fay
ISBN: 0132850656

- The Good Guide: A Sourcebook For Interpreters, Docents, And Tour Guides
Published by Ironwood Press
Author: Alison L. Grinder
ISBN: 0932541003
- Selling Destinations: Geography For The Travel Professional
Published by Delmar Thompson Learning
Author: Marc Mancini
ISBN: 1401819826
- How To Start A Home-Based Travel Agency
Published by Tom Ogg and Associates
Author: Tom Ogg
ISBN: 1888290056
- Guerrilla Publicity
Published by Adams Media Corporation
Author: Jay Conrad Levinson, Rich Frishman, Jill Lublin
ISBN: 1-58062-682-3
- Marketing Without Advertising
Author: Michael Phillips, Salli Rasberry
ISBN: 0873376080
- The 22 Immutable Laws of Marketing
Published by Harper Business
Author: Al Ries and Jack Trout
ISBN: 0887306667
- 6 Steps To Free Publicity
Published by Career Press Inc
Author: Marcia Yudkin
ISBN: 1-56414-675-8
- Endless Referrals: Network Your Everyday Contacts into Sales (New and Updated Edition)

Author: Bob Burg
ISBN: 0070089973
- How To Become Your Own Publicist
  Published by McGraw-Hill
  Author: Jessica Hatchigan
  ISBN:0-07-138332-8

Marking/How To Get Business

Hunting for business for your Tour Operating/Management Firm is about the same thing as searching for a job in your field. As such, you have to apply all the job search skills discussed in the early chapters of this book, customizing them to suit your present need and position.

a. Cold calls to Schools, Organizations and Conference/Convention Organizers for information interviews about who may need the services, and provide them with reasons why they may need the services of your Tour Operating/Management Firm.

b. Networking

Network with other tour operators nationally and internationally—including tour operators in your country of origin and countries around it. You can be exchanging tour packages, sending and receiving tourist groups to and from these countries.

c. Yellow pages advertisement

d. Brochure/Flyers

e. Business Cards

f. Create a Website

g. Join Associations/social clubs

h. Distribute gift certificates and discounted tour packages to your clients to give to their friends

i. Send out tour package offers for special days and seasons like Christmas, New Year, Easter, Canada Day, Valentine day etc.

j. Keep in touch with your clients and call the clients who have not used your services for some time and remind them of your good services and new discounted offers available.

k. Find out and incorporate the marketing methods and approaches of other professionals in your field into your own method and approach.

l. Call your clients—new/old/regulars, a day or two after they use your services to thank them for using the services of your tour management firm, but above all, to ask them how they are feeling, and if they enjoyed the tour trip.

m. Offer discount to your regular clients and offer them free tour package if they bring in four or more new clients—referral reward

n. Send out a discounted tour package offer for students, seniors, couples, singles, teenagers, and some specific professions/professionals like lawyers, truck drivers, factory workers, teachers etc, including a lecture session on a particular topic.

o. Develop a weekly newsletter, write in the local newspaper and or magazine giving tips on how to increase awareness, enrich ones cultural sense, love and promote the environment and cultural heritages, and use tour and sight seeing to manage stress. Act like the professional you are.

Good luck!

Public-Relations Professional/Publicist

A public relations professional/publicist is a person who is in the business of creating, generating and or drumming up publicity through the media for the client, the client's product(s) or the client's service(s) with the sole intention of improving the client's public image.

The clientele of a publicist may range from celebrities—

singers, sportsmen, movie actors, to politicians, governments, businesses, industries, companies and organizations.

The Publicist stages a goodwill campaign for the client during the client's heydays and during crisis period. At every campaign the publicist aims to earn a favourable public image/opinion for the client.

A publicist may choose to specialize in one or more of the various areas of specializations in the field of public relations, including:

    a.   Celebrity affairs
    b.   Entertainment
    c.   Government affairs
    d.   Political affairs
    e.   Organizations
    f.   Public affairs
    g.   Industry/Company/Business affairs
    h.   Science/Technology/Research
    i.   Crisis management/Damage control
    j.   Racial/Multicultural affairs
    k.   Fund raising/Charity
    l.   Events
    m.   Environmental affairs
    n.   Private practice

At all times, the members of the above mentioned specialized areas seek the services of the publicist to gain positive publicity.

However, a publicist could be contracted to spread/ stage a negative campaign about a competitor on behalf of a client with the sole aim of earning negative publicity for the competitor.

As a publicist, you need to:

    a. Be persistent, persuasive, confident and diplomatic

    b. Have a craving for trends—the ability to read a lot to know the current trends (Trendy)

    c. Have contacts in the media (editors)

d. Know the kind of story each editor/contact works with
e. Have excellent communication skills
f. Be people smart
g. Have team work skills
h. Excellent telephone skills/manners
i. Excellent writing/report writing skills
j. Be very creative—be able to package a story/report to make it as attractive and newsworthy as possible
k. Have presentation skills
l. Be able to meet deadlines
m. Be very professional
n. Have a craving for information—be addicted to the act of seeking and searching for information

You may choose to specialize in an area related to your field of expertise.

What You Need To Start-UP

a. A Computer (with Internet connection)

Use a desktop or a laptop computer with a 56k modem. Install the following software:

Word processor (MS Office)—Use this to write letters, create mailing labels, address envelopes. In the MS office you've got MS word, Excel, Access, Outlook, and Powerpoint.

Spreadsheet—You can create charts and do your finances with spreadsheet program. Use MS Excel for your spreadsheet needs.

QuickBooks Pro—With this you can create custom invoices, compute sales, do electronic banking, bill payments, control inventory and payroll. Use it for all accounting and bookkeeping.

Database—Use the Database program to keep record of clients, sellers, vendors and all your business contacts/links. With the database program you can keep record of phone calls, faxes, meeting, conferences, seminars time and dates of events and incidents. You may want to use Dbase or Fox Pro for your database needs.

Graphic—Use this to create flyers, announcements newsletters and advertisements. You may want to use PageMaker, QuarkXpress and Clarisworks for your graphic exploits.

Scheduler—Use this to manage your schedules.

b.   Phone, Fax, Printer, Scanner, Copier (can buy all-in-one)
c.   Office Furniture (including office supplies and office accessories)
d.   Insurance
e.   Fees payable to become a member in professional and or trade associations (if any).
f.   PR Software systems
g.   Video Camera (Digital preferably)
h.   Photo Camera (Digital preferably)
i.   Tape Recorder (Digital preferably)
j.   Marketing/advertising cost.
k.   Books
l.   Personal image improvement cost and other miscellaneous expenses

The total cost of your start-up needs will not exceed $20,000 Canadian.

Professional/Trade Associations You May Like To Join/Know

- Canadian Public Relations Society
  220 Laurier Avenue West, Suite 720
  Ottawa, On
  K1P 5Z9
  Phone: 613-232-1222
  Website: www.cprs.ca
- International Association of Business Communicators

1 Halladie Plaza, Suite 600
San Francisco, CA 94102
USA
Phone: 1-415-433-3400
Website: www.iabc.com

Books you May Need to Buy
6 Steps To Free Publicity
Published by Career Press Inc
Author: Marcia Yudkin
ISBN: 1-56414-675-8
- Endless Referrals: Network Your Everyday
Contacts into Sales (New and Updated Edition)
Author: Bob Burg
ISBN: 0070089973
Guerrilla Publicity
Published by Adams Media Corporation
Author: Jay Conrad Levinson, Rich Frishman, and
Jill Lublin
ISBN: 1-58062-682-3
- How To Become Your Own Publicist
Published by McGraw-Hill
Author: Jessica Hatchigan
ISBN:0-07-138332-8
- How To Open and Operate A Home-Based
Communications Business
Published by Globe Pequot Press
Author: Louann Nagy Werksma
ISBN: 1564406318
- The Practice Of Public Relations
Published by Prentice-Hall
Author: Fraser Seitel
ISBN: 013613811X
- Public Relations: Strategies & Tactics
Published by Addison Wesley Publishing Company

Author: Dennis L. Wilcox
ISBN: 0321015479

- Effective Public Relations
  Published by Prentice-Hall
  Author: Scott M. Cutlipp, Allen H. Centre, and
  Glen M. Broom
  ISBN: 0132450100
- Lesley's Handbook of Public Relations and
  Communications
  Published by NTC Business Books
  Author: Phillip Lesley
  ISBN: 0844232572
- The Handbook Of Strategic Public Relations and
  Integrated Communications
  Published by McGraw-Hill
  Author: Clarke L. Caywood
  ISBN: 0786311312
- Public Relations Writing: The Essentials Of Style
  and Format
  Published by NTC Publishing Group
  Author: Thomas H. Bivins
  ISBN: 0844203513
- Guerrilla Selling: Unconventional Weapons and
  Tactics for Increasing Your Sales
  Published by Houghton Mifflin
  Author: Bill Gallagher, Orvel Ray Wilson and Jay
  Conrad Levinson
  ISBN: 0395580390
- Guerrilla Teleselling: New Unconventional
  weapons and Tactics To Sell When You can't Be
  There in Person
  Author: Jay Conrad Levinson, Mark S.A Smith, and
  Orval Ray Wilson
  ISBN: 0471242799
- Teleselling: A Self-Teaching Guide

Published by J. Wiley
Author: Porterfield James D
ISBN: 0471115673

Marking/How To Get Business

Hunting for business for your public Relations Firm is about the same thing as searching for a job in your field. As such, you have to apply all the job search skills discussed in the early chapters of this book, customizing them to suit your present need and position.

a. Cold calls to Companies, Businesses, Schools, Organizations and Events/Conference/ Convention Organizers for information interviews about who may need the services, and provide them with reasons and leads why they may need the services of your Public-Relations Firm.

b. Find out and incorporate the marketing methods and approaches of other professionals in your field into your own method and approach

c. Networking
Network with other professionals who are into private practise in your professional Organization to find out who needs a plug for his expertise and practise.

d. Yellow pages advertisement

e. Brochure/Flyers

f. Business Cards

g. Create a Website

h. Join Associations/social clubs

i. Distribute gift certificates and discounted publicity packages to clients to give to their friends

j. Send out publicity package offers for special days and seasons like Christmas New year, Easter, Canada day, Valentine day and special events etc.

k. Keep in touch with your clients and call the clients

who have not used your services for some time and remind them of your good services, new leads and discounted offers available

l. Call your clients—new/old/regulars, weeks, months and or years after they use your services to thank them for using the services of your Public-Relations firm, but above all, to ask them how they are doing and how satisfied they are with the result of the earlier publicity campaign.

m. Offer free publicity package to your regular clients for referrals—if they bring in four or more new clients

n. Develop a weekly/monthly Newsletter, write in the local newspaper and or magazine giving tips on how to increase awareness, and public relations. Act like the professional you are.

Good luck!

General Brief about the Dozen And One Businesses

The dozen and one businesses you can run from your home as discussed in this book is not a definitive list of businesses you can run from home as a Foreign Trained Professional who is relatively new in Canada. Rather, they are good examples amongst thousands of other businesses you can run from your home. Selecting them for discussion in this book was based on:

a. Suitability for a relatively new immigrant

b. Suitability for a professional and or skilled person

c. Relatively easy to access/launch

d. Income Potential: Businesses that will not bring in a steady and somewhat an above average income are not included in this edition of this book. As a professional, you merit more than ever to earn a high enough income to meet the demands of the minimum standard expected of you. The dozen

and one businesses have the potential of limitless
expansion depending on what scale it is operated
and or on what one wants.

e.   Convenient to Operate from home
The dozen and one businesses discussed in this
edition, are the businesses you can conveniently
start and operate from your home without any
employee at least for the first year of operation.
Without violating any zoning/community privacy
and or residential regulations.

f.   Non-Seasonal and Viable
The dozen and one businesses discussed here are
evergreen businesses. They thrive throughout the
year and in all seasons. A Toronto-based Canadian
expert in home-based business who was consulted
during the course of writing this book said thus—
'Depending on how you operate them, they could
be immune to economic fluctuations and probably
recession'.

g.   Low Stress
You have enough stress already, having been
through several refusals in the corporate corridors.
The dozen and one businesses discussed here could
be operated with minimal stress.

h.   Low Start-up Cost (less than $20,000 CAD)

i.   Service-based Business
The dozen and one businesses discussed here
are all service-oriented businesses because a large
number of Foreign Trained Professionals in
Canada are service oriented professionals. Service-
oriented business saves you money, because you
wont spend lots of money buying lots of tools,
equipments and storage. You have yourself, your
skills, your expertise, and your services to market,
rather than a product—relatively easier right? Much

similar to searching for a job.

j.   Accommodating

Most of the dozen and one businesses discussed here are extremely accommodating—any professional can pitch his/her flag and specialize in his/her area of expertise within the businesses.

However, there are many more businesses you can start from your home that are not listed in this edition. Do not despair if I did not list any business that suits your interest or aptitude. There are many books on home-based businesses. Most other home-based businesses you may think of can be started and operated using about the same methods and modalities pointed out for the dozen and one home-based businesses.

Points to consider before choosing any of the dozen and one businesses

a.   Are you resolved to, and do you believe in the business?

b.   Will you enjoy the act of conducting the business?

c.   Will you enjoy the type of crowd and clients the business will attract to you?

d.   Will you be able to weather any setback and or crisis that may arise in the course of conducting the business?

e.   Will you be able to believe and resolve to doing the business, enjoy the act and process of conducting the business, enjoy the type of clients the business will attract to you—be satisfied? Are you ready to remain the steadfast captain of the business during thick and thin?

In answering the questions, do not let your enthusiasm blind you to the obvious.

If your answer is yes + yes + yes + yes + yes then you are set to take off. It is that simple.

Believe + Resolve + Happy indulgence + Joyful Client-Business owner relationship + Readiness for crisis management + Satisfaction = Total Success

The human community is ready for you and your business.

My sincere congratulations!

Irrespective of the business you choose to start and operate, there are general requirements that any person in business must meet and they include:

  a. Self-Management—As a self-employed business owner, you need control, restraint and motivation
  b. Time management—Manage your time skilfully. Time is money
  c. Money Management—Manage your in-out flow of cash skilfully
  d. Organized Office—Organize your office for optimum operation
  e. Marketing/Advertising/Publicity—Whether it is Product(s), Service(s) or Expertise that requires selling, you need to market/advertise/publicize it to the market.

Advertising/Marketing/Publicity are simply the act of making a product, service or expertise known to the public with the sole intention of getting the public to buy and use it. People only buy the products and use the services and expertise they know about, heard about, read about or see around. Getting your product(s) or service(s) known to the public could be achieved through:

The newspaper, television, radio, internet, journals, magazines, yellow pages, signs, flyers, direct mailing, referrals, networking, brochures, business cards, door-to-door, seminars, conferences. Failure to stage a successful advertising/marketing/publicity campaign will relegate the opportunity of getting the public to know, hear, read or see your product/service/expertise.

If you do not advertise your product, nobody will advertise them for you. And nobody can advertise your product better than yourself.

Newspapers/Magazines/Journals—In the local newspaper/magazine/journal, you will find the ad hotline of the company. Or call the company and request to be directed to the marketing/advertisement department.

Television/Radio—Call the company and request to be directed to the marketing/advertisement department.

Internet—Create your own Website and use Web marketing techniques to increase the traffic to the site. Promote your site.

Yellow Pages—the phone company that set up you business line may help to tell you the advertising rates in the phone directory. Be sure to place your ad under the correct heading.

Direct Mailing—contact the mailing list companies and buy lists of people that fit into your niche-target. In your yellow pages, go under the heading 'mailing list' and you will find list of mailing list companies.

Networking/Referrals—always dispense excellent service and product(s) so that clients who have used the product(s) or service(s) will refer others to you. Network with every client that comes your way. Organizations, Associations, Social clubs, Seminars, Conferences are excellent arenas to network.

Signs—Signs can attract lots of clients in your area as well as people passing by. People can also use the signs to locate you more easily.

Flyers/Brochures—They contain the literature and photos about your product(s) and service(s), your contact address, phones, fax, email, and website address. Flyers and brochures can be mailed to your clients, distributed in the malls, seminars and conferences.

Business Cards—Business card makes you look

professional and serious. By giving a person your business card, you are telling him/her to remember you professionally with the card. Your business card is your mini resume, brochure and flyer. Make a good one with the right contact address, phone, fax, email and website address.

Thirty seconds Self-selling—In all the sections of how to get business for all the dozen and one businesses, I repeatedly said that finding business for your firm is pretty much like searching for a job in your field and you must apply all the job search skills you learnt from the facilitators in the job search centre you attended. Remember the act of telling the employer about yourself in 30 seconds?

Yes you do.

Good!

Do you agree that the question 'what do you do?' is a very common question from people we are meeting for the first time?

Now imagine yourself sharing a seat in a plane, metro, public transit—city bus, tram/street car, in the stadium, conference hall, cinema, restaurant, bar/pub, in a party and the question 'what do you do?' was directed to you. Most people answer this question without making proper use of the opportunity. People answer this question not giving a positive image about their profession either by omission or commission. But it is an invitation to sell yourself professionally and dish out your business card.

Consider the following lines:

'These days Companies turn to information professionals for information on competitors, solution to a specific problem, vetting an innovation, to increasing productivity. Because it is time and cost effective, and they get the exact information they need. I am an Information Broker. Here is my card'

'When most Companies, Businesses and Organizations want to recruit a professional, they seek the services of an

executive search firm/headhunters because it is far less expensive and more effective than advertising in the newspapers. I am a Headhunter. You can have my card'

'It is an entrenched fact that relaxation and touch therapy is not only good for the body and the mind but also cures aches, pain and stress. I am a Massage Therapist. You may have my card'

In just thirty seconds you told your audience not only what you do, but also the advantages, and how a prospective client may benefit from your services.

You can practice saying it out loud in the privacy of your office, car, washroom, kitchen, balcony, living room, study room etc, so that when confronted with the question 'what do you do?' It will flow smoothly.

The end point of Advertisement/Marketing/Publicity is to sell.

Selling has been described to be the business of convincing a person(s) to buy a product(s), service(s) and or idea(s). Selling is an act, and like most acts, it could be learnt and applied to any field by any interested party.

However, there are some sacred steps involved in Sales. The steps are sacred because they have to be followed religiously to achieve the desired result. The steps includes:

a. Identifying your Market—This is pretty simple, you have to identify your client(s) before selling to them

b. Introduction—introduce your product(s) or service(s)

c. Qualify your client—Find out if he/she/they are suitable for your product/service

d. Presentation—Tell all the pros of your product/ service

e. Close—make the sale.

The following is a list of books on Marketing, Advertising and Publicity:

- Guerrilla Publicity
  Published by Adams Media Corporation
  Author: Jay Conrad Levinson, Rich Frishman, and Jill Lublin
  ISBN: 1-58062-682-3
- Marketing Without Advertising
  Author: Michael Phillips, Salli Rasberry
  ISBN: 0873376080
- The 22 Immutable Laws of Marketing
  Published by Harper Business
  Author: Al Ries and Jack Trout
  ISBN: 0887306667
- The 22 Irrefutable Laws of Advertising
  Published by John Willey and Sons
  Author: Michael Newman
  ISBN: 0470-82106-X
- 6 Steps To Free Publicity
  Published by Career Press Inc
  Author: Marcia Yudkin
  ISBN: 1-56414-675-8
- Endless Referrals: Network Your Everyday Contacts into Sales (New and Updated Edition)
  Author: Bob Burg
  ISBN: 0070089973
- How To Become Your Own Publicist
  Published by McGraw-Hill
  Author: Jessica Hatchigan
  ISBN: 0-07-138332-8
- Guerrilla Selling: Unconventional Weapons and Tactics for Increasing Your Sales
  Published by Houghton Mifflin
  Author: Bill Gallagher, Orvel Ray Wilson and Jay Conrad Levinson

ISBN: 0395580390

- Guerrilla Teleselling: New Unconventional weapons and Tactics To Sell When You can't Be There in Person
  Author: Jay Conrad Levinson, Mark S.A Smith, and Orval Ray Wilson
  ISBN: 0471242799
- How To Become A Marketing Superstar
  Published by Hyperion Books
  Author: Jeffrey J. Fox
  ISBN: 0-7868-6824-4

That a business is being run from home does not make it inseparable from your family, household chores and activities around your home. Working from home could be very difficult because of distractions, and there is no boss watching over your shoulder every time. You require lots of discipline to run your business from home. Discipline to separate working hours from family and friends.

Distractions may include children, friends, Television, Radio, and other household chores. Having screaming, crying, giggling of kids and barking dogs in the background while on a phone conversation with a client is very unprofessional and distracting. When on the phone with a client keep the dogs away in the kennel or kennels. Keep the children quiet and or out of the office with their baby-sitter/nanny and or in the day care.

You have to run your home-based business like any other business that is run from an executive office in Bay Street, Toronto, Canada or from an executive office in Wall Street, New York, USA.

Good luck!

GLOSSARY

Academic Bridge Programs

Academic programs, which may make the new immigrant, Foreign Trained Professionals and or Skilled Immigrants more employable. Some of the academic bridge programs provide paid and or unpaid internship and co-op placements.

Academic Credentials Assessment

The evaluation of one's academic qualification, as compared to the Canadian academic qualification standard, for employment and educational purposes.

Accreditation Program(s)

Program(s), which renders a person's academic, professional and practical experience(s) as being of satisfactory and or of acceptable standard.

Canadian Corporate Culture

The business culture as it relates to the Canadian corporate circles.

Canadian Experience

This means that one has professional, practical, work experience and or academic training inside of Canada.

Career Bridge Program(s)

Program(s) that provides the connection between Foreign Trained Professionals and or Skilled Immigrants with the workplace of their respective fields of expertise, Canadian labour market and the Canadian corporate culture. The programs are designed to offer the new immigrants 'Canadian experience'—Canadian workplace/practical work experience they need to secure employment in their respective fields of expertise.

CaRMS

Canadian Residency Matching Services

Chamber of Commerce

A union and or association of businesspeople in a community, region or area with a common interest geared towards improving the trade and commerce of such a community, area and or region.

Cold Call

Making contact with a company, organization and a person through telephone, email, and letter or in person, without prior introduction, invitation, or referral is called Cold Call.

Commissioned Agent

An agent who makes commission only on the sales he/she makes for the company.

Community Settlement Agencies

Agencies that help new immigrants settle in their chosen communities.

Co-op Placement

The act of working in a cooperative, company, organization and firm on a temporary basis to acquire workplace and practical experiences as they relate to the field of study and or expertise.

Co-signer

A person that acts as a guarantor for another by jointly signing a legal document

Credit history

The history of how a person borrows and pays back his/her debts.

Direct Mailing

A publicity strategy that enlists sending information, advertisement materials, marketing,
Sales pitch and flyers etc., by post directly to the targeted audience and or prospective clients.

Door-to-Door

The act of going from house to house, knocking at every door in a neighborhood, area and or region to sell, advertise and or publicize a product and or service.

Entrepreneurial Trait

The inherent qualities and skills, which distinguishes a person as an entrepreneur and or a businessman.

Evergreen business

Business that thrives throughout the year and in all season.

Factoring

A type of financial service where a seller transfers a debt to another firm (the Factor) that acts as principal. The factor turns to the buyer to collect the debt. All credit card transaction is a form of factoring.

Flyer

A flyer is a sheet of paper advertising products and or services.

Foreign Credentials and Documents

Credentials and Documents obtained outside of Canada and United states.

Foreign Experience

Experience obtained outside of Canada and the United States.

Foreign Trained Professional(s)

A person(s) and or professional(s), who obtained his/her academic degree and professional training and experience outside of Canada and United States.

Functional Plan

A plan that is implementable and designed to achieve the desired result.

Goal Setting

Making a list of objectives (must-do) to be attained and or achieved within a time frame.

Hidden Job Market

The hidden job market consists of jobs that are not advertised and it comprises of about 80% of jobs. Networking is the best way to secure a job in the hidden job market.

IMG's

International Medical Graduates

Interview Skills

Skills needed to successfully attend and undergo an interview.

Irrevocable Letter of Credit

This type of letter of credit, cannot be altered, amended and or cancelled by the issuing bank (the buyers bank) usually at the request of the buyer, without the consent of the beneficiary (the seller).

Job Leads

Resources, directions and paths that may lead one to a job/employment opportunity.

Job-Specific language/terminology

Language and terminology used to represent things, conditions and situations in a specific job.

Letter of Credit (L/C)

It is an instrument of business transaction, a safe method of ensuring payment in a business transaction. A letter of credit is an undertaking and or guarantee for payment of a specified sum of money within a stated time frame, issued by a buyer's bank at the buyer's request. The undertaking contains conditions that must be met by the seller within a stated time frame before receiving payment.

Liability/Trouble Shooting Ability

The ability to foresee and prevent a liability and or trouble before it becomes a problem.

Line of credit

A revolving type of loan/credit, with an established maximum that the borrower may have access to, the maximum amount becomes available as soon as the borrower pays the previous borrowed amount.

Literate Culture

Culture replete with literate values.

Mailing Labels

Labels you can use to personalize your mailings. You can have your company logo and or mascot on your mailing labels.

Mailing List

A list of people's names and addresses in the possession of an organization, company and or a firm, used to mail information, advertising materials and or products to these individuals. One can also compile a mailing list from the phone book.

Malpractice Insurance Coverage

An insurance coverage that undertakes any liability, which may be incurred by a professional in carrying out his/her professional responsibilities.

Mentorship Program

A program that employs experienced Canadian Professionals to advice and guide new immigrants, Foreign Trained Professionals and Skilled Immigrants, in similar fields/ professions as the mentors in their job search, professional life and the Canadian labour market and corporate culture.

Merchant Account

An account, which enables one to accept credit card payments for goods, services and or debts.

Monoculturacial

Comprising of one culture and one race

Monocultural

Comprising of one culture

Monoracial

Comprising of one race

Networking

Networking is the act of making and establishing contacts and exchanging information for the purpose of career advancement. It is the most effective tool of job searching and securing a job in Canada and elsewhere in the world. Truly, whom you know fetches you jobs much more easier than what you know.

No Canadian Experience

This means that one does not have professional, practical, work experience and or academic training in Canada.

Non-Transferable Letter of Credit

This type of letter of credit cannot be transferred to a second and third beneficiary.

Occupation-Specific language/terminology

Language, terminology and or nomenclature employed in a specific occupation to represent things, conditions and or situations.

Overqualified Labourer

An individual engaged in a job that he/she is overqualified to do.

People Smart

The skill and or ability to charm and deal with people in an effective and endearing way that keeps the people comfortable while doing what is required of them, and earns you their respect and or likeness.

Presentation Skills

The ability to make presentation(s) in a very attractive and interesting way.

Professional Enhancement

The horning, sharpening, improving and or upgrading the professional status of a professional is known as professional enhancement.

Professional Liability Insurance Coverage

An insurance coverage, which covers a professional while undertaking his/her professional responsibilities, is known as professional insurance coverage.

Prior Learning Assessment (PLA)

The assessment and or evaluation of a person's previous academic, professional, and practical experiences.

Qualifying Examination/Test

A pass in this examination and or test qualifies one for licensing in a designated regulated profession.

Referrals

The act of referring a person and or persons to a place to obtain help, information, service and or purchase product(s).

Retainer Agent

A retainer agent is paid a fixed amount of money to work for a company/manufacturer for a particular product in a particular period of time.

Resume

A summary of your education and training, professional experience, work history, technical and soft skills, accomplishments, interests and activities/hobbies as they relate to the job position you are targeting.

Revocable Letter of Credit

A revocable letter of credit, can be altered, amended and or cancelled by the issuing bank (the buyers bank) usually at the request of the buyer, without the consent of the beneficiary (the seller).

Sales Pitch

A prepared and rehearsed speech which a salesman and or sales representative presents to the prospective buyer when trying to sell a product and or service.

Small Business Administration Act

The government of Canada supports and assists small businesses as contained in this act. The SBA provides financial, technical, advice and consulting services to small businesses.

Soft Skills

Soft skills are the skills outside of your technical and professional skills. They are the inherent skills that relates to your everyday interaction with people, the public, and handling of situations. Soft skills are transferable.

Start-Up-Capital

The capital needed to start a business and or a venture

Success Strategy

A laid down game plan to achieve success in an endeavor

Survival Job

A job, that though one is overqualified to do, but, has to do it to pay bills while searching for a befitting job.
- A doctor working as a taxi driver is engaged in a survival job.
- A lawyer working as a security guard is engaged in a survival job.
- An Engineer working as a general labourer in a factory floor is engaged in a survival job
- An Architect working as a waiter in a bar is engaged in a survival job.

Telephone Skills

The ability and manners needed to conduct a telephone conversation/communication for the purpose of presentation, interview, research, sales, advertising and or marketing.

Term Lenders

Term lenders lend money to individuals, companies, organizations and firms for a fixed period of time, for profit.

Time Management

The act of managing ones time by allotting a task to every bit of a person's time.

TOFEL

Test of English as a Foreign Language

Transferable Letter of Credit

This type of letter of credit can be transferred to a second and third beneficiary.

Un-Canadian

Not Canadian in nature

Upgrading Course/Program

Program(s) and or courses designed to erase the deficiencies in a person's academic, professional and or practical status as compared with the Canadian standard.

Volunteer Work

An unpaid work and or service related to your field of expertise.

Wage Subsidy

This is a type of Student employment program where the government subsidizes the salary/wage of the student while he works in a company.

APPENDIX

Career Bridging
Certificate Course (3-6 months)
Undergraduate Courses related to your field (may be short considering transfer credit)
Volunteer Work
Some Private Practice (In Your Field)
Acupuncture Clinic
Architectural Workshop
Chiropodist Clinic
Chiropractic Clinic
Dental Clinic
Dietetic Clinic
Fitness Counseling
Fitness Trainer
Legal Consultant/Clinic
Nutritional Counseling
Physiotherapy Clinic
Podiatric Clinic
Prescription Orthotics
Rest Clinic
Veterinary Clinic
In all, do not lose focus.

Other Businesses you may start
Automotive Painter
Bakery (Baker)
Business Plan Writer
Business Broker
Book Cover Designer
Carpentry Workshop
Copywriter
Desktop Publishing
Electrical Workshop
Estate Agent
Freelance Editor, Proofreading, Indexing
Funeral Director
Graphology
Hair Stylist (Hair Products)
Home Appraiser
Immigration Consultant
Insurance Broker
Interior Decorator
Landscaping
Mediator
Microbrewery (Microbrewer)
Newsletter Publishing
Painter & Decorator
Photographer/Photography
Private Tutoring
Sprinkler System Installer
Tax Preparation Service
Technical Writer
Tile setting Services (Tilesetter)
Travel Agent
Travel Consultant
Website Designer
Welding Services (Welder)

EPILOGUE

Morph into an entrenched member of your profession. Evaluate every option, opportunity and lead. Reach forth to touch the skies of your profession and or trade by employing the best of positive thinking...

"What can I do for Canada, the Canadian Corporate employment procedure, and the Canadian labour market? What can I do for myself in Canada?"

Empower your foreign degree and or experience with any of the options outlined in this guide. Give your best to the system and obtain the very abundant best it has to offer.

Good Luck!

ABOUT THE AUTHOR

Obi Orakwue is a Foreign Trained Professional in Canada, a Nigerian Trained Biochemist. Mr. Orakwue had been through various 'Survival Jobs', interviews, and first hand encounters with the bully barrier "No Canadian Experience". He earned additional insight by closely following the plight of other Foreign Trained Professionals in Canada, in the journey to employment in their chosen professions. He has written other books including:

Fiction
- Overqualified Labourer
- Corrupted Ambition
- The Comedy of Time
- The Terrorist Creed
- The Councilor and The Municipal Mafia
- The Lost Gene: Victim of Want

Presently, he is putting pruning touches to his latest work entitled 'The Career Spouse' while keeping pace with a Post-Graduate program.

He lives in Toronto Canada.

ISBN 1-41206198-9